THE HIDDEN WHISTLE AND FLUTE
Stitch One

THE HIDDEN WHISTLE AND FLUTE
Stitch One

George Major

ATHENA PRESS
LONDON

THE HIDDEN WHISTLE AND FLUTE
Stitch One
Copyright © George Major 2008

All Rights Reserved

No part of this book may be reproduced in any form,
by photocopying or by any electronic or mechanical means,
including information storage or retrieval systems,
without permission in writing from both the copyright owner
and the publisher of this book.

ISBN 978 1 84748 170 2

First Published 2008 by
ATHENA PRESS
Queen's House, 2 Holly Road
Twickenham TW1 4EG
United Kingdom

Printed for Athena Press

Foreword

I first met George in 1995 when I was invited to visit the Cockney Museum in Stoneleigh. It brought back a lot of memories of my own childhood when talking to George as I then also realised that he had a very similar struggle to survive as I myself had.

George has come a long way since those early days and even with a disability such as his deafness, it did not hinder him. His charity work is commendable and I am pleased to know him. I am also the proud owner of a pearly cap presented to me in 1995.

Q: Why did I choose to support a charity with proceeds from my book?

A: I'm not fully dressed in my pearly whistle and flute without a collecting tin in my hand.

Q: Why support Capital 95.8's Help a London Child?

A: It is a reflection of my childhood. We all need to help right the wrong which takes place on our doorstep.

Prologue

Here I was looking in the mirror feeling very proud of my new pearly suit covered in thousands of pearl buttons. It took me twelve months to hand sew on each button. It's traditional that all pearly kings sew on their own buttons, with each sewn with love.

My mate Bruce pulled up in his jam jar to pick up Granddad Fred, Brian and myself to take us to a pub called The World Turned Upside Down on the Old Kent Road where our other mates had arranged to meet us.

No turning back now, I thought as I was on my way to the jam jar. As I arrived, Bruce was busy giving the jam jar a final polish. As I walked up to him I said, 'Lot of spit and span bullshit you are doing with that jam jar. Have you been in the Kate Karney [army]?'

'Piss off,' he said. 'Anyway, I'm taking royalty in my car so it has to look fit for a king.'

Bruce always had bees and honey (money) and knew how to spend it. He was a car dealer and this Ford Prefect 100E was his best toy. I felt honoured to be chauffeured by Bruce in his pride and joy.

We arrived outside The World Turned Upside Down to begin our celebration party. As I walked in a big cheer greeted me and drinks were shoved in my hand. It was a real smoky old pub, almost as old as the Old Kent Road itself, and was surrounded by lots of Peabody flats occupied by the working class in its Victorian-style buildings.

The beer was flowing freely and not once was I allowed to pay for a drink, as this was to be my night and my mates were not going to have it any other way.

Brian always fancied himself as a singer and he got up and started singing 'When you're smiling the whole world smiles with you' and as you can imagine it got everyone joining in. Then followed songs like 'The Lambeth walk', 'Knees up Mother Brown' and so on.

I decided to have a go at 'Maybe it's because I'm a Londoner'. It was fantastic; the party was in full swing.

My mates had arranged for jellied eels, mussels and dry rolls to be handed around for all to enjoy. Everyone was having a great time in celebration of me taking up my birthright as the Pearly King of Peckham at last. It would have been even better had my Auntie Iris been there with me. She would have been so proud as she was the person who had encouraged me at the age of seven to take up my crown. Unfortunately she was too ill and frail now to be there in body, but she was there in spirit. She had said it was God's intention; at this moment I thought of that and felt that she must have been right and that's why I was here. I was so filled with emotion and I remember thinking the name of this pub summed up my life as a young boy whose life was turned upside down.

I came alive and realised that this was my world, this was what I was born into. I was at home now, I belonged to a family. I was so proud to belong to the family of the pearly kings and queens who stood with me that night. It's really hard to believe that I had taken so long to come to the decision to take up my role as a pearly king. This was it: I would use my role to raise money and increase awareness of the plight of children being abused and ill-treated.

In one sense it was frightening because of my ill-treatment as a child: this would be a reminder of it. On the one hand I wondered whether this memory of my childhood would destroy my vision: what if I came across another boy or girl who had gone through what I had gone through? Would I break down? Would I turn my back on them or would I understand and give that loving hand?

I was now someone, and I made a vow to myself that, if I could help it, no other child would live like I had lived and have to endure what I had endured.

At 10.20 p.m. the bell went for last orders before the pub was to close. Brian stood up on a table and brought everyone to silence and said, 'Raise your glasses to George, the Pearly King of Peckham. Long may he reign!'

Then everyone shouted together, 'Long live the king! Long live the king! Long live the king!'

The king was about to start his reign and, as I listened, the memory of my childhood came flooding back, a childhood I thought I would never survive. The pain was still there but I knew at that moment that I would always extend a loving hand to stem the flow of pain of every child if I could. I was one of a few who had survived and what a life I had, and what a different life I was to live in the future. Now is the time to tell others about those days.

★

Chapter One

My earliest memory as a child was back in 1942 when I was just four years old, travelling to a new home with my father. He was trying to find a tram stop in Nunhead Lane, Peckham in South London.

As I was small and could not walk fast enough, my father scooped me up in his arms and carried me to find the tram stop.

My father was a big bloke the size of a heavyweight boxer. He was six feet tall, which seemed like a giant to me. His hands were rough and calloused, the hands of a working man. They looked like shovels to me, and a thump from him would send you to kingdom come. I know because I experienced it many times.

He wore size eleven boots and his feet always stank, his nose was big and always stood out like a door knocker, and his dark brown hair was going a bit thin on top, about right for a thirty-seven-year-old man.

He had a straight back and a very flat stomach, which was surprising really considering that he drank beer like water from a tap.

Nunhead Lane in South London was made up of cobblestone roads, and the tramlines ran through the centre of the road. That was about all you could see, as the air was full of the London smog, which came in so thick you had trouble seeing where you were going.

I couldn't see all the people but I could hear them all coughing and talking at once, most probably about World War Two, which had escalated very rapidly, and who would be bombed next.

So here I was in the arms of my father walking down Nunhead Lane. As I looked around me everyone who passed close to us in the smog seemed to be dressed in uniforms.

Eventually we found our tram stop and, although I did not know it at the time, we were on our way to another new home, the fourth in as many years. Then suddenly my father dropped me and gave me a clout around my head with his big shovelled hand because I had wet myself on his best 'whistle and flute'.

'You little bastard!' he yelled. With that I started crying, so he gave me another clout around the head. All I could hear was ringing in my ears. I felt rejected.

It was freezing cold and the warmth of my pee on my legs instantly turned very cold. I was shivering and trying hard not to cry again, in case I got another clout. I couldn't understand why my father hated me so much. Why did he have to be so cruel and violent towards me?

My father often aimed at my head when beating me, which at first made my ears go numb, then I would get strange noises develop in my ears like a loud whistling sound, then the whistling would turn into a roar like a train rushing through a tunnel.

The sound was so frightening after a beating about the head; this caused me to hold my tiny hands and arms over my head, so that my body could take most of the blows rather than my head. At least it was less frightening. This was the start of my hearing loss. Even at that young age I felt lonely, unloved and so insecure, and that feeling grew worse through my childhood.

My mother's name was Maud and my father's was George. They got married at the Camberwell Registry Office in Peckham, South London, in 1934.

Both my parents were born and brought up in Peckham; my mother was twenty-four and my father was twenty-nine. There were three children from that marriage: my eldest sister, Violet, who is mentally handicapped; myself – George – and my youngest sister, Joyce. All three of us were born in Colchester Military Hospital in Essex. My father at that time was a regular soldier and they soon got married and got a military house at his army base in Colchester. Perhaps that was the reason why they had married.

The marriage broke down six weeks after my youngest sister, Joyce, was born. This could have been because my father was abroad fighting in the war leaving my mother on her own to raise three children, one of whom was handicapped. She was also missing smoky London.

Our mother abandoned all three of us, leaving us all at the Great West Hatch Public Assistance Home in Essex. Then she disappeared back to London, leaving no forwarding address.

So here we were at our second home at West Hatch, my youngest sister at six weeks, myself at twenty months, and my eldest sister Violet at thirty-three months. Violet, being severely mentally handicapped and diagnosed as an imbecile, was unable to care for or defend herself in any way. Knowing this, I was not going to neglect her; but of course I didn't know then that I was to spend the best part of my life looking out for her.

My father was discharged from the army on medical grounds. He found out that his family had disappeared, and having found us took us out of Great West Hatch Public Assistance Home to bring us back to London.

My father arranged with his sister, who was my Auntie Vi, and her husband, Uncle Fred, to look after my younger sister, Joyce, and my eldest sister, Violet.

Auntie Vi had two children of her own, Stanley and Jean, who were eight and ten at the time. Auntie Vi must have found it very hard and difficult bringing up four children, one of them severely handicapped.

Just a few weeks later, Violet became seriously ill and was admitted to hospital. My Auntie Vi could not cope with Violet's mental illness and the problems that it caused. My sister was having convulsions and having to see the doctor on a regular basis and make frequent visits to the hospital. She was unable to communicate and her eyes were rolling in her head.

Admittedly it was a lot to cope with. Furthermore, Violet was admitted to hospital with pneumonia and also had an operation on her back.

She was then classified as an 'imbecile' with no specific diagnosis, except to say that her eye movement could be nystagmus.

When she was well enough she was admitted to the Fountain Hospital in Tooting, South London, which was a hospital for male and female mental and physically handicapped people, including children.

Violet never came home again; she is now over seventy years of age and has been institutionalised all her life.

That was a problem solved for my father. He never saw her again, and it was as if she was dead as far as he was concerned.

Later, I was able to find her and help her. She had inspired me as a pearly king and as a person. I just wanted to help her and others (more of that later).

My younger sister, Joyce, who was always the lucky one, was now on her own living with Auntie Vi and Uncle Fred, after the tragic deaths of their own children in Boswell Road, Thornton Heath, South London: another problem solved for my father.

Now that left me with my father, open to a future of abuse and beatings. My father and myself had been staying with his eldest half-sister, Auntie Ethel, and Uncle Jack, but we were now leaving Kimberley Avenue, Nunhead, for yet another new home.

I could see a large flame coming towards us. As it got closer I saw this old bloke carrying what looked like an Aladdin lamp with the flame coming from it. He was leading the tram along the tramline, as they did in those days for safety reasons, because of the thick smog.

We boarded the tram and took our seats. I was now feeling colder due to my wee and wet short trousers. I began to shiver even more with the fear of going to another new home.

The seats in the tram being wooden made it even colder with my wee starting to freeze around my legs. The further our tram travelled the more the smog cleared. The tram journey took us to Selhurst Road, South Norwood, a stone's throw from Norwood Junction station in South London.

As we got off for a short walk down the main high street of South Norwood I was amazed as I saw this big clock tower in the middle of the road. I had never seen a clock as big as that before; the middle hand must have been as big as my leg. It was like being in a new world to me.

I was wondering where our new home was. Then, at the bottom of the high street that joins onto Selhurst Road, my father suddenly stopped outside this large Victorian house. 'This is it,' he said, 'your new home.' I looked up at this big house. It looked very impressive from the outside. It had very wide concrete steps leading to a double Victorian front door. It was the first house leading from the high street with its many shops. Opposite the bank was this large clock tower standing gracefully on its own.

As I climbed the large concrete steps, it felt like I was climbing up a mountain, towards the double Victorian front door. I looked over to this graceful clock that was to the right of me. It seemed to be winking at me and saying, 'Come in.' The welcome was to be short-lived. Once we stepped behind the double Victorian door it was not so impressive anymore.

As we walked into the main hallway the first thing that I noticed was the smell. The whole place stank of decay. There was rubbish everywhere and children about my age running up and down the stairs, shouting. As I ventured further in I could feel this very impressive house was just a slum, a run-down place only fit for down-and-outs, though even that was to give them credit.

When I first saw the children I thought, Good, there will be other children to play with. But one of them shouted to me, saying, 'What do you want here?' in a very unfriendly manner.

My father had answered for me and said, 'You mind your own bloody business or I might have to give you a good hiding!' A saddening look of fear rushed into the little boy's eyes as he quickly ran up the stairs and out of my father's sight.

The building was divided into separate rooms, with one family in each room. There were about seven other families living in this Victorian building. There were other people standing about looking at us in an unfriendly way. The children, half naked, were running about the landing and stairs. Some of them were much bigger than me, which made me feel a bit frightened. As we made our way up the stairs to the second floor I saw an open door. I peered into this room and I could see it was supposed to be a kitchen. The smell there was worse than the hall. It was so small that with just three people in there it would be overcrowded.

The only fittings it had in it were an old glass china shallow clip sink and draining board, an old gas cooker that was black with grease, and one old dirty kitchen cabinet. The walls were covered in grease and dust. You could see the dust clinging on to the grease. The floor was covered in oil cloth, the door mats and lino were well worn and in places completely worn away showing part of the floorboards. They were just as greasy and dirty. You could see that it had never been washed. This was the only kitchen for the use of all the families living in this house. Had there been a fire we all would have been burnt alive before reaching the front door.

The room that we were to live in was right next to this filthy kitchen. My father knocked on the door of the room that we were to live in, and it was opened by my father's girlfriend, Rosy Lea. No connection to a 'cup of tea' – her name being cockney slang for tea. Rosy Lea was a tall, slim blue-eyed blonde. She had long legs, and this lovely smile that lit up like a Christmas tree, which made me feel welcomed.

'You must be Georgie,' Rosy Lea said.

I looked at her and said, 'Are you my mum?'

'No, Georgie,' she replied, 'but if you want me to be your mum I will. I always wanted a little boy like you.'

I felt warmth from her straight away, and the fear I felt from my father and this house just melted away for a while. There seemed to be a bond between us right from the beginning.

Rosy Lea was already living here and had agreed that my father and I should come to live with her. This was known as 'over the brush'. In those days, for example, if a couple were living together and not married it was 'over the brush', which was not done in those days; it was frowned on by society. So a slum place like this would be the only place they could get away with living over the brush. Another name for it was living in sin. Being a young boy I didn't know about that sort of thing, so it didn't bother me, and I learned to love Rosy for being my mother.

We entered our room, which we were to sit and eat in, and also sleep. But we were quite lucky, as our room was fairly large and with only three of us using it.

Other families in the house had four or five children all living in one room. Our room had flowered paper on the walls, which was peeling off. It was very dark and shabby. The floor covering was the same as the kitchen but much cleaner; I suppose Rosy Lea had washed it.

The ceiling was high with a creative ceiling rose. Although our room was shabby it was also quite clean. It was lit by a gaslight hanging from the ceiling, with gaslights hanging from the walls. They had to be lit with a match and gave out a dim glow. In those days electricity wasn't readily available to the working class and gas lanterns were the normal things.

There was an enormous window to the front of the room – the only window that overlooked the high street.

The only furniture in the room was two old armchairs, an old sideboard with its doors half hanging off, and a tallboy for storage. There was a double bed in the corner of the room, which was to be shared by all three of us. I don't know if they got up to any hanky-panky, as I was a heavy sleeper and oblivious to what adults do. I was to sleep by the wall so I could never be shoved out of bed.

In the corner was a chamber pot. It was a really nice blue patterned one. We had to use a pot because there was only one toilet. It was on the ground floor that was used by everyone in the house. It was not at all pleasant, it was as dirty as the house, and we probably would have got dysentery if we had used it. Most of the families in the house used a bucket or a chamber pot, and used the toilet to empty the pot, which would result in spilling most of its contents over the seat and floor. That made the room wet, dirty and stinking.

This was to be my home for a few months. It wasn't much, but I believe it was a better place than the Great West Hatch Public Assistance Home in Essex. For the first few days of my living here I was left alone while my father and Rosy Lea went out to work, locking me in the room. They went out very early in the morning, leaving me asleep.

My father was always the first to leave, but because I was a heavy sleeper they did not disturb me and they would return home late in the evening.

I was locked in this room all day long, which was in itself a terrifying experience for me, with no food or heat. I felt so very lonely and frightened. The positive start I had had with Rosy Lea now seemed to be a figment of my imagination. I felt rejected once again; first my own mother had left me and now it seemed Rosy Lea was rejecting me. The house was very noisy; it seemed that the whole street lived here. People were always clattering up and down the stairs, and rushing about in the rooms above, and shouting up and down the stairs. I wished that I could go out and play with the children and run up and down the stairs like they did.

As people passed my door, sometimes stopping, it frightened me, as I thought that any minute someone was going to come into my room and murder me.

I could hear the adults talking while they cooked in the kitchen, and I could smell the hot food being cooked. I was very hungry and the smell of their food just stayed in my nostrils, which made it even worse.

My stomach ached for food and the boredom made me want to use the pot all the time – or worse still, I would fall asleep and wake up shivering.

There was no TV or radio then, just the sound of the other tenants above, who sounded like a pack of live elephants stamping around. I felt sick, hungry and very cold, unable to run around and warm myself up, and as the day dragged on I had to do something to amuse myself. I would stand on the tips of my toes to reach the big window to look at the street below.

From the window I could see the large clock on the tower. My eyes wandered to the main high street, and saw the trams racing by. I would listen to the loud noise that they made over the track lines, at times drowning the noise of the people; but as the trams passed into the distance, the sound of the people in the building would take over again.

It was nice for me to watch all the people going about their daily lives. I noticed an old lady over the road, she was selling newspapers and shouting, '*Evening Standard, Evening News*! Get your papers here… Read all about it!' Every now and then she would stop to chat and laugh with her customers. She had a big smiling face and you could see that she loved every minute of it. For a moment she looked up at me and gave me a wave. It was as if she was saying, 'Come on down and join me.' I wished that I could have done so, after returning her wave.

Then my eyes struck this barrow boy, a market trader to the left of the clock tower, standing by his barrow, which was full of fruit and vegetables. He was wearing a cap, which was a common thing in them days. His age seemed to be catching up on him; his face lit up just like the old lady selling her newspapers. He had big rosy cheeks and his complexion seemed to be used to the cold weather. He wore a long overcoat to keep the cold out. Over his coat he wore a leather apron with a front pocket for his money. As he stood there he was looking so happy as he shouted his wares. 'Last few left!' he was calling, holding up a handful of oranges, with his broad grin spread across his face. There was no need to shout to attract people as he already had a queue of people waiting to be served, but by shouting perhaps it kept his mind off the cold. Fruits and vegetables were scarce, as it was wartime.

South Norwood was a very select part of London in them days so that's why our paper lady and barrow boy stood out more amongst the better-dressed people that they were serving. I was enjoying watching and listening to my paper lady and barrow boy as they carried on shouting; you could see that they were used to it all their life. I was thinking how I would love to do that, not knowing at the time that I would be doing just that very soon.

After a few hours of watching them I became restless. I then ran around the room and pretended I was playing with other children in the house, and that I was selling from a barrow, and then I got exhausted and lay down and cried because I was hungry, tired, lonely and frightened. Then I fell asleep. I woke up feeling wet and found I had peed myself again; this was something I did on a regular basis until I was thirteen. There was no heating on in the room and I was freezing cold and felt miserable. Being cold was one of my abiding memories of when I was a child wherever I lived.

I went back to the window to see if the paper lady and the barrow boy were still selling their wares. Yes, they were still there with the same old smiling faces, and still as fresh as when I had first started to watch them hours earlier. When darkness fell and the gas lamps were lit, it gave the streets this magical atmosphere; it was eerie and magical at the same time.

I watched them until it was time for them to go home. I saw the old lady walking away, in her long dress to her ankles with an old overcoat draped over her shoulder, and she faded into the distance. My heart began to bleed and I started feeling lonely again.

I turned to the barrow boy, who was now packing the last of his empty boxes, then watched him move away with his barrow until he was out of sight. I now felt even more alone, as my only form of entertainment had now disappeared.

I turned back into my room, which was like a prison, and as I looked around me I saw the room was very dark. It was terrifying, the lights outside from the road were casting shadows in the room and it seemed like there were people hiding in the corners of the room and moving about. I thought they were going to jump out at me so I quickly turned back to the window. I was afraid to leave the relative light of the window. As footsteps came along the passage outside my door my heart took an extra beat. I was expecting the door handle to turn and someone to come in to jump on me. My fear was growing with every sound and I was thinking the worst. Again I looked out of the window for some form of comfort, and waiting for me was my own form of fireworks display. I would watch as trams passed, with their passengers chatting amongst themselves. I also enjoyed watching the trams' overhead electric cables from the conductor poles giving off sparks, some bigger and brighter than others. With the glow of the gas lamps, the sparks from the trams and the buzz of people rushing home, it was magical and gave a great atmosphere.

I stood there mesmerised and felt less lonely and frightened, not wanting to turn around into the room and back to the frightening shadows. I was just dozing off at the window when I heard the key turn in my door. My heart was racing, sweat was building up in me as the door opened. I then gave out a loud scream, but there was no need to scream because it was Rosy Lea.

I fell against her long legs and held them tight, sobbing. 'What's the matter?' she asked.

'I'm frightened,' I said.

She moved to light the gas lamps with me in tow; I kept on clinging to her leg. Rosy then sat down and put me on her knee and gave me some apples to eat. She said, 'I'm not going to leave you on your own anymore, Georgie. I am sorry, Georgie,' she said, 'I didn't think to leave you any food. You must be starving – we can't wait for that lot to finish in there.' She pointed to the direction of the kitchen. 'Let's go and get some pie and mash – we can get some for your dad as well.'

Still clutching to Rosy Lea, I took the tram with her to the pie and mash shop.

By now I was beginning to feel much happier and more secure with Rosy. Stepping off the tram, we arrived at the pie and mash shop, with its marble-topped tables and wooden benches each side of the table that seated twelve to a table. Rosy brought over my pie and mash with the hot steam rising from the top. I wolfed it down as if there was no tomorrow, feeling the lovely hot food going to my hungry tummy. As I ate the last spoonful I picked up the plate to lick it dry. 'Do you want another one, Georgie?' Rosy asked. She must have seen how hungry I was. Before I could say thank you, my next pie and mash was in front of me, which was eaten just as fast. I was now full and feeling warmed up from the pie and mash. Rosy could see that I was now full and showing signs of tiredness. On my way home, with Rosy carrying the pies for my father, she put her arms around me and I fell asleep, feeling very contented and happy.

Rosy carried me to our bed and there I slept until morning, waking up to an empty room again. This same loneliness carried on for a few more days, and every day I watched my paper lady and barrow boy from the window.

After a few days Rosy Lea was getting concerned for me. Arriving home one evening her concern turned to my legs, which were chafed where I had wet myself so much and had not washed. She boiled some water and put me into a little tin bath. Tin baths were common in those days, as the poor class had no bathrooms.

She gently gave me a wash. She soaped me all over with her soft hands. She was doing it so gently and I remember feeling very much loved by her. While she was doing this I felt more loved than I had ever been loved before in my short life, not knowing that I would ever be loved like this again as a child. I wanted her to soap me for ever I felt so warm and loved.

She put some ointment on my tiny legs and wrapped me in my father's army coat and sat me on her knee and cuddled me. It was a moment in my life that I felt an excitement of love stir inside of me. A very memorable moment that remains in my life to this day. As she cuddled me, she said, 'I'm not going to leave you on your own anymore, Georgie. I know that your dad doesn't want you to go to the market, but I just can't leave you alone anymore. So tomorrow morning, when your dad's gone to work, you can come with me to the market and help me. Your father doesn't need to know, it will be our secret.'

I was to hold many more secrets in my young life in order to save others and myself from being hurt.

I started to cry as I sat on Rosy's knee, for I was now relieved that I was not going to be alone anymore and that someone was now caring about me. I jumped off her lap and went to the window to see the paper lady. She was gone, but the barrow boy was still there.

I waved to him and for a moment I thought he had waved back shouting, 'Welcome to our wonderful market life, boy.' But when I looked up to the clock tower, the face of the clock seemed to smile at me. I did not understand what a market was, apart from my barrow boy across the road, and Rosy Lea explaining earlier that there were lots of my barrow boys selling in a street. I was so excited and couldn't wait for the next morning to arrive. I was woken by Rosy Lea saying, 'Come on, Georgie, time to go.' It was still the early hours of morning. 'We are off to the market.'

My father had already left for work much earlier, as he had done each day of the week, except Sundays. I did not know what my father's line of work was at the time, but I knew it was not market work, as he really hated markets.

We ran for the tram, which had pulled up half full with people, mostly women. Nearly all of them wore long aprons and shawls wrapped around their shoulders. There was a lot of chatter and they seemed to be talking all at once, and knew each other.

As we neared East Street Market in Walworth Road, South London, other people were getting on the tram with broad grins across their faces. 'Morning, love,' they called on boarding the tram. 'Morning, ducks,' the conductor would say, while he was busy charging for their tickets. Everyone seemed so happy that it gave me a sense of happiness and enjoyment. Better than spending my first four years in an army base and a children's home, or living on my own in our room in South Norwood. I had never seen an early morning life before that had so much friendliness about it. I turned to Rosy Lea and said, 'Are they all going to the market as well?'

'No, Georgie, those ladies wearing shawls are charladies going to work in the city, where they clean offices.'

'Aren't they happy!' I said.

'Yes, Georgie, all early risers are happy.'

Our tram pulled up opposite East Street Market that runs from the Walworth Road to the Old Kent Road, near the Elephant and Castle. The street was packed with market people preparing for a hard day's work. Holding Rosy's hand, I walked with her through the mass of stalls and traders. 'Morning, ducks,' traders called to Rosy. 'Morning, love,' was her reply. I could not believe my eyes – there were all kinds of stalls and barrow boys selling everything from fruit and vegetables to caged animals.

There were cages and cages of puppies, kittens and home-bred canaries. It was noisy, good and exciting, which I loved. What a difference it made from my dull, cold room on my own, just being here surrounded by all the colourful barrows and the streets full of these happy people, some even singing. It just captivated me and I never wanted it to end.

I wanted to dance but was unable to, with every inch taken up with people, barrows and boxes, and the customers had not yet arrived. It seemed to take hours to reach the stalls where Rosy was to work, but finally we arrived and were met by Rosy's father. He looked at me with a big smile on his face and said, 'Good morning, Georgie. Rosy has told me all about you.' He stroked my hair as he talked to Rosy.

Her father had this fixed smile on his face; he was a bit on the fat side with rosy cheeks and blond wavy hair. He was shorter than Rosy Lea, coming up to her shoulders. His skin was tanned and leathery, most probably from being an outside worker in the rain and hail and sunshine all year round.

I had noticed that he was holding Rosy's hand and kissing her a lot, something that I never saw my father do to her. All this was making me feel more secure. Rosy's father's stall was being dressed by him with fruit and vegetables, all the spuds at the front were piled up on top of each other like a stone wall. Next to them the cabbages and cauliflowers were built in the same way, showing the whites of the heads; then the runner beans and the peas in their pods were laid out like pairs of soldiers.

Then the carrots, all cleaned, were laid on top of each other with the green stalk facing out towards you, the colours all coordinating to catch the attention of the customer. People were served from the back of this colourful and striking display, and by the end of the day the lucky customer would get the contents of the display.

My first day was taken up learning to clean the carrots by putting them in a bucket of water and cleaning off the mud, then trimming the cauliflowers at the top to show off the white heads, then cleaning up and running to the café to get tea for Rosy and her father.

For every day that passed my interest was growing. The new day could never come quick enough. Every day as I was learning more I felt that I wanted to live on a market amongst the happiness. I was enjoying the people around me, mostly Rosy and her father, as they gave me a sense of being wanted and loved. I felt that this was home, a home that I did not want to leave. After a while Rosy's father let me have a go at selling and following all that I had heard and picked up from Rosy, her father and other market traders. I would shout out 'my wares'. I had watched in awe as Rosy shouted, 'Come on, loves, best spuds here!' Or, picking up a bundle of carrots, 'Come on, ducks, carrots at half a penny a pound. They make you see in the dark!' You learn to say anything, shouting for a sale.

I was getting on well with Rosy's father but I got on better with Rosy, all the time sharing our secret of me helping her on the market, and I found myself learning to be loyal, which is a high thing in market life.

You learn to stick together; it is all built on learning the secrets of market life. I also knew that if I had told my father about helping Rosy on the market my market days would finish, and no way was I going to risk that. It would mean being locked in that room again.

Rosy continued to take me to the market six days a week. She had a soft spot for me and I for her. She made me happy, she cared for me, she would sew up my grubby clothes, and when the soles of my shoes got worn out she would put cardboard inside to keep out the wet and cold. She would not be much better dressed herself, but at least we were happy and enjoying our market life, and as poor as she was she always had that lovely smile fixed on her pretty face.

Rosy saw in my face how I enjoyed going to the market each day, but always reminded me not to tell my father. I also found markets a great source of entertainment, a place to make friends, a place to socialise and also a place that gave me love. As I walked down the market lane I would stand and stare and listen and learn the patter of the trader, each one of them having this great gift of the gab, talking people into buying whatever they had on offer. Again I would start my selling of carrots, copying what I had learned from listening to the market traders. With Rosy's father shouting in the background, 'Best cabbage of the year!' I shouted, 'The best carrots you've ever tasted – makes you see in the dark!'

I will never forget my first selling experience. I loved it. I was now over five years old, and at this young age I felt the pull of the market life. Even though I didn't know it at the time, this was part of my heritage. 'You are good, Georgie,' Rosy often said, and gave me money – probably only a few pennies, but it meant much more to me. As always, Rosy would call out, 'Come on, Georgie, time to go home!' But I never wanted to rush to go home: why should I? I was enjoying my life there on the market.

On one particular day my attention was fixed on a market trader who was just ready for the kill with a customer, but she was not quite sure whether to buy the shoes she was being offered. 'Come on, ducks, real leather soles, last you a lifetime. Tell you what, I'll give you a free shoe brush, all that, just two shillings to you – have I got your business?'

'OK,' said the old dear who looked like she had just months to live.

Taking my hand for the journey home, Rosy said, 'You love coming to the market, don't you, Georgie?'

'Yes, I really love it,' was my honest reply, but that was coming to an end very soon, much to my disappointment.

Whenever Rosy and my father were together they were always shouting at each other. I don't know what it was about but it did frighten me. The only time Rosy ever shouted at anyone was my father. I was getting closer to Rosy and was enjoying her being my mum. I could not remember my own mother and I felt that Rosy was my mum. Rosy was a nice person and so easy for me to talk to; she was a kind market trader's daughter. She had that sparkle in her eyes and a lot of rabbit to impress you.

She had a gift for the patter and was a no-nonsense woman. If you did upset her she would give as much as she got, as my father would find out. She was brought up herself on the markets and had learnt the hard way about life, but she coped with whatever it threw at her. So in the rows with my father she would get the better of him and he would retreat to the pub, slamming the door behind him, and it would be me she would cuddle after, perhaps to take the fear from me.

I never saw my father much, as I was asleep when he came in. He worked long hours and went to the pub a lot before coming home. It did not bother me much, not seeing my father, as I hardly seemed to see him at all throughout my early years, with him being in the army for the first four years of my life. One evening after arriving home in the late evening we found my father was already waiting at home. Normally, Rosy and I would always get home first. As always I felt very pleased with myself and proud of being part of the market, seeing I was happier than I had ever been. I was so happy; I thought this was my life now and thought it would never end for me.

As my father was waiting in the room, I was so excited at myself that I told my father about my wonderful day at the market. This was the worst thing that I could have done. First I had broken a secret with Rosy and wrecked my chance at going to the market with Rosy. I waited for the worst. My father's eyes filled with rage, and his hair seemed to stand on its ends as he said, 'Say that again!' I froze with fear and guilt. My father was in a rage and hit me very hard over the head. It sent me almost across the room. My head was spinning, my ears were ringing, the frightening sounds had returned.

Rosy came rushing to my aid and picked me up and put her arms around me. I was still in a daze. My father's rage then turned to Rosy. 'Why did you take him to a fucking market?' he shouted. He repeated the same words a few times. 'You know I don't want him anywhere near a fucking market!'

Rosy shouted back that it was terrible to expect a small boy to stay locked in this room all day on his own without food or warmth, and that she was going to take me to the market whether he liked it or not. 'We will see about that,' my father said.

Rosy was now turning towards my father to give back more than he gave her. She lashed out at my father with full force, hitting him on the mouth. Blood started to show from his lip. I was so terrified that he was going to hit her back, but he didn't; he just rushed out holding his handkerchief to his mouth and slammed the door behind him.

For a split second I was proud at my father for not hitting Rosy back. To me that shows a man, as only a coward hits a woman. I was crying really hard. This was my fault for saying that I had been at the market. I then started to cling on to Rosy's coat. 'Don't leave me,' I was crying, 'don't leave me. I'm sorry. I don't want to be left on my own again. I want to come to the market with you. Don't leave me!'

Rosy bent down to me and said, 'Don't worry, Georgie, you can still come to the market. Your father will not get his own way over this. Now, off you go to bed and stop crying. I will care for you. Now you go to sleep while I go to the pub and tell your father that he can't leave you on your own, and that's why I must take you to the market.'

But after falling asleep, crying, I was woken up when they came back from the pub. The row continued into the night, and the tenants were banging on the floor above. *All my fault*, I kept saying to myself. *I must never share a secret again*. With Rosy standing up for me throughout, my father was having none of it.

I lay on the bed holding my hands to my ears to shut out the shouting. I was so frightened that I would be left on my own again, and I was crying because I thought I would not be able to go to the market again. I then drifted into a sleep, with the sound of my ears ringing and hurting. The next morning Rosy woke me, stroking my face. 'Come on, Georgie, we are going to the market.'

I was very relieved. Our market visits carried on every day, and the past experience left me as I started to enjoy my market life as usual; but this enjoyment had to be between Rosy and me because if my father found out there would be hell to pay. Rosy Lea had got the better of my father, and I don't think he liked it. I think he knew that I was still going to the market but pretended that he didn't – maybe to save another cut lip. Rows were still going on whenever they were together, and my father seemed to be getting more and more agitated as time went on. Rosy too was not her usual self.

The rows were now getting worse as the weeks went by. Then, one morning, I was not woken by Rosy stroking my face in a loving way but was woken by my father shaking me and shouting, 'Come on, you lazy bastard, get up. We are moving!'

'Is Rosy coming with us?' was my first response.

'No,' he said. 'Now get dressed, you lazy bastard, get dressed and make it quick. You are coming with me, and you won't be seeing Rosy Lea again. Now hurry up!'

I tried to get dressed slowly in order to delay our departure. I did not want to leave, but if I said that I didn't want to leave I know that I would have got a hiding for saying it. 'Come on, hurry!' my father was now shouting again. When I completed dressing I just stood there frozen, not by the cold but by fear. I stood there frozen like a block of ice, staring at Rosy Lea, hearing those words again in my head, 'You are not seeing Rosy Lea again.' But I wanted to see her again, I wanted her as a mum. I didn't want to leave. At this point, while staring at Rosy, I wet myself. I was thinking of all the good times I had had with Rosy. I did not want to leave her, and would have been happy if my father had decided to leave me with her; but that was not to be.

I knew that I would never see Rosy Lea again or go to the markets, and as the tears began to flow down my cheeks, Rosy came over to me to kiss me and catch the tears running down my face. She held me so tight that for a moment I thought that she would not let go. 'I'm sorry,' she said, 'but if I can I will see you again.'

My father then got hold of my hair and pulled me towards him. I felt as if my hair was going to come away from my scalp. Rosy was calling out as she disappeared from my sight, with my father almost dragging me towards the front door and away from a woman who I had wished was my mum. Little did I know that another nightmare was about to start for me, but this time without a caring mother's support that I had with Rosy. She was the only mother figure I ever had or would ever have again. Little did she know how she had influenced my life.

My father dragged me out of that house away from Rosy. I was crying for Rosy and did not understand why my father was making me leave her. I was heartbroken. She had become a mother to me and I had felt closer to her than my father. This was the second mother to leave me in my short life. As we walked along the road I turned around to look up at the window that I had looked out of so many times, now seeing Rosy Lea standing there alone, crying and looking so sad. I started to cry again and pulled away from my father's hand, but he had tightened his grip. As we rounded the corner and went out of sight of Rosy, my father gave me a belt around the ear and told me to stop being a baby. Dragging myself behind my father, I was struggling with a sack over my shoulder that held all my clothes, some of which had been picked up by Rosy from second-hand stalls at the market, and some belonging to my father.

So now I had a little more than what I had started with when I first arrived. All my belongings I carried felt like a heavy weight on my back. My father had to stop every now and then for me to catch up. I was feeling ill with fright and too hungry to move. In my mind the only thing I wanted to do was to run back to the arms of Rosy Lea. My father was shouting, 'We ain't got all day, now keep up!'

This was proving very difficult for me with my heavy sack, still crying for Rosy Lea, and I had no motivation to hurry away from her. I was just hoping that this was a bad dream. I felt as if I had lost everything in this world, alone again. Rosy had given me so much love, so much caring, so much fun. Now it was fast disappearing from my life. Now I was heading to Thornton Heath in South London; but this move was to be my biggest nightmare – a nightmare that gave me a nightmare to even write about it.

Chapter Two

From the high street of South Norwood it took my father and me a good hour to walk to Boswell Road, Thornton Heath, South London. This would normally take fifteen minutes but I was in no hurry to leave Rosy Lea, and I also dragged behind my father, struggling with the sack of clothes over my shoulder. He had to stop every now and then in order for me to catch up with him and the two suitcases he was carrying. He was shouting, 'We ain't got all day – now bloody keep up!' This was very difficult for me with the heavy sack that I had to carry.

I was a little scared of the idea of living in yet another new place where I had never been before, and I was still heartbroken about leaving Rosy Lea. Finally we had turned into Boswell Road where we were to live and this was the road and home that was to witness the start of my traumatic childhood. It was also to be the start of my ducking and diving in order to survive.

On either side of Boswell Road was a long row of terraced houses, with every sixth house having a side alley that led you to the back of the houses. Each house had a pretty front door that made the road appealing and welcoming. There were about one hundred houses in Boswell Road, which all looked the same except for the paintwork of each house. They were painted in a different colour; some were blue, green, cream and black, and looked very well looked after, with nice clean fronts and pretty clean curtains on the windows – a very big difference, not like I was used to having. At first I thought my father must have come into a lot of money to be able to live here.

As I walked along Boswell Road I felt intimidated, as this was a very well-to-do area, with no kids half naked and dirty here, so we must have stood out a mile, especially me with my dirty raggedy clothes, and my feet hanging out of my old second-hand shoes.

The house we were to live in was halfway down Boswell Road, and finally we arrived at our front door. My father opened the front door with the key that he had in his pocket. As he opened the door facing us was a short passage leading to a flight of stairs. 'We are upstairs,' said my father.

I dropped the heavy sack that I was carrying and ran up the stairs, leaving my father still standing at the front door. I ran into the top room facing the stairs and looked out of the window overlooking the back garden. Then I came out onto the back landing and into a hall that led to the kitchen, which was half the size of the one at Rosy Lea's place. Then, next to that, there was a toilet.

From the hall I went down one step, then up two steps going towards the front of the house. On my left I peeped into another room then finally into the front room. I was observing everything and wondering which bedroom would be mine. Now I looked out of the front room window as my father came into the room and I said to him, 'Who else is living with us?' I was expecting to meet another Rosy Lea, hopefully.

'Just us two for now,' he said.

When my father spoke to me he would never call me by my name. If he were in a bad mood he would call me anything from a 'useless shit' to a 'trouble-causing bastard'.

'Where am I going to sleep?' I asked, searching for an answer from him. He pointed to the next room, which led to the middle room next to the front room. In it was a single iron-framed bed. On the floor was worn-out lino; the walls were covered with a dark, dirty, patterned wallpaper with a picture rail around the top. It had an iron-framed fireplace and then, at the side of the fire breast, were two old built-in wardrobes.

I was excited at the thought of having my very own bedroom: no more sleeping with anyone, which pleased me. There was no handle on the bedroom door, so I was safe from being locked in here. My father's bedroom was to be the front room, which also had an iron fireplace. There was lino in the centre of the floor with painted edges, and a double bed that he was to sleep in, and a small chest of drawers. The walls looked the same as my bedroom but a bit cleaner.

The other back room was to be used as a sitting room. It had a small wooden table and four chairs. Then there was a sideboard and a fireplace, which had a built-in oven and a small fire in the middle that was used to heat up the top of the oven and a hotplate to boil the kettle. Just like the other rooms, the patterned lino was also old and worn, crying out to be cleaned.

The passage and stairs leading to the front door had lino down the middle with painted sides. So often I had wished that the stairs had carpet and not that hard lino, because I was thrown down them enough times, with nothing to cushion my fall.

As for the kitchen… well, if you had put a standard bath in it you would have filled the room up, that's how small it was, and in this very small kitchen there was a dirty old electric cooker, a six-inch-deep brown glazed sink with a wooden draining board, and that was it.

This was our new home, a flat within the house, which my father had rented for five shillings a week. There I was to live and get a taste of a traumatic childhood.

The flat below us was rented by a couple who were to change my life and became my friends. The house front door was shared with the tenants downstairs, and there were no locks on our door or the tenants' door downstairs, so really it was like living in one house; the only difference was we had our own kitchen. But it was like living in a house; you could hear what was going on downstairs, and what was going on upstairs.

Like where I had lived in South Norwood, the only means of light was by gaslights. Every room had a gaslight, and the dull glow from it would make the place look haunted; even the small toilet had a gaslight, and the passageway had just enough light to enable you to see your way up or down the stairs.

My father's family had found this flat for him and pooled together to get a few bits and pieces of essential furniture, which was not very much. All the furnishings were grubby and in a shabby state. There was no television in those days, just a radio run by battery that had to be charged every two weeks or so. My father seemed very pleased with our new home.

After my first night sleep of tossing and turning, and feeling upset at the thought of not being with Rosy Lea and the adventures at the market, I woke up to find myself on my own again, my father had left for work. So I dressed myself, as I often did, and decided to explore my new surroundings. As I was walking around the local streets I had the feeling that people were staring at me, obviously because I looked out of place in the posh neighbourhood with my torn and dirty clothing, and my uncombed hair. I can never remember having my hair brushed by my father. Rosy Lea did brush my hair now and then, but not on a regular basis. As people stared at me, I would say, 'Ain't you seen a kid before?' Deep down I really wanted to meet up with some of the local kids and play with them. Often I could hear the kids playing outside while I was locked in the room in South Norwood.

I needed to find other kids to cut out the boredom and have some friends to talk to; this seemed difficult in this posh neighbourhood. But I could see that there was lots of community spirit, as I had explored around the local streets and the back alleys. Doors were left open and the keys to the front doors were in the letter boxes hanging on a piece of string; if you wanted to let yourself in you would pull the string from the letter box and use the key hanging on the end. At the rear of the terraced houses there were gates between the back gardens to the next-door neighbours'.

I was really bored. I had not spoken or seen anyone since six o'clock the evening before, as my father had left me on my own to go to the pub, so I had put myself to bed.

I was getting very hungry and wanted food so my mind was taken from finding kids to play with to finding food. Then I saw a baker's horse and cart delivering bread to the local houses. I waited for the baker man to deliver his bread to a house then crept up to the baker's cart and stole a loaf of bread. At that moment someone shouted, 'Look thief!' I was terrified and just ran, not knowing where I was running to, and finished up on an old bomb site, where I sat down to eat my bread.

I had eaten that loaf of bread as if there was no tomorrow. Having finished all my bread and cured my hunger, I lay back on the rubble of the bombed site, thinking of Rosy Lea and how much I was going to miss her and her father, also no more going to the markets. My father would be pleased, and the thought of it all made me cry with deep sadness.

As I lay crying I felt someone touching me. I froze with sheer fright, as I looked up there was this middle-aged man with a humpback. He was touching my leg and moving his hand towards my private parts. I knew this was wrong and I tried to move away but he seemed determined to touch my private parts. Then, with all my strength, I kicked at his private parts as he hovered over me. As he held himself where I had kicked him, I could see pain and agony he was feeling written all over his face, but I didn't care, and took that opportunity to escape and run as fast as I could.

I finally found my way home and safe, but as I had no key to our front door my only chance of getting in would be if the downstairs tenant were in, so that I could get to the safety of my own home.

I gave the door a very demanding single knock. It was opened by the tenant downstairs, who was to change my life. The door was opened by a small lady who was very thin and partly crippled, she had large clear blue eyes that looked very welcoming and friendly. She had a round-like sweet face with short hair that was light brown in colour. She wore a full dress and a flowered apron. She had tiny hands and feet, and stood about 4' 9" from head to toe. When she spoke her voice was very kind and gentle. 'Can I help you?'

I replied, 'I live upstairs.'

She then said, 'Oh, you must be Georgie.'

'Yes,' I said, 'I'm here with my dad.'

'I know,' she said, 'I have heard all about you. Do you like your new home?'

'Yes, its all right, I suppose, but a bit of a posh street.'

'Oh, it's not, really, but you will get used to it. But always remember when you knock on the front door it's one knock for downstairs and two knocks for upstairs… Can you remember that?'

'Yes,' I said.

'You look very tired,' she said. 'Would you like a drink?'

'Yes please,' I said, and followed her to her back sitting room.

As I followed her, I noticed how slow she walked, and that her hands were a funny shape. The knuckles and balls of her hand were sticking out and you could see that she was in constant pain. The glasses that she was wearing made her eyes look even bigger than what they were. As she moved you could see the pain in her eyes, that's why she must have explained to me how important it was that I remembered, one knock for downstairs and two knocks for upstairs – to save her walking to the front door unnecessarily and so avoid further pain.

She sat on one of the two easy chairs; the one she sat on had a lot of cushions to raise her higher in a sitting position. The other chair was a rocking one, which was for her husband. She invited me to sit in the rocking chair, and I enjoyed rocking in it as she was talking to me. Under the window overlooking the side of the garden was this big wooden table that almost took up half the sitting room. I noticed it was spotlessly clean, and it must have given her a lot of suffering and pain to keep it like that. The furniture was old but in good condition, and she had proper curtains at the window. I had never seen proper curtains at a window before, but realised that it made the room look and feel cosy; not like the other house we lived in, where we had put any old rags at the window during the blackouts.

Again she reminded me that one knock on the front door meant that it was for her flat, and two knocks was for us upstairs. She explained that she used to have a string tied to her key so that her doctor, husband and daughter or friends could let themselves in, obviously to save the pain that she would get by going back and forth to the door; but when the last upstairs tenants left after many years she removed the key from the string while she got to know the new tenants, who were my father and myself.

It was not uncommon in those days for many houses to have their front door key on a piece of string, because everyone felt quite safe; also we never had anything of value for anyone to rob.

I had started to feel at home with her as she talked to me and I felt how warm and kind she was towards me. Her skin looked so soft, and straight away I felt that this woman was kind and gentle. She told me that her name was Iris Thompson. Here I was, talking to and facing the woman who was to change my life and become my friend and my angel, who I called 'Auntie Iris'.

After being offered another drink and some biscuits, it felt like we had been talking for a long time. I was feeling quite relaxed talking to this woman, who had a way with children. I felt comfortable enough to begin sharing my feelings about Rosy Lea, and how I was going to miss her and the markets. She was listening sympathetically and said how sorry she was to hear my story. She understood and said, 'You will soon settle down and make some new friends around here and hopefully be happy.'

That word – happy – was to prove not the right word for me. Mrs Thompson must have realised that I was very hungry, as she kept getting up to get me bits of food and watching me wolfing it down.

She had given me bread with home-made jam on it. Seeing how quickly I had eaten it, she then gave me cakes, and still for all the food that she was giving me she watched me eat it all like there was no tomorrow. She was looking at me with sympathy and understanding. I must have spent two or three hours with this small angel of a woman, talking and sharing with her the details of my short five years of life and how I felt. Then her husband, Mr Alfred Thompson, walked in through the door with their only daughter, Deirdre.

Deirdre was on the large size and about a couple of years older than me with a reddish face. She wore glasses that, like her mother's, made her eyes look bigger than they really were. Mr Thompson, whom I was to later call 'Uncle Alf', was a real handsome man with the look of Errol Flynn and a pencil-like moustache. He was about 5' 9" tall with black wavy hair.

He was a real gentleman, kind and loving to his wife and daughter. As he cuddled his wife with a gentle hold and a loving kiss, I thought at that time how lovely it was to see it. I had never seen this before and it made me feel so secure with this family.

Mr Thompson was a very good plasterer and was respected by all who knew him. He always worked hard and supported his family to a high standard. So I was very pleased at meeting my new neighbours and future friends. I found out later that Mr and Mrs Thompson had a stillborn son who would have been my age, and I think that is why a bonding had started between us.

Mr Thompson had told me how he had made a very small coffin for his only son and buried him because they could not afford a proper burial; maybe they took me on as a replacement to their own lost son, and I hope that I had given them a replacement of that love.

I then went upstairs to our flat, which was empty, with no father to greet me. As usual he was still at work; just as well I had eaten downstairs, because there was no food in the cupboard. Even at that age I felt lonely, unloved and insecure, and that was to prove more so in my early young days ahead of me.

I lay on my bed and felt happy that I had met Mr and Mrs Thompson. My thoughts were, What a lovely family. The thought of them cuddling and kissing each other made me wonder if my parents had been like that – able to show affection to each other in that way. I began wondering if my mum was small and kind like Mrs Thompson or if I would even meet my mum. The thoughts filled me with emotion which led to more tears and the feeling of wanting and needing a mom, one like Mrs Thompson, a mum who could love me and care for me. I cried louder and shouted out that I wanted my mom, and I wanted her now, but at the time this was not to be. Then I drifted off to sleep.

I woke up in a room filled with complete darkness. It was quiet and lonely as my father had not come back home, and if he had I would not have known, as I was fast asleep.

I tried to find my way to the kitchen because I was starving again. As I tried to find my way along the passage, feeling along the wall, my hand had caught my father's overcoat that was hanging on the wall. Not knowing what it was it frightened me. I thought it was the man with the humpback. In my fright I ran, and forgetting that there was the two steps that led from the passage to the upstairs landing, I fell and must have made a big noise and screamed. At that moment, Mr Thompson had run up the stairs to see what was wrong, using his torch for light. He picked me up and shouted my father's name with no response; then he carried me downstairs to their dining room, which was lit with the gas lanterns.

Mrs Thompson, with her arms outstretched, took hold of me and Mr Thompson placed me on her lap. There she cuddled me and rocked me and said, 'Do you want something to eat?' She must have known that I was starving again. So once again I was being fed by Mrs Thompson, who must have known that you can't leave a young child like that without food; but in them days this form of child neglect was common, and people were afraid to comment on it, even more so if they knew the child had a big father like mine.

For a few days this was the way in which I lived, and when I did ask my father if I could have something to eat because I was starving, he would reply, 'Get yourself a bit of bread – it's all we've got for now.'

He was like a bear with a sore head and I felt he didn't want me there. I knew I was in the way, so I just sat there and didn't say anything to him. When I told him about our new neighbours he just grunted, for he did not care if I was there or not, and neither was he interested in our new neighbours. My father just wanted his night out in the pub to drink himself silly.

Being left alone in our new flat was not so worrying to me this time because I was not locked in, and I felt some security knowing that Mr and Mrs Thompson were living downstairs. Within two or three weeks my father had got himself a new job. I think it was to give himself more leisure time or maybe more time in the pub.

His new job was driving an open-back lorry. He was able to drive because he had learned while in the army. I was glad that he had this job because it enabled him to take me with him, so I was no longer left on my own. He was either told about leaving me on my own by Mr and Mrs Thompson or he was afraid that he would not get away much longer with leaving me on my own all day and night, especially in this type of neighbourhood – knowing he could not lock the door to keep me in.

But whatever the reason, it suited me because at least I was out and about and less bored by being stuck at home. In fact, going out in my dad's lorry was exciting to me. It was like sitting on the top deck of a double-decker bus, where I could see everything that was going on around me. We travelled all over London, stopping to deliver building materials, and besides that it gave me an opportunity to go in the cafés with my father to eat. Although I mostly had lemonade and sandwiches, it was good.

We would go all over London, going west, east, north and south, and this gave me a chance to see more of the city. This joy of being in my father's lorry six days a week driving every day was an adventure to me.

This went on for a few weeks and I must have been the most travelled young boy in London at the time.

As it was nearing the end of the working day, my father was unloading the last of his orders down the Old Kent Road. I noticed nearby a few people wearing clothes which were covered in buttons. I was curious and took a keen interest, as I had never seen anyone dressed like that before, and I didn't understand what they were about; but I realised a couple years later that they were in fact pearly kings and queens.

Two of them approached my father and began arguing with him. I thought this was strange at the time. Why should my father be arguing with them pearlies. Then one of them pointed at me and I became afraid and thought any minute now my father was going to have a punch-up with them. He was the biggest of them all, but fortunately it never happened, my father walked away from them to get into our lorry.

As my father drove away I kept staring at them, mostly admiring their pearly suits, which seemed to fascinate me. Then the same two pearlies who'd been arguing with my father were staring back at me and pointing their fingers at me with their eyes fixed on me. As we drove out of sight from them by turning a corner, I turned to my father and said, 'Why were you shouting with those people?' trying to find out more.

'None of your bloody business – and don't ever go near people dressed like that!'

'Why?' I asked; but he gave me a clout around my head and said, 'Look, if you say another word I will give you a bloody good hiding. Now shut up!'

I did as I was told; I knew what would happen if I did not. I was only young, a five-year-old child, but this altercation stuck with me. I wondered why should my father be arguing with those people, and then shouting at me because I was asking questions about them…

Meeting those pearlies had put my father in a very bad mood, and he seemed to know them very well, but I was hoping that we would not be meeting them again as it was really frightening for me at the time. Going out with my father in the lorry made me feel closer to him, even though he never talked to me. When he did speak to me it was to shout, but I had got used to the shouting, with my mind fixed on enjoying the scenery and the hustle and bustle of the London streets.

There were very few cars around; in fact Boswell Road would be lucky to have two cars parked in the street, with yellow lines not thought of in those days. If you parked on the street in the hours of darkness you had to leave your lights on. That was law then. We still had mostly horses and carts delivering beer to the public houses and coal to homes that could afford to buy it. Then we had the milkman, the baker and the greengrocer all delivering with their horse and cart; some days you would see more horses than people.

My journeys with my father on the lorry seemed to come to an end a short while later and I never met them pearlies again while out in his lorry. So I was back on my own again. My father must have got another job, which did not allow him to take me with him, but it now gave me more time to see Mrs Thompson. Our friendship was growing by the day, as I was staying in her flat almost all day, watching her doing her housework with the pain showing on her face. I watched her put out the washing on the line, holding the pegs in her mouth while she held her painful hands on the washing line. This I found her doing all the time without complaining but with a loving heart.

I began to help her by polishing the floor for her, helping her to sit down and to get up. I learned how to make cups of tea for her, clean her windows, and would do all I could to reduce her pain.

She would put me on her lap and gently cuddle me, stroke my hair and talk to me. I just so wanted her to be my mum. She was treating me not only as if I were her son, but as a real human being, and Mr Thompson was becoming more like a father to me, which often made me wonder how things would have turned out if he could have kept me to himself as he was doing as much for me was he would have done for his own son, had he lived.

I had been living in Boswell Road for about nine weeks and up to then did not know that my father's sister, Auntie Vi, and her husband, Uncle Fred, were living only a few doors away with Joyce, my youngest sister. They had just lost their son, Stanley, and Jean, their daughter, in an accident involving a runaway horse and cart that went into the back of the car that Uncle Fred was driving, killing both children.

My father never told me that I had an auntie and a sister living in the same street as myself. It was only a time later that I had found this out. But I thought, Why should I bother about who lives where and when? I've got Mr Thompson and Mrs Thompson, and I now started calling them 'Auntie' and 'Uncle' anyway.

I had been helping Auntie Iris with her housework when she asked me to sit on her lap. As always, I made the best effort to place myself on her lap lengthways in order not to cause her any pain when I got on her lap. She always cuddled me, and as she did I could see the pain in her face, so I lessened her grip by pushing her arms away from me, but held her arms gently, as I thought this would ease the pain that she was having.

We stayed like that for quite a while. I heard her sniffle and felt her body shudder. I turned to look up at her, my loving angel, and asked, 'Why are you crying?'

She then responded and asked me, 'Are you all right, Georgie?'

I felt a little puzzled, and not sure how to answer, so she then said, 'I just don't want to lose you.'

Trying to reassure her I said, 'I am not going anywhere, I'll be all right.'

What she meant by those words – 'I don't want to lose you' – I don't know. Perhaps she was worried about the war and the London Blitz, as this was still going on, and not a night went by without the air-raid siren coming on and having to take shelter with her and Uncle Alf at our neighbour's house. She was worried, knowing I had no loving mum or dad to protect me and be concerned about my safety or well-being during the air raids.

I had dreaded the lonely time left to save myself, and also my fear of the bombs, but Auntie Iris and Uncle Alf were my guardian angels. At least they cared for me... or did Auntie Iris mean something else? Did she know something that I didn't?

I always went to Auntie Iris when I was desperately hungry or cold, but my lonely days spent with Auntie Iris were soon to turn to a hide-and-seek game. My life was about to change again.

It was Sunday morning when everyone was at home and resting and not working when I heard two very loud knocks on our front door. I had remembered Auntie Iris saying one knock for downstairs and two knocks for upstairs. This was the first time anyone had knocked two times since we lived here. My first thought was, Perhaps Rosy Lea wants to come and live here. This would be great because then I would have two mums, Auntie Iris and Rosy Lea.

I had rushed downstairs to open the front door but when I opened the door it wasn't Rosy Lea standing there with her suitcases in both hands, as I had hoped. No, it was a woman I had never seen before.

She said, 'I am your Auntie Hilda.' Hearing this caused my brain to lock. I could not blink from looking at her. 'Is your father in?' she asked. This most certainly was no Mary Poppins standing there to click her fingers and all would be well; no, in fact she was quite the opposite. The woman standing there was to be my nightmare – someone you would rather forget.

She was my father's youngest sister. She was tall, like my father, and as I stared up at her she looked like a skinny giant; she was so skinny that if she stood behind a lamp post you wouldn't be able to see her.

She had this large pointed flat nose, her short brown mousy hair flapped around her ears, and her cold sharp blue eyes were boring into me.

She repeated her question, but in a very loud aggressive voice this time. 'Is your father here? I'm your Auntie Hilda!' she said, and brushed past me.

'Come on up, Hilda!' my father called from the top of the stairs. As her lanky body cast a shadow in the hallway, even the spiders seem to run from her in fear. My only first thought was that she looked and sounded like a witch, without her broom and black cat.

I seemed to know from that moment that this woman was going to be a nightmare. That initial thought I will never forget. She looked older than her age of forty-seven years, as she climbed our stairs I followed her and felt a cold shiver come all over me. I was wondering to myself, What on earth is she doing here? To my horror I was to find out very soon.

As soon as she reached the top of the stairs, she took full charge of the flat. The first thing she did was to give me a new name – 'Melsham'. Looking in the *Oxford Dictionary* years later, I could not find a meaning to that name. It had no meaning, it meant nothing, and that's what I was to her: nothing.

'You, Melsham,' she said, 'you are sleeping with your father.' She ordered my father to take my iron bed out of my room, and replace it with the double bed that my father had been using in the front room, with its saggy mattress.

My iron bed was then put in the front room, which she laid claim to as her bedroom. With sarcasm in her voice, she said, 'Joyce – my darling – will sleep in my room.' I had not yet met my sister, Joyce, who had lived a few doors down the road. Auntie Hilda had hardly ever spoken to me, but when she did she referred to me as 'Melsham'. I just couldn't understand why it was necessary to give me a new name.

So once again I was to share a bedroom and bed with my father. Just when I was enjoying being on my own in my own bed, Auntie Hilda had to come along and change things.

Unknown to me, a family conference had taken place and it had been decided by the family that Auntie Hilda would come and live with us so she could look after me and my sister Joyce, who was her pet love.

Little did I know then that she would stay for many years, and they were many, many, painful years for me – physically, emotionally and mentally.

My sister Joyce had already had a lot of contact with Auntie Hilda due to Auntie Vi and Auntie Hilda seeing each other a few doors along, and they were very close.

Due to their regular visit and my auntie's close relationship, Joyce had become a firm favourite of Auntie Hilda before she had even met me. I was happy that my sister was coming to live with us, as it meant that I would have someone to play with and cut out the lonely time spent on my own. This hope was to be short-lived, because Auntie Hilda was to keep Joyce close to her and push me out, which really divided us for many years after.

Later that day, Auntie Hilda ordered my father around, getting him to move this, move that, move this and so on, which he dared not question.

My Auntie Hilda had not said a word to me and passed me by as if I was a part of the furnishing; not once did she look at me, either. This made me feel even more rejected than I had ever been. I wanted to shout and scream, 'I am here, I am not part of the furniture and my name is Georgie, *not Melsham*!' But if I did, my father would have dealt with me.

There was another two knocks at the door. Fear took over, and I was reluctant to answer it this time just in case it was another Auntie Hilda.

Auntie Hilda looked at me with her cold staring eyes. She didn't actually tell me to go and open the front door, but you could see it in her cold staring eyes. I made my way as slowly as I could, full of dread, but luckily as I opened the door it was my Auntie Vi and Uncle Fred with my sister, Joyce. Auntie Vi was carrying some of Auntie Hilda's other belongings, and Uncle Fred was carrying her singer sewing machine. Phew, what a relief!

Auntie Hilda was a dressmaker and earned her living by making all kinds of women's clothing. Her work was brought around to her, mostly from the Old Kent Road. This would mean that she would be indoors most of the time, to my disappointment. But at least it would give my father added extra income for running the home.

As I looked at my Auntie Vi for the first time, I saw she was completely different to her sister, Auntie Hilda. Her hair was golden and draped to her shoulders. She had a round face with a lovely smile that seemed to make her even prettier and friendly. She had an average build and was about 5' 6" tall and nearing fifty in age. I had taken to her straight away; she was like a princess, whereas Aunt Hilda a witch. Uncle Fred, who stood an inch taller than his wife, was a very handsome man, with straight black hair and an average build. Then there was my sister, Joyce, who was much taller than me even though she was eighteen months younger. She was attractive and slim – mostly bones – with a very pale complexion.

'Come up,' Auntie Hilda had ordered, and I had followed them up the stairs. Joyce kept looking back at me and smiling, and I was returning the smile. 'Now you come with me, darling,' Auntie Hilda had said to Joyce. Which she quickly did, but Joyce was still smiling at me, which pleased me.

Auntie Hilda pulled Joyce behind her to break the eye contact between us. Auntie Hilda kept on saying to my father and Auntie Vi and Uncle Fred how good Joyce was. All I could hear was Joyce this, Joyce that, and this upset me, as I had been thinking how great it was to have my sister with me. I thought we would be a happy family, but no this was not to be.

I watched Auntie Hilda unpacking Joyce's bags and noticed that she had lots of nice clothes and toys; she had obviously been well looked after. Not like me; I had no toys and only had the clothes that I stood up in, and small number of other second-hand clothes, but nothing like what my sister had.

When Auntie Vi and Uncle Fred had left, Auntie Hilda said to my father, 'Tell him to go out and play on the streets.' She did not talk to me or even look at me, so my father told me to bugger off. I skipped downstairs to see Auntie Iris. I just had to get away and talk to someone who cared about me I told Auntie Iris what had happened and how scared I was. Picking me up and putting me on her lap, which was very painful for her, she gave me her usual cuddle and said in a very sweet gentle voice, 'You will be all right, Georgie, your father needs someone to help care for you and your sister.'

I looked up to her face as my tears were rolling down my cheeks. 'She hates me! She hates me! She doesn't even look at me or talk to me, she calls me "Melsham". My name is not Melsham. I need answers to questions that go running through my mind, like, "Am I bad?" Is that why she won't talk to me? Why didn't my father tell me she was coming here to live and order us about, and make things worse?'

I looked at Auntie Iris for the answers to my searching questions, and then explained that I'd tried to be so nice and to please her, but she still hated me. Why?

I noticed that the more that I was thinking and talking about Auntie Hilda, the more I could feel my body tightening up in fear. My hands started to form into a fist ready to fight my way out of the house. This feeling only began to change with reassurance as Auntie Iris told me that all would be well. Then I began to feel a little bit better and calmed down.

Uncle Alf, seeing how upset I had been, said, 'Come on, Georgie, let's go out for a walk.' Holding my hand, he took me to the local park so I could play on the swings and the see-saw. Then we went off to the local sweet shop to get me some sweets, and his usual five-in-a-packet Woodbine cigarettes, which he often smoked.

He always brought his cigarettes in a packet of five, but I never understood why. As we were walking back, with Uncle Alf still holding my hand like he was holding the hands of his lost son, he started to explain more about the reasons why Auntie Hilda was the type of woman she was. He explained, 'She is a maiden aunt, Georgie, and only ever had one boyfriend that she loved, who was cruelly taken from her some years ago when he died of TB.' This was a known killer in them days. 'It has left her afraid to love another man; in fact she's grown to distrust men; perhaps for other reasons she also don't trust or like boys like you.' My father must have explained this to him when drinking with him in the local pub just around the corner to where we live.

Having heard this, I thought that perhaps I could try and win Auntie Hilda's trust by doing my best to please her; then perhaps she might begin to like me. When we arrived home I took myself upstairs to Auntie Hilda and took hold of her hand and smiled at her. She pulled her hand away from me as if I had done some dreadful thing. 'Go away!' she yelled, and I watched her to see if she had a smile on her face, but no it was not to be. I was very disappointed at her reaction; she had that cold look in her eyes as she stared towards me. I was still determined to try and please her, so I followed her to the kitchen and watched her make a cup of tea, six heaped spoonfuls of tea leaves in a small teapot. Then she poured the boiling water into the teapot and I watched her stir it like soup. She then poured the tea into her cup, and it came out black, as if the tea was in full mourning. Then she put the milk in, which could not have been more that a teaspoonful, then stirred it, with no sugar. Had she had left the teaspoon in the cup, the teaspoon would have stood up on its own!

All the time that she was making her tea she had a cigarette hanging from her bottom lip. Not once did she look at me or talk to me. I felt sick. This was a day I shall never forget, as if a sudden curse had entered my life. She then walked into the sitting room, while I followed, with her fag still hanging from her lips and the ash still clinging to the end for dear life. She still did not acknowledge me. She then put her cup of tea on the small dining table and picked up Joyce and put her on her knee.

She started to talk to my father. She was telling him that he had to get his life in order and that no women were to be brought to the house. His wages had to be handed over to her so she could look after the family.

I remember my father arguing with her and told her he would see that she had enough money but he would never hand over his wages to any woman. She then pulled out her packet of John Players cigarettes and lit a fresh fag from the still burning dog end of the last fag. I watched her smoke that fag, she then pulled out another new fag, and did the same. This was how she smoked – like a long chain, from the time of waking up in the morning until the time of going to bed. During the seven days of the week she would use seven sticks of matches, one for each day to light her first fag. She had a constant smell of stale cigarettes about her and there was a sour sickly stench on her breath, which I did not like. She also had this horrible cough, and she often coughed with the fag still hanging from her mouth, as if it was glued to her bottom lip. Without coming up for a breath of life, she would continue to cough, and sometimes I would think that at any minute she would fail to take another breath and stay alive. It was just frightening to watch; she only ever smoked John Players untipped. I often thought that it was because she must have liked the picture of the sailor on the cigarette packet. From her upper lip a nicotine stain travelled up her nose to her forehead, and then to the centre of her hair, which made her even more frightening to look at.

This was the very person who was to share in my upbringing, giving me no security or love, only misery and heartbreak. So here she stood, almost six foot of her, with her worn down shoes and grubby little apron with a packet of cigarettes in it, where she kept her stash of John Players cigarettes – which soon filled the whole flat with the smell of tobacco and smoke. There was ash on the floor in spots where she had stopped to cough and it had fallen from her lips.

Having put myself to bed with still no word uttered from Auntie Hilda, or even a glance from her, I lay on my bed to be shared with my father. I was thinking to myself, I could be dead for all they care! And with the arrival of Auntie Hilda, I was wondering if she could just go away and leave us, like every other woman in my life had. I wanted her to go away and Rosy Lea to come back and live with us.

It was a nice flat, and I was sure Rosy Lea would love it there. I was thinking that I would go to the market the next day and ask her to come and live with us, and maybe Auntie Hilda would go away. But then I remembered Rosy Lea saying that she always wanted a boy. I was not sure if she would want a girl, and I did not want my sister to go away again. My mind was full of all these thoughts racing around.

My bedroom door was open and I overheard Auntie Hilda and my father talking. Auntie Hilda was saying that I needed to be taken in hand and was out of control, and should be taught to do as I was told. My father was agreeing, and said he knew how to handle a little bastard like me. Auntie Hilda told my father that he would have to be the one to discipline me, and if she found out that I had done wrong, my father was to act at once because she could not handle me.

With no hesitation my father had agreed, and said that if I did wrong then he would come down on me hard. 'Make sure you do,' she said. 'You will have to use a very hard hand with him. He has got a wilful look in his eyes, that Melsham, and I don't trust him as far as I can see him. It's Joyce who we should care for more, because she is a girl, and also Vi and Fred like her as well.'

I had heard enough and covered myself in bed with my hands over my ears. I just didn't want to listen to anymore. My stomach was churning with terror and I wished that this were some bad dream that would soon go away – but no; that terror was a premonition of what was to come.

When my father came to bed I was still awake. He had been to the pub and came home stinking of stale beer and burping like a pig. As he climbed into bed, the smell was even worse with the sweat of his body hovering over me. He had pulled the only thin blanket from me, as I tried to pull some of the blanket from him to try to recover the warmth that I had before he came to bed. He was too strong for me to recover any part of the blanket. I was now shivering, so I decided to move nearer to his body to get the rays of heat from him, only to be met with a thump from his elbow.

I was tossing and turning and trying to get some of the thin blanket over me. Many a time I was cold, without any blankets, as my father would turn over and take the thin, papery blanket with him. He also often had his old army coat over him, so he was all right but I was freezing. I would pray for a good hot summer, but then I had to endure the smell of his body, which would be worse. I just could not win.

If I ever did get some of the blanket, it was accompanied with a thump, but was well worth it just to get some warmth. We could not afford pyjamas so I slept in my underpants, but it was very cold – especially if I had to get up during the cold dark nights to put on some extra layers of clothes to get warm. This was also difficult, because without any electricity, and only gas lanterns for lighting, I was unable to see. The long and cold winter nights were a constant battle.

At the foot of each door there was old clothing rolled up to stop the cold draughts. We would put newspapers around the windows to help keep out the draughts and cold. These were the lengths that people would go to during those days to try and keep warm during the winter.

I woke up the next morning feeling very tired due to the lack of sleep and still feeling frightened of Auntie Hilda.

I did not want to stay in the flat with her, as my father had already left for work. As I sneaked downstairs to see Auntie Iris, I heard Auntie Hilda call Joyce, saying, 'Your breakfast is ready,' while coughing at the same time. 'Coming, Auntie,' was the reply from Joyce.

I knocked very quietly on Auntie Iris's sitting-room door and then opened it.

'Hello, Georgie. How are you getting on with your Auntie Hilda?' asked Auntie Iris. Deirdre was sitting at the big dining table eating her breakfast. 'Come and sit down, Georgie. Have you had any breakfast?'

'No,' I said, 'I am too frightened to stay in the flat with Auntie Hilda, and anyway she wouldn't make me any breakfast because she doesn't like me.' I then burst into tears and started to shiver.

Again, Auntie Iris put her arms around me and said, 'I am sure she will get used to you, Georgie, when she sees what a good boy you are. And anyway, she has not had children before, so it must be hard for her.' Auntie Iris was very fair-minded, and a kind and forgiving person with a heart of gold.

I then said, 'She does not like me and I could be dead for all she cares.'

Auntie Iris sat me down and gave me a welcome drink of lemonade and a boiled egg with slices of bread cut into soldiers. It was so warm and so peaceful in her flat and I was wishing that I lived down here rather than upstairs.

I then went back upstairs, to find Auntie Hilda pedalling away on her sewing machine, with Joyce sitting near her on the floor surrounded by her toys. Auntie Hilda had her fag hanging in her mouth.

'Where have you been, Melsham?' she asked. She didn't wait for an answer, but just went on shouting at me. 'You had better watch out, Melsham! If I have any trouble from you I will tell your father to give you a good hiding, so watch you don't get under my feet! And I don't want you getting in the way of my work. The sooner you start school, the better. It's enough that I have to work and look after your sister!'

As she said her last word she began coughing again, and it seemed ages before she could take her next breath. It was just frightening to watch. 'Get out of my sight,' she said while still coughing, and I gladly obeyed her and took flight to the streets outside that were to be my new home.

After searching the streets for some kids to play with, I at last found my first friend, Raymond. He lived just a few doors along, wore glasses and had a runny nose. He was about my age and spent most of the day playing in his garden and home. His mum was a very big woman who must have weighed sixteen stone, but her heart was just as big. We had grown to like each other. Raymond had a bigger and older sister whose name was Hilda. The name sent shock waves through me, but the girl was nice. She and her mum took an interest in me and said that I could come round anytime. Raymond was a bit slow, but that did not bother me. Other kids did not want to play with him, but I found him all right. On returning home, I found my father was in front of the mirror, combing his hair and getting ready to go down to the pub. Not once did he or Auntie Hilda enquire as to where I had been all day, or show any concern, knowing that we had already had an air raid that day. I'd gone for my safety with Raymond and his family into their air-raid shelter.

My father then left to go to the pub, leaving me with Auntie Hilda, the person who was to share my upbringing. Right from the beginning she had given me no security or love, only misery and heartbreak. I sat there looking at this woman. There was an ugliness about her that I will never forget. And this was just the beginning.

Chapter Three

Auntie Hilda was now becoming more hateful towards me. She showed no motherly love, and simple things like teaching me how to brush my teeth, wash myself or take pride in myself she found it unnecessary for me to know. She probably thought, why should she? I meant nothing to her. Why paint a picture if you don't like painting?

She was more concerned about telling me what a shit I was, and by rubbing my nose in the bed sheets and my underpants when I had wet myself, which was now happening more frequently, due to my feeling of insecurity and fear.

Auntie Hilda found great pleasure in constantly telling me what a shit I was, and how ugly and useless I was. That was the only time she ever spoke to me, to disgrace me and to put me down and disown me. These were the sort of things she would tell me, day in and day out.

Being told these horrible things about myself at such a young age was quite soul-destroying, and made me start believing that what she was telling me about myself to be true and real.

I was now nearing six years of age, and to my relief my first day of school had arrived. This exciting day had been brought forward due to my Auntie Hilda, not because she had good intentions for my welfare, but because she wanted to get me from under her feet.

My father had not bothered to find me a school, for he was not interested in my education or welfare. I think the pressure of me being at home and in the way had decided that school was best for me.

My first day at school was a very lonely time for me. There was no one there for me to hold my hand and take me to school on that special and exciting first day. I was yet again all by myself. There I was, standing on my own, watching the new arrivals with their mums and dads, holding hands while walking and talking to each other and showing lots of affection. Parents were giving words of comfort and cuddles to those children who were finding the idea of being left to face their new experience of school upsetting.

I felt sick inside watching them and seeing how lucky they were. In my mind I was wishing if only Rosy Lea or Auntie Iris was here, if only I had a mum here with me…

The loneliness left me feeling drained and ugly. I cried and cried – that was all I seemed to be doing in my young life. As I sat there crying I heard someone ask, 'Why are you crying? Have you lost your mom?'

Hearing those words gave me an excuse to say, '*Yes*, I have lost my mom!' Well, it wasn't exactly a lie. I really had lost my mum – lost her to my life.

The speaker introduced himself to me as a teacher and then asked, 'What is your name?'

Not thinking about what I was about to say, I replied, 'Melsham.' So often I had been called by this by Auntie Hilda that I was now beginning at times to think it was my real name.

With a puzzled expression, the teacher repeated the word 'Melsham', and questioned the name that I had given. This suddenly jogged my memory. 'No,' I said, 'I mean Georgie.' I was still crying my eyes out.

I wasn't crying because I had to go to school but because of the loneliness and sadness I felt. When I got myself up that morning I felt a sense of relief knowing that I was going to school for the very first time. I had hoped that it would give me a chance to meet and play with other kids and get away from the flat.

Now, seeing all the kids with their mums and dads had taken that short-lived excitement from me. On my first day at school I must have stood out, by looking like the poorest child standing outside by the railings of that school within such a classy area, which you would not find all over London in those days. This is why I must have stood out even more amongst the other children.

There I was, standing with the soles of my shoes almost hanging off. I was very skinny due to the lack of decent food. You could have counted the ribs around my chest. My clothes were always dirty, as Auntie Hilda was not interested in my appearance, which helped to emphasise the poverty we had at home.

The teacher then said, 'Let's go and find your mom; she must be worried sick about you.'

'No, I will be all right,' I said, trying my very hardest to stop crying. I didn't want my lie to go any further, because the end result would be another good hiding for me.

I asked the teacher, 'Which class do I go to?'

Looking at his notes he said, 'Over there,' and pointed to a queue.

My school was a two-storey brick building, with a very large playground at the front. The school was split into two parts. To the right were the infants, and to the left of the building were the juniors. The classroom had basic dull cream-coloured walls with no pictures or anything on the walls to liven it up. At the front of the classroom was a large blackboard, and then arranged in rows were small wooden double desks with lids.

I got the impression that the other children were trying to avoid sitting next to me, probably because I must have had a smell about me. I often wished that I had better clean clothing like the other kids.

I met Raymond in the playground, which really made my day. At last – a friend. This also meant I had some company to walk home with after school. Even better, I knew that Raymond's mum would be there to meet him after school, so I would be able to tag along and share the excitement that a child enjoys, knowing that mum or dad will be waiting at the school gates. I felt a bit of pride in myself, being a schoolboy, and also I was happy knowing that I had a friend at the same school, which stopped me feeling so out of place and lonely.

On arriving home, I went through the back alley to Auntie Iris's door to share my first day's experience at school. I sat on her lap, something that I was never able to do to Auntie Hilda or my father. Putting her pain-filled arms around my waist, I told her all about my day at school and how I enjoyed it. I shared the excitement I felt at having seen so many kids in one place, and how good it was to be able to play with Raymond and his friends in the playground.

She asked, 'What did you learn today?' I replied by saying, 'Not much' – not aware that I was losing my hearing and failing to understand what was being said in the classroom.

Later I went up the stairs to Auntie Hilda. Not once did she ask how my first day at school was, or if I had enjoyed it.

I was now being pushed out more on the streets from early morning to late at night, with only my schooling giving me the chance to share the company of friends and a chance to warm my cold body during the day.

On evenings and weekends the streets would become my oyster, and the playground leading to my survival, where I would either steal or starve – for I had no choice at the time. My Sundays were the loneliest day of the week as I travelled the streets trying to find something to eat as all the shops and cafes were closed. All I could see were my mates and everyone dressed up in their Sunday best attending Sunday school. Most kids were brought up to do this on a Sunday but of course I was excluded from such learning. Auntie Hilda said I was too evil to go into a house of God. Such days were also bad since as I passed the rows of houses I could sense the family life that other kids were experiencing. I could smell the most important meal of the week, when the family came together to eat their roast beef, roast potatoes and Yorkshire pudding with gravy. This was then the traditional Sunday meal, which is sadly disappearing now, along with table manners, and being replaced by a trip round to the curry house to eat as much as you like.

Back in those days, my sister, Joyce, had just a few days earlier come back from hospital suffering from malnutrition. It was not unusual, because the national shortage of food caused it to be rationed to each household; but in our home it was even worse.

Auntie Hilda's sewing-machine work had dried up, and my father was short of work, which meant that you had to cook as cheap as you could and make things go even further. For the first time our standard of living had actually declined, and we were really on the poverty line, which did not make things easier for me with Auntie Hilda's cooking. They say that if you are starving you will eat anything; that was definitely not true in my case.

Auntie Hilda only ever cooked a meal in the evening because my father needed at least one meal a day. Sometimes she would make porridge for breakfast. To feed the four of us all she would make anything that was cheap to prepare.

My father had dirty habits, one of which was picking his nose. Often after watching him as he picked his nose I'd see him roll the product into a ball then flick it anywhere, regardless of who was watching. Watching this would leave me feeling sick in my stomach and disgusted to see him behave like this.

Another one of his bad habits would be using his dirty handkerchief, which would be full of dirty snot and bogies. It would be so stiff like it had been starched, and black from all the smog that passed through his nostrils. Never was there an empty spot of clean space on his handkerchief.

I would then watch Auntie Hilda put my father's used hankies in the cooking pot to boil them. After that, I would watch her use the same pot to cook our dinner in it, when the family budget could stretch to a meal.

It would make me feel even more sick, just thinking of those dirty hankies that had been in the same cooking pot as our dinner. Her favourite and cheapest meal for dinner was a bacon pudding, which is a suet pastry with layers of bacon lined up on top of the pastry like soldiers, then wrapped up in a cloth and boiled – using the same pot that my father's hankies had been boiled in. Then she would serve it with boiled potatoes.

It was a very cheap meal in those days. But when my dinner had been placed before me, the only thought that was going around in my mind was not the hunger I felt, but my father's hankies that had been boiled in the same pot. My first reaction was to turn my nose up and not eat it, regardless of how hungry I might be. I would be there poking at it and pushing it around the plate with my fork after Auntie Hilda had dished it up.

The smell was sickening with the steam rising up my nostrils and staying there, causing my stomach to turn, and the toes on my feet would curl up.

By now Auntie Hilda realised how much I hated this dinner and used it as the perfect opportunity to see me suffer; and that was exactly what she did, without a doubt.

'You are going to sit there till you have eaten every last bit!' she yelled. On the back of that she yelled it again, but still I would refuse, just poking at it with my fork. While shouting she would also say, 'Eat it, you dirty no good-for-nothing, eat it – now eat it!'

I was too afraid to explain why I couldn't eat it, because should I even attempt to, it would give Auntie Hilda more bullets to put in her gun. She would just keep going on, and on, and on, saying it over and over again.

For some unknown reason, my sister Joyce seemed to just love bacon pudding. Perhaps it was because she never took any notice of what went on in the pot it was cooked in, or it could be because she chose not to think about father's dirty habit of picking his nose.

With my stomach now becoming more like a ship on a rough sea, up it came. I was sick, and sick again. Being sick on an empty stomach gets very painful, but Auntie Hilda carried on yelling, 'Eat it!' I couldn't believe it – she was not referring to the bacon pudding, but started pointing to the vomit. Yes – the vomit – all that had spilled over my dinner plate and onto the floor! 'Eat it, eat it!' she kept shouting. By now I felt ill and weak and my legs became numb. Sweat started to pour off me and my eyes began to close. 'Eat it, eat it, you dirty good-for-nothing!' By now I felt that I needed to go to bed, as I felt tired and weak. As I tried to take myself off to bed the dreaded words were uttered by her: 'Wait till your father gets home!'

I had heard it so many times I knew what to expect on my father's return: another bloody good hiding again.

True to her word, as soon as my father came into the dining room she blurted out, 'He won't eat his dinner, that has taken me all day to cook, and he has been lippy to me. He is out of control – do something!'

At that my father pulled me from the chair by the roots of my hair, with my legs hanging in mid air and threw me across the room. He then threw my dinner and the vomit that was on the plate in my face and began hitting me around the head.

I did not move. I was too weak. All I could hear was Auntie Hilda shouting, 'You no-good-for-nothing!' Somehow I managed to get myself to the sink and washed away my dinner and smell from my hair and face and take myself to bed.

My little ears were ringing. It sounded like the sound of a train going through a tunnel, which was now getting louder. All fell silent – not the flat but my hearing. I'm not sure if it was the result of the beating around my ears or natural deafness, but all I know is that slowly but surely I was losing my hearing.

Auntie Hilda knew that I did not like bacon pudding but enjoyed humiliating me, so out of spite she would make it regularly, just so she could see me suffer at the hands of my father. I know that she got great pleasure out of this, because you could see the smirk on her face when I was being punished. Her pleasure was in watching my suffering.

Another pet hate of mine that she found out was porridge. I could not eat it – not that I didn't like porridge, but it was the way in which she made just for me. She would boil the water, then pour in the oats and add salt, which was fine, but after serving a portion for everyone apart from me she would add extra salt to my portion and force me to sit and eat it.

I'm sure that she put loads of salt into the porridge to make me sick, and sick I was. Her famous words would fly from her mouth: 'Wait till your father gets home!' And I'd get another good hiding from my father.

I remember one particularly bad meal I had struggled to eat. I had brought up more vomit and the pain in my stomach was growing by the minute. Auntie Hilda got hold of a spoon and started to shovel my food and vomit into my mouth.

'Open up!' she said, pulling my jaw open with force. My mouth was already dry as I tried to swallow what she was shovelling in. Wow! I was choking with the vomit coming from my tummy that was blocking my windpipe.

'Eat up, you good-for-nothing!' she was shouting, and I was heaving even more. I was trying to catch my breath as my eyes were stinging with tears. That evil face of hers was boring into me and I could feel her hatred staring into my eyes. Somehow I managed to kick my chair backwards so that my body landed on the floor and I ran downstairs into the street, still choking and trying to catch my breath. I needed water, I just needed water.

I turned into the alley where there was a large puddle. I threw myself down onto my belly and drew in the water from the puddle. I had to get rid of the horrible taste of my own vomit. I then tried to get up but was too weak to stand, with the pain in my stomach increasing by the minute. I knew then that I could never eat Auntie Hilda's cooking again. I would rather starve and die.

I stayed outside in the alley until darkness so that I could creep into my bed without Auntie Hilda knowing. Once I managed to get in (a key was now hanging on a piece of string just inside the letterbox), my head started to boil and my body was shaking from the pain in my stomach. I could feel running poo coming from my bottom but I just lay there in bed unable to move. I told myself that I was getting better, and just to rest and forget the pain. *Rest, rest, no pain, no pain*, I was telling myself as I fell asleep (or was it a fever that made me pass out?).

In the morning I was woken by Auntie Hilda. 'Have you shit yourself, Melsham?' she said, picking the bedclothes off me. 'You have, you dirty, good-for-nothing! Get up!'

Still feeling very weak and ill I dragged myself up from my bed and as I stood up she put her hand behind my neck and pushed my head onto the wet and pooey bed without warning. Now I was almost fainting, and I had poo around my mouth and nostrils but was still too weak to pull myself up. By now I felt exactly like the name she always called me: the scum of the earth.

Today I am still suffering from my experience of those days. It has left me with a phobia about food and where and what I eat. I find it almost impossible to go to anyone's home and eat, regardless of how clean his or her home may be, or how well I know him or her. Maybe it is because I do not have a choice in someone's house, and it feels like Auntie Hilda is still there, forcing me to eat. The only place that I can eat food comfortably is in my own home, knowing that my wife has cooked it.

Sometimes I can go into a clean café or restaurant, but only one of my own choosing, and that's about it. To many of my friends, I would like to apologise to them, and hope that after reading my story they will understand the reasons behind my excuses not to eat at their homes.

Auntie Hilda was eleven when she lost her father. She was in her late twenties when she lost her one and only boyfriend. He was cruelly taken from her and died of TB. Tuberculosis was very common in those days; perhaps this is why Auntie Hilda had no feelings for men or boys after. But whatever the reason I was getting the full brunt of it. Auntie Hilda's cooking gave me reasons to find any excuse not to attend dinner or eat at home again, so I was forced onto the streets for company and food. No one would miss me anyway.'

Almost daily, Auntie Hilda would find some excuse to tell my father about when I was in and what I had done wrong that day. If it was not about eating my meal, it would be some made-up story that I may have lied about or gave Auntie Hilda some lip. I was even wrong for living.

Whatever reason she had thought of, she would be waiting for the return of my father. She would enjoy concocting stories and telling him her version of events. I never had a chance to give my side of the story. My father would then hit me with his giant hands or another weapon that was within his reach, like a boot or a rolling pin. So often I felt like a rag doll with the stuffing knocked out of me. My natural reaction was to curl up like a ball on the floor, trying desperately to cover my head with my hands. This made no difference to the pain. I would be shouting, 'Sorry, sorry!' but still the blows rained down onto me. It seemed to continue for ages, while all the time Auntie Hilda was standing there and enjoying it. To me this was to become the normal way of life. I felt like nobody's child.

I don't know if my father was cruel by nature or just to me. Maybe Auntie Hilda got on his nerves so much that he had to take it out on me;

but then there were many times when I would watch him get a poker and catch the mice as they ran along the skirting. He would hit them until they were dead. I found it uncomfortable because even if I trod on a spider I would feel guilty and go cold inside, so seeing the way my father killed the mice would upset me and leave me feeling that it was only a matter of time before he would use the same poker and punish me also.

In the beginning I would go into Auntie Iris's flat for my cuddles, warmth and food, until Joyce found it necessary to tell Auntie Hilda that I was going into their flat.

One day when I came home from school Auntie Hilda was waiting for me and told me to come downstairs with her to see Mrs Thompson. Auntie Hilda never knew of the close relationship that we had, and why I called her 'Auntie Iris'.

Auntie Hilda knocked on Auntie Iris's door and grabbed me by the neck and began asking, 'What has he stole from you?'

Auntie Iris said, 'What are you talking about? He has never stolen from me – he is a very good boy!'

Hilda had a look of anger on her face because she didn't like what she was hearing in those words from Auntie Iris. She went into a rage, shouting, 'You don't know what he is like! He is evil and rotten to the core, he is a thief and a liar.'

Auntie Iris knew me better and was not having it. She stood up for me, saying, 'No, he is a good boy, Hilda, he is God's child.' Auntie Hilda then realised that there was no getting Auntie Iris on her side, and told her that if she caught me there again she would be sorry, so she had better watch out.

I felt so good because someone had just stood up for me, and Auntie Hilda did not like that. From that day on Auntie Hilda never ever spoke to Auntie Iris again. I was now banned from seeing Auntie Iris and Uncle Alf again. Rosy Lea and Auntie Iris, the two motherly loves whom I had found, had now been cruelly snatched away from me and my loneliness was restored.

I could not bear to lose another kind person from my life, so I decided to sneak in through the back door to see Auntie Iris after a few days. I explained how sorry I was for what had happened. She told me that I had nothing to be sorry about. It was so nice to hear her call my name again.

'It's not your fault, Georgie, and God will forgive her. You can come anytime, Georgie.' I was so happy to hear those words and to know that I had not lost my angel.

We decided between us that it would be best for us both if we kept my visits to her flat a secret. In order to do so I would need to sneak in through the back in future. (I was to keep a lot more secrets later in my childhood.)

Auntie Iris had always welcomed me into her home; she would save all her bacon rinds and a little fairy cake or a jam tart for me. I didn't realise at the time, but it being wartime, food was very scarce. As I got older I realised that everything she gave me was a sacrifice for her.

I was beginning to get to know most of the neighbours, young and old, down our road.

There was Mr and Mrs Crookshank. Mr Crookshank was an ex-policeman who worked in the local church around the corner as a caretaker. I got on well with him, and his wife who often welcomed me into their home. They had a grown-up daughter who often came to visit them. The road we lived in had a lot of professional people like Mr Crookshank.

Often he would take me to the church to help him clean.

I used to enjoy sitting on the bumper of a large heavy polishing block. It had a handle that was bolted onto it. I would sit on it with my light weight and hold on to the handle as he pulled it along while the block was polishing the floor.

I would help him put the chairs out in the hall that was at the side of the church. He always praised me and made me feel good within myself. He was big, like my father, with silver hair, and seemed to enjoy my company as much as I enjoyed his.

He managed to get me into the boys' clubs that were held in the church hall. This gave me the chance to play with the other kids who attended, which I enjoyed. I had no uniform, so Mr and Mrs Crookshank pooled together to get me my uniform with its cap.

After being a member for a few weeks I now had my new uniform, which I had changed into, in their home. When I put the uniform on and stood there, a combination of feelings came over me. I felt so proud and rich – it was the smartest that I had ever been! I was so excited and overjoyed I felt like a soldier and proud to wear my uniform.

Mr Crookshank had taken me by the hand in my uniform to the

local church hall to join my cub team. I felt wanted and big, because unlike going to school on my own I was going to my church hall in my uniform to cubs with someone holding my hand. I was filled with the pride of being part of a club and wearing a uniform to prove it.

My thoughts were that Auntie Iris would be proud of me, together with Auntie Hilda and my father, thanks to Mr and Mrs Crookshank, who had made it so real. I sneaked in to see Auntie Iris first to show her my uniform; she complimented me by saying what a smart boy I was, and how proud she was of me. She had a tear in her eye, which was a tear of excitement for me. She put her arms around me and kissed me and said, 'You are such a darling. I have never seen you so smart!' She was pulling up my socks, which had slipped to my ankles.

I then went upstairs to Auntie Hilda to show her my new uniform. On reaching the top of the stairs there was an outburst from her. 'Where did you nick that uniform from, Melsham?' she shouted. Then my father came to the top of the stairs where I was standing. 'Look,' said Auntie Hilda, 'he has nicked some nice boy's uniform!'

At that, my father swung out his right hand around my head, causing me to lose my balance, and I fell down the stairs, landing on the bottom stair. 'Get that bloody thing off!' he shouted.

Somehow, I managed to get myself up and made my way to Mr and Mrs Crookshank and returned the uniform to them.

Mr Crookshank asked what was wrong, and I explained that I must return my uniform to them, as I was not allowed to take things from people. He said, 'But it is yours, Georgie – to keep.' I repeated, 'But I must not accept it – I am not allowed to accept it.' I then changed into my old clothes and left, very upset and lost.

A day later, Auntie Hilda made it clear that I was not allowed to see Mr and Mrs Crookshank ever again. They must have had a row over my uniform. Auntie Hilda never spoke to them again as they passed each other in the street or at church; they would look away on seeing each other.

Mr and Mrs Crookshank were not the only neighbours whom I was seeing in secret. There was Mrs and Mr Squibb, the brother of my Uncle Fred and sister-in-law of my Auntie Vi, who lived further down the road. By now, Uncle Fred and Auntie Vi had moved to Eastbourne to start a new life after the death of their two children, Stanley and Jean. Mr Squibb was tall and handsome with a very pretty wife. I always thought of them as film stars. Mr Squibb's first name was Frank, but I called him Uncle Frank. He would take me out on his motorbike in the sidecar, which was attached to the side of his bike. I would often help him to do up his back garden and clean his bike.

Upstairs to them was Mr Squibb's mother, who lived in the back room, which was like a granny room with its own gas ring. I would go up and talk with her for ages and run little errands for her. She was always grateful for my help, which was often rewarded by a kiss and praise for what I had done.

I was encouraged by most of the local grown-ups in my road.

Then there was Mr and Mrs Newbury, who had a son called Douglas, who was one of my friends whom I played with. Then there was Mr and Mrs McCarthy, whose son, Frank, was another friend. Then there was Nelly and her husband, and Irish couple who had no children; I used to go into their home and watch Nelly's husband do carpentry and help him in his workshop at the bottom of his garden. There were many more neighbours I knew, and I used to pop into their homes and lend a hand. They all helped me to be part of a community, helped me to see life from a different point of view, and helped me to forget my real home life. I felt that everyone liked me and I liked them too; no longer was I seeing them as posh people, but nice everyday people.

My friendships with them all had to remain a secret, because if Auntie Hilda knew I would be in for it; so I had to run two lives – one at home and one outside – which made me very confused about life. I was most certainly not happy at home; I felt that the way in which I was treated wasn't about discipline, it was about Auntie Hilda accusing me of imaginary crimes that I was supposed to have committed; and most of the time I did not do anything wrong. I was just an innocent child crying out to be loved.

It is really strange when you are being misused by your parents. As bad as they may be, you don't learn to hate them. Maybe at the time of being punished you do, but you seem to accept it, and you learn more about life. I suppose that is why it is hard to understand why a woman who is being beaten up by her husband, or partner, accepts more rather than leaving. So when I hear people say, 'Why doesn't she leave him?' I understand why. I suppose that is nature, really. You can't seem to escape from yourself. Only a person who has had the same or similar experience to what I was going through can understand that, and it's the reason why I still loved my father and Auntie Hilda in my own little way and sometimes miss them both – even today.

My hearing was getting more difficult as the weeks and months went by. I started to notice it when people began asking, 'Are you deaf, or can't you hear me?'

What didn't help was when anyone came to see my father or Auntie Hilda and they were having a conversation. Auntie Hilda would say, 'Don't listen to our conversation! You shouldn't be listening to us.' Then, after a while you tend to shut off like turning off a radio. I knew that if I appeared to be listening it would end up with me getting a good hiding.

You start to believe and convince yourself that you can't hear them talking. By doing this the nerves in your ears become confused, which can create nerve deafness. Even today if two people or more are having a conversation in close earshot of me, I am not able to follow their conversation even with my hearing aids.

Most people tend to think that being deaf means the volume is turned down; well, it isn't. There are different types of deafness. In my case I can't hear high-pitched sounds, and at a short distance I hear nothing.

When people talk to me I need to watch and read their lips, otherwise if I don't they sound like they are talking an unknown language to me.

You can imagine the problem that I had trying to hear and listen to the teachers at school and at that young age! I hadn't mastered the art of lip-reading on the other side of the fence. It is an unusual disability. People can't *see* you as deaf. It is not easily recognised, like having an injury. Sometimes people assume that you are stupid, or rude, by not speaking when you are spoken to.

So school was my biggest problem. There I was at the back of the class, mucking about and not learning anything; but how can you learn if you can't hear what is being said in class?

Nowadays if you make no progress at school, the first thing that you can expect to happen is that an ear test would be carried out; but back in them days that never happened. Then the parents would highlight their concern at their child's learning, which would be discussed with the teacher.

In my case I didn't have parents who were concerned about my welfare or my progress of learning, so I was left behind, with no one showing or taking an interest in my learning. I did not understand at the time how bad my hearing was, or the effect that it was having on my learning. What I do know is that I was getting the cane on my hands more times than any other child in the school, for mucking about in the back of the classroom. What would you expect from a six-year-old child who can't hear, and is also having problems at home?

When my sister started school, on her first day Auntie Hilda was very happy to take her to school. This trend continued from the first day and every single day after that, without fail, while she was in the infants' school. Auntie Hilda took a full interest in the progress of Joyce's learning. With me, no one cared, so I was either mucking about at the back of the class or gazing out of the window into the playground just waiting for playtime.

When playtime came I just ran around to rid myself of the boredom of sitting at the back of my classroom. I would run like a mad thing on my own, until one of the older boys shouted, 'Titch!' – another name I was given. 'Do you want to play with us?' they would ask, while running around with their arms outstretched going, 'Vroom, vroom, vroom!' and 'Bang, bang!' pretending to be airplanes dropping bombs on the house. I would just run around copying them; that was what I liked about school – not the lessons, just playtime with other children to play with. It gave me a really good buzz and I felt I had been accepted. I was one of them. I felt like a normal human being while playing with my friends at school; but even that was to change later.

I had a tendency to always mix with older boys, and being the smallest of the gang they decided that the name 'Titch' was an ideal nickname for me. The name never bothered me. It seemed like an endearment to me, and at least I was being noticed; also I could understand the reason behind the new name. I was really enjoying going to school, but for the wrong reasons. I wasn't learning anything, but playtime was the highlight of me going to school.

I still hadn't fully realised that I was deaf. My deafness was not so acute at this time, but I still had great difficulty understanding what was being taught or said. It was at this point that my deafness really started to affect my life. The school had no idea that I was deaf, and I was thought to be stupid or insolent when I didn't reply when spoken to. I was constantly being shouted at for not listening and not doing as I was told, so the playground was my joy. At playtime I was always grazing my knees or my arms, like boys do. I was always up to mischief. We didn't have bats and balls to play with, so we would use whatever we could lay our hands on to play games.

In the school playground there was a big heap of coke that was stored there for the school heating system. The coke was made from some form of processed coal.

One day at school, one of the boys was mucking about with this coke, while the other boys were throwing the coke about like boys do, pretending that they were playing cricket.

I, being the batsman, had a plank of wood that I was using for a bat. I shouted to one of the boys to throw the coke in my direction, intending to hit it for a six to play a game of cricket, but it missed and hit me on the head by accident. I fell over, with blood pouring from my head wound. I didn't cry, as I was used to getting hurt at home and crying meant more punishment, so I was getting hardened to pain. I just lay there, stunned and still so as not to get hurt again, thinking that I was being attacked by my father again.

The teachers must have thought I was dead. Teachers came from all directions to attend to me. One of them, seeing all the blood said, 'Call an ambulance.' This meant someone had to run to the headmaster's room to use the telephone. The pain was setting into me and it felt as if my head was about to explode. While waiting for the ambulance, the teachers were talking to me in a very tender way. This was unusual, because for the first time I was seeing grown people showing a lot of concern for my wounds and showing kindness to me. No one had ever shown kindness to me when I was hurt before, but now for the first time it was happening to me.

I was baffled and began thinking, Why should other people show concern for me when my family didn't? The concerns for me were very moving for me; the pain in my head was fast disappearing and being taken over by the joy for their concern and their attention. For the first time I felt as if all the angels of God were taking me to heaven and lasting peace.

I was taken to the hospital, and I found that again I was being fussed over, but this time it was by all the nurses. Then I thought that now maybe Auntie Hilda and my father would be just as concerned and show me some kindness.

The blood was cleaned away from my head. It revealed a deep cut, which needed to be stitched, and then a bandage was put around my head. The kindness and concern was so powerful for me that I wanted it to last for ever. I felt at peace; I felt like a person.

One of the teachers had accompanied me to the hospital which was about a ten-minute walk from home. She walked back with me to make sure that I went home and rested. When I got to the end of my road I said to the teacher, 'Thank you, Teacher. I will walk home from here,' and made an excuse why she should not take me to my front door.

As I walked down my road I was getting even more kindness and concern shown towards me from the neighbours. When they saw my bandaged head, they were saying 'Oh dear, Georgie, what has happened to you, my poor dear?' So I told them my story. I was feeling like the hero, and I enjoyed this day that was filled with love being shown towards me by everyone.

I arrived home and went upstairs feeling very happy with myself and full of self-respect. I had hoped that Auntie Hilda would show me some sympathy and kindness when she saw me, but oh no! There was no sign of concern, only bitter disappointment. The first thing Auntie Hilda said to me when she saw my bandaged head was, 'You've been in trouble and fighting, haven't you? You are always causing trouble wherever you go!' This was followed by her favourite words, yet again: 'Wait till your father gets home!' Even on this one occasion, she just could not find it in her heart to try and show just a little concern, or maybe enquire about what had happened, or at least ask me why I was wearing a bandage. She was only bothered about making sure that there was going to be added punishment on top of the pain I had already endured.

My heart sank. It was back to the old times. I would have loved her to say, 'Oh, Georgie, what has happened to you?' and then to put her arms around me and give me a cuddle. But no, that was not in her nature; that was too much to hope for. Sympathy and understanding were not things Auntie Hilda did, especially where I was concerned.

'It was an accident,' I said.

'Don't lie to me, Melsham! You're a little troublemaker, a no-good-for-nothing. I've had enough of you. I can't stand you,' followed by her usual, 'Wait till your father gets home!'

True to her word as soon as my father came home she just couldn't wait to tell him – tell him that I had been causing trouble again at school. He then got hold of me and pushed me up against the wall.

Then he shouted, 'I am warning you, you little bastard, if you keep bringing trouble to your Auntie Hilda I will kill you, you little bastard!' Then as a final warning of what he would do he hit me unexpectedly around the head and ripped of my bandage, causing my head to bleed again.

Again, I was on my own, with no one to give me any of that comfort or show concern just when I needed it most.

I was trembling and feeling sick, so I took myself to my bed. As I lay there with toilet paper pressed on my wound, I started to feel alone again; at least they could have gone to my school and found out exactly what had happened if they doubted me. Instead they just didn't care or think I was worth the trouble, as it gave them more satisfaction to punish me even more.

I was lying on my bed still trying to stop the blood on my forehead and thinking, Where is my mother? She would look after me and love me and care for me. I was beginning to feel that I needed to find my mum and get her to take me away; and it is times like this that make you more determined to find her.

It seemed that everywhere I looked I was seeing more children at school. I could see friends playing happily down my road with their mothers; they all seemed to have mothers with them, who were watching over them and sharing the fun and sometimes joining in as they skipped and played down the road.

I often lay on my bed all by myself, and I so wanted to find my mother. As I watched my schoolmates going hand in hand with their mums I felt loneliness, because I went to school on my own.

I was only six and a half, but at this point I vowed that Auntie Hilda or my father would not get the better of me. This was the start of my fighting spirit that has stood me in good stead for the many battles I have fought throughout my short life. My deafness was becoming a problem to me. I could not really understand why my mates had learned so much at school and not me.

I had thought at the time that they had bigger brains than me, not realising that it was due to my deafness. More and more I was being asked, 'Did you hear me?' or, 'I asked you to do this or that.' But I hadn't heard what they had asked me to do. I think the teachers just looked on me as either backward or stupid, or even both. I also felt that the teachers were picking on me. I was constantly getting the wrong end of the stick because I had not heard right, finding myself in trouble and getting the cane for it, but I still felt safer with them than Auntie Hilda or my father.

The teachers were so much nicer towards me. They gave me better treatment than I was getting at home, and even when I was caned at school it never hurt like it did at home from the hands of my father. The blows from his giant hands would burn my skin and cause excruciating pain.

Slowly Auntie Hilda was brainwashing me by telling me every day how rotten I was, what a shit I was and how ugly I was. When you are told this daily you begin to be like the person in the picture she paints of you. While brainwashing me about my ears, telling me that I am not to listen when company arrived, she must have known that I was deaf and took pleasure in making it obvious when it suited her, especially when my sister, Joyce, was talking to me and I could not hear her. Auntie Hilda would say, 'He can hear you, he is just stupid,' and encourage Joyce to annoy me.

I was turning more and more to Auntie Iris, telling her of my feelings and asking why other children had a mum but not me. I didn't go into details of my suffering at the time; I felt that if I told her she would agree with what Auntie Hilda kept telling me about myself, and would not want to see me anymore. So the feelings that I was expressing to Auntie Iris concerned my mother and my school, but not the true feelings I had about my home life.

I was also in fear of Auntie Hilda finding out about Auntie Iris still seeing me; the last thing that I wanted was to have her upset. Had I told her or given details of what was really happening to me upstairs it might be possible that Auntie Iris and Uncle Alf would confront Auntie Hilda and my father, which would possibly cause a war of words to develop. It was not worth it, because at the end of the day I would be blamed for causing trouble, which meant another good hiding for me. So I carried on bottling up everything inside me, trying to put it to the back of my mind.

My problems at home were between Auntie Hilda, my father and me. It seemed that there was no limit to Auntie Hilda's hatred towards me, for every opportunity she had to mistrust or degrade me she would take it. I didn't get washed on a daily basis; nobody was interested enough to teach me the importance of personal hygiene. Having a wash was a boy's pet hate anyway, and I was no exception to that.

Sometimes she would look at me and say, 'Melsham, it's time that you had a wash.' She would then lift me onto the draining board in our small kitchen, where I was told to wash myself in the big butler's sink. There I would wash myself with cold water under the cold-water tap that hung from the wall over the sink, using a bar of carbolic soap, which smelt like chemicals.

Auntie Hilda was unable to cope with the fact that anyone inside or outside the family could like me or love me. Whenever we had contact with members of the family she would lie about me, desperately trying her best to convince them into thinking and agreeing that I was a troublemaker always bringing home trouble. 'Have nothing to do with him,' she'd say. I became a complete outcast from the family – always was and always would be. Perhaps that's why I need reassuring that I am not really that person. So all of this did not help my learning at school, and coupled with my deafness my learning was non-existent. How can you learn when you are constantly being brainwashed into thinking that you are useless?

How can you learn when you are suffering pain?

How can you learn when you are lonely?

How can you learn when you are deaf?

All this was against me, with nothing for me, so often I really wished that I was dead. I had lost count of the number of times the thought entered my little innocent mind, but I felt a coward that I could not take my own life. I spent hours working out a plan of how best to end my life – without pain or suffering, as I did not want to have any more pain. I even asked people what it would be like if someone hanged himself or stabbed himself – would he feel pain? Or how quick would it be to die if you drowned? I even thought of jumping in front of a tram – but then I thought that might turn out to drag me along the road in agony.

Had it not been for Auntie Iris and Uncle Alf, Mr and Mrs Crookshank, Mr and Mrs Whitby and Raymond's mum and dad, and many more neighbours, maybe I would have been dead. During my life the tears I shed could have filled a pool.

I was now getting a lot of fantasies. I think they helped me keep going. One of my most frequent fantasies was that I would find my real mother and that she would hold me in her arms and kiss my tears away, reassuring me. She would tell me it was a very big mistake and that she always meant to come and take me and my sister with her. Or if that were not possible, the next best thing would be for Rosy Lea to take me to the markets every day.

I often thought that I would find my sister, Violet, and that she would be made better, also that Uncle Alf turned out to be my real dad. For everyday I had these fantasies, hoping that one of them would become true; and some of the fantasies did come true, as you will find out.

I felt that almost everyone around me was against me, and these fantasies would help me to cope with the harsh, cruel realities of life. But for now anyway I had to carry on regardless with my life.

The Blitz was still in full swing, and many a time I didn't hear the sirens and would find myself being dragged to an air-raid shelter by the neighbours while out on the streets on my own. The war was scary for me. It was only when I saw people running around for a safe place to hide that I would realise that the sirens had or were coming, or when someone grabbed me to take me to their air-raid shelter, or when I saw the smoke and fire in the distance. I had noticed how everyone was concerned for each other and always looked out for each other. The war was drawing to its end, but my war with life was far from ending and still a very long way off.

By the time I was seven, having not known when my birthday was and never having a chance to have a birthday or even a card, a birthday for me would come and go without me even knowing about it. But I was beginning to understand more of my surroundings and getting much closer to Auntie Iris and Uncle Alf. I found it very hard to even attempt to ask Auntie Hilda or my father for anything, fearing a good hiding for asking, or an evil blank look.

Just looking at Auntie Hilda's face was enough to tell me that her heart was filled with hatred for me. So I began to put questions to Auntie Iris, questions that I dared not ask of Auntie Hilda or my father. I was fully aware that I had a handicapped sister, and I wanted to know where she was. Did my mother take her back, and if she did perhaps she would take me back as well? I was also hoping that maybe I could play with Violet. So I asked Auntie Iris if she could find her for me.

She knew how much I had wanted to meet Violet. I had told her so many times, but this time I must have been more forceful in my words. It was after her telling Uncle Alf that between them they must have decided to find out where Violet really was. Uncle Alf always drank in the same pub as my father – The Railway Telegraph – and had learned later that when my father drank he talked a lot, and the more he drank the more he talked. So one evening Uncle Alf, after waiting for my father to down a few drinks, and choosing his moment carefully, asked him out of the blue, 'Where is Violet, George?' Without any prompting or hesitation, the answer was forthcoming. 'She is in the Fountain Hospital in Tooting Bec.'

From the information Uncle Alf got, he had checked it out to see if she was there. Uncle Alf had it confirmed and arranged for a visit.

I popped into Auntie Iris's flat, as I always did. On this particular occasion I noticed that Auntie Iris had a brighter than usual broad grin on her face. She held out her arms for me to sit on her lap, with Uncle Alf holding his arm around her shoulder, and said, 'Would you like to meet your sister – Violet?'

Full of excitement, I answered, 'Yes, yes, yes, please!' I just could not contain the joy I felt as I said this. I carried on shouting while she still held me on her lap. When I calmed down she told me that this must be our secret. 'You must never tell anyone,' she said. She knew that I could keep a secret, because I was doing this on a regular basis in order to survive.

I had no idea at the time where Violet was, so the first thought that went through my mind was that perhaps she was living with my mum. 'Is she living with my mom?' I asked.

'No, Georgie, she is in a hospital… would you still like to go?'

Without hesitation I replied, 'Oh, yes, yes, yes!' But I felt a little bit sad that she was not with my mother. It was arranged that Uncle Alf and myself would go to visit my Violet on the Sunday, as it was a day that he was not working.

I was counting the days before I could see Violet. I felt so happy, for at last one of my wishes was to come true, and each night I was tossing and turning in bed thinking of all the things that I was going to say to her. My excitement had to be held inside me as I dared not let Auntie Hilda or my father know that I was to meet my sister. I knew what that would have meant: no visits to Violet, and the chance that my father would not trust Uncle Alf anymore with the information that he had given to him. As a young kid it is very hard to hide one's excitement and secrets, but my life depended on it.

My big day had arrived – a day that was to change another part of my life for ever. I sneaked downstairs and left our flat while everyone was still asleep. I quietly knocked on the door and Auntie Iris opened it. Auntie Iris and Uncle Alf were up and dressed, and both of them put their fingers on their lips to indicate that I keep very quiet.

She had packed some sandwiches and cakes in a tin box, as we could be gone all day. They explained that Uncle Alf would leave first, and I was to follow and meet outside the Railway Telegraph pub. When I arrived at the pub he held my hand as if I was his son, to catch a bus to the Fountain Hospital at Tooting Bec to meet my handicapped sister, Violet.

When we arrived I noticed how big the hospital was, with lots of open ground and a large Victorian building. It was quite scary and frightening, but having Uncle Alf with me made me feel more relaxed and secure. I was then taken aback at seeing all shapes and sizes of funny-looking people. They were of all ages. As we entered the building some were lying on the floor in a sleeping position, but others had their legs and arms in the air while lying on the floor. Others were standing with their backs to the wall, rocking themselves back and forth. Others you could see had wet themselves. Some were staring at the walls, others were asleep on chairs, and some were walking around half naked.

There was a lot of noise with a lot of shouting, screaming and coughing. A young person like myself one would expect to take one look and run, but in my case I was not shocked or afraid. In fact I went up to one of them who was having trouble trying to sit down on a chair, and I helped him. I seemed to have had a strong desire to help others; maybe it was because I had never had a loving family that cared or loved me.

I felt very concerned for them. But I was here to meet my sister, Violet. Uncle Alf had gone off to find the Matron's office to fetch Violet. After what seemed ages, I saw Uncle Alf holding the hand of a girl. I stared at her, not expecting to see what I saw. 'This is Violet,' he said, and a cold shiver came over me. My heart sank, and my bottom lip dropped as she stood before me.

She was a lot taller than me, with very short hair as if a basin had been put on her head and the hair cut around it. She had a runny nose and with her bottom lip dropped down, her chin was dribbling from her open mouth and down her bottom lip. Her eyes were just rolling in her head without stopping once. Her whole body seemed to be twisted; just everything about her did not look normal. I had never seen her before, only when we were babies, and that memory of her had faded. A sudden cry for help had entered my mind; no tears, just shock and disbelief.

I was shocked at seeing her like this. Why didn't my father bother with her? Why didn't he care? Why did Auntie Hilda not care? Why didn't anyone in my family care? Why should my sister be left on her own with nobody in the family waiting to see her? Why should my sister, Violet, be on her own with no family to care for her? Why was she like this? Why, why, why… and most of all, why didn't my bloody family care?

My anger had taken hold of me after the shock, and from that first moment I felt that I should care and I should help her. She needed someone to, and that someone was to be me.

Uncle Alf could see by the look on my face when I took Violet's hands how I must have felt. I spent the rest of the day taking Violet around the hospital grounds with Uncle Alf. I was talking to her but she could not understand. I was getting to know my sister; she could not understand me, but I could not understand her either. I was also trying to find answers to why anyone could just leave someone like Violet on her own. It wasn't her fault that she was the way she was. I found that for all the state she was in Violet had a sweet nature.

It was a very sad and upsetting departure from my sister. I promised her that I would come back to see her. I pledged to myself that I would never let her down and that I would always see and help her. On going home on the bus with Uncle Alf I was not excited as I was when coming to meet my sister. The shock left me staring into space. Uncle Alf sensed the effect this had on me and kept on saying, 'Don't worry, Georgie, we will come again. It was nice coming with you to see your sister, and I shall help you all I can with her.'

When we got off the bus, Uncle Alf said, 'You go first to Auntie Iris.'

I knew what that meant. We were not to be seen together going home in case my father saw us. Uncle Alf knew that the first thing that I wanted to do would be to see Auntie Iris and share my experience.

After I'd crept into Auntie Iris's flat I ran to her and flopped into her lap with tears running down my cheeks, saying, 'I must help Violet! No one wants her – she hasn't even got a nice auntie like you. She has got nothing! I just want to help my sister.'

I burst into tears again. Auntie Iris didn't care, she simply took me on her lap and held me tight and rocked me back and forth, comforting me, and whispering in my ear that everything was going to be all right. She kissed me and told me that God would help as well, because God loved little children – but I said, 'Only the good ones.'

She asked, 'Who told you that, Georgie?' and I replied, 'Oh someone…' I did not tell her that it was Auntie Hilda who told me.

It had only been a few weeks earlier that I had asked Auntie Hilda if I could go to church with her and my sister, hoping that my request would please her, as she always took my sister to church every Sunday near the Old Kent Road at the Elephant and Castle.

'No, you can't go,' she said. 'God only likes good children, and you are too bad and wicked to go to church. Your place is in hell.'

Auntie Iris was very religious, and church members would come to her home to pray, as she could no longer go to church due to her illness. So here I had two people who went to church, and one of them was saying that God loves me, and the other was saying that God does not love me. Like a lot of other things, this confused me.

Almost every Sunday, Uncle Alf would take me to see Violet, and I was now getting more and more determined that I should help my sister. I got to know Violet's friends and would talk to them and make them laugh. Although Violet could not communicate with me due to her health problem, I was getting so close to her that I understood her more; after all, we were both in the same boat, not being wanted by our family, so perhaps I was trying to make up for it to her.

Uncle Alf had noticed how Violet's teeth were growing outwards and needed attention. He made a complaint about it, hoping that something could be done about it, but that fell on deaf ears. I also noticed how the patients were being treated, and on one occasion I saw a male nurse hitting an old woman who was unable to feed herself due to her mental state, but he kept hitting her. I then went over to the nurse and told him, 'Stop, or I will hit you!' When Uncle Alf came over to support my action, we were told to mind our own business. In those days things of that nature were not considered important.

One day, Uncle Alf told me that his firm had contacted him about a big job plastering up north, which meant that he would not be able to take me on my weekly visit to my sister's hospital. This news was good for him but heartbreaking for me. What was I to do? I knew that Auntie

Iris wouldn't be able to take me, due to her health, and I knew there would be no hope with my own family. Besides, they knew nothing about me seeing Violet; if they did, that would be the last time I'd see her.

So I decided to take myself. After all I knew the route, as I had travelled there enough times. I could go there blindfolded and still find my way, so it was a case of either walk or bunk on the bus or a bit of both to get there.

On my first journey to the hospital I walked and ran all the way. It took me about 1½ hours. Well, walking and running with the soles of your shoes hanging off can be a bit painful, but my sister Violet was worth it. Then I started to get more daring and bunked on the bus, jumping off when the conductor shouted at me to get off. I had explained to Auntie Iris what I was doing, walking and bunking, and like any mother she was not happy about this. So she began giving me my bus fare, which I kept and spent on taking Violet to the café, which she really loved to do.

A few weeks had passed by when Uncle Alf came home for a long weekend rest from his contract up north. He caught me walking back from the tobacconist, which stood on the corner of Thornton Heath railway goods yard. At the rear of this tobacconist was a hairdresser's shop for men, which was owned by a tall Jewish man. He was always smoking a pipe, which left aromas of different flavours as you went in which made a good advert for tobacco. He knew me well as a regular, as I was always getting Auntie Hilda's supply of John Players untipped cigarettes.

The tobacconist shop was opposite the Railway Telegraph. Uncle Alf had just come out of the pub. 'Hello, Georgie,' he said. 'I've got a nice surprise for you in my back garden shed.' Then, taking my hand, he walked home with me. My heart was pounding with excitement. What was this surprise in store for me? All kinds of thoughts entered my mind – a bit of bacon rind, maybe. Auntie Iris always surprised me with it, as she knew how much I loved it. Or some sweets, or maybe a comic, because she knew I liked *Desperate Dan*… As we turned into our road, Uncle Alf let go of my hand, because if Auntie Hilda had seen him holding my hand or showing any concern towards me he knew that he would be heading for a row, and he didn't want that.

'You go on, Georgie,' he said, putting me in front of him, 'I will catch up with you in a minute. Meet me at Auntie Iris's.'

As I crept into her flat from the back alley, as I now always did, Auntie Iris put her finger on her lips indicating for me to be very quiet. Then Uncle Alf came in from the front door. Auntie Iris was sitting in her usual chair with an excited smile on her beaming face.

'Uncle Alf has something for you, Georgie.' She indicated for me to close my eyes and not open them until they said 'ready'. It seemed like a lifetime waiting for the magical word – something that would never happen in my flat upstairs. Auntie Hilda or my father had never given me anything, only heartache and pain.

'Ready!' they said. I opened my eyes, and there before me was Uncle Alf with the biggest grin I had ever seen written across his face. He was holding a second-hand bike.

'It's yours, Georgie!' they said together. It sounded like they had been rehearsing the words together. 'It's yours, Georgie!' they repeated.

I had never been given anything before in my seven years.

I could not believe that this was happening to me. It seemed so strange. I just did not understand why anyone was giving me something. The only thing that I was used to getting was a good hiding – or a face of hatred looking down at me.

My mouth was locked wide open and then my eyes started to fill with water, and before I knew it the tears were running down my cheeks. I'm not sure if it was due to the shock of having something given to me for the first time, or just happiness or a feeling of how lucky I was to have a bike! This was my first ever gift, a day I would remember for ever, something just for me to keep.

'Let me show you how to ride it, Georgie,' Uncle Alf said, trying to convince me that it was not a dream, and this was really happening to me.

'Can you?' I said, with tears still running down my cheeks. 'My bike, my bike!' I was saying. I was still asking myself if this was really true, or was I dreaming?

'It's your bike,' said Auntie Iris, 'and it's your bike to keep. So you don't need to walk to the hospital to see Violet anymore, but you will need to learn to ride it.'

The next day I was seeing Violet, so I was determined to learn to ride the bike by tomorrow so that I could ride to the hospital on my own. Uncle Alf would go ahead of me first with the bike. He took me to the local recreation ground, which was a ten-minute walk for my first, very first, lesson. I think he took me there because there was open space and lots of grass that would be able to cushion me should I fall off the bike.

In no time whatsoever I had mastered the art of riding a bike. 'It was meant for you, Georgie' Uncle Alf said. Then he started shouting, 'You have done it, you have done it!'

I rode my bike back, feeling full of pride that I had learned to ride it so quickly, and this was my bike my pride and joy. As I was riding, Uncle Alf was ready to grab me should I fall or lose my balance, and I was shouting, 'Look, Uncle, I can ride my bike without falling and with legs outstretched, whoopee!'

When we arrived home, Auntie Hilda was standing at the front gate paying the milkman the weekly milk bill. Seeing me on my bike, laughing with the enjoyment of riding it, she took one big cold look and shouted, 'Where did you nick that from, Melsham?'

Before I was able to give her any answer to her searching question, Uncle Alf replied, because he knew what she was hoping to hear – that I had nicked it. But he made a point of letting her know what a big mistake she had made. 'I got it for him,' he said loudly, 'and he did not nick it from anyone. He is a good boy.'

That was the first time that I had heard him shout at anyone, and he wanted to give me a verdict of 'not guilty' for nicking a bike. But I felt bad that Hilda was put in her place. She looked at me in a way that gave me a cold shiver of fear, and I knew that somehow she would get her own back on me, as she always had done.

Taking my bike like a proud owner to the back garden, I began to wash it. I scrubbed and polished it and spent hours cleaning it. In the end I stood it against the fence, gleaming clean. This was my bike a first ever – a present – and no one was going to take it from me. Tomorrow I would ride it to Violet's hospital.

As I rode to the hospital I felt that I just wanted to ride and ride and never stop and then share my excitement with my Violet – not that she would understand, but at least I had someone who to share my joy with.

I arrived at the hospital in quicker time than I would normally travel, I placed my bike against the wall knowing it would be safe; unlike today, when locking your bike to a lamp post or railing is a must. Even then, you can find your wheels are missing. I spent the entire day with Violet and her friends. For five enjoyable weeks I was just as excited about my bike as the day it was given to me. I didn't even let my sister, Joyce, ride it, and I was still taking good care of it and keeping it clean just like new. Any old excuse was all I needed to go out on my bike.

Auntie Hilda told me to get her usual John Players cigarettes at the tobacconist, and armed with 1s 6d – the cost of twenty John Players – I took my bike on the short journey to the tobacconist. I rested my bike outside the Railway Telegraph pub on the kerbside and walked across the road to get Auntie Hilda's fags. On my return, I was just a few feet away from my bike when I saw a motorcyclist coming over the bridge from Thornton Heath railway station on my left.

All of a sudden the motorcyclist lost control of his bike. He flew over the handlebars of his bike towards the tobacconist, where I had just come from, and then landed in the road just by the shop. His bike carried on and headed towards my bike, just missing me by a whisker; but my bike had taken the full impact.

I looked over to the bike rider, who was lying only a few yards from me on the road with no crash helmet, which was not needed by law then. His eyes wide open with blood running from a head wound. His right leg was twisted behind him. 'He is dead!' someone shouted, as I rushed over to help. This was the first time that I had seen someone dead, which was very frightening for me at the time.

I was told to leave the scene, as it was not a place for a boy, so I went over to my bike. I stared at it in a complete daze of disbelief, while people were running up to me asking if I was all right. I just burst into tears, firstly because of the thought of seeing someone dead and realising that it could have been me, and then secondly at seeing my lovely bike all buckled and twisted. The very first gift that I had ever had was now destroyed before my eyes. I just sat on the pavement, crying my eyes out, unable to speak to answer the question, 'Are you all right, son?' I was thinking, No I was not all right! My first gift that I was given by Uncle Alf has been destroyed, together with my pride and joy.

How could I explain this away to Uncle Alf and Auntie Iris, who had put so much effort into getting my bike so I could see Violet? By now the ambulance and the police had arrived. An elderly copper said, 'Hello, son, are you all right?'

'No, I am not,' I said, now getting angry at losing my bike. My blood was boiling. 'Look at my bike!'

'Don't worry about that, I'm sure that you will get a new one,' he said, after asking me what I saw of the accident and assuring himself that

I did not need medical help. He wrote down all the information about the driver, time of accident and date and so on. Then he said to me, 'Give this to your mum and dad,' and handed me a piece of paper. 'They will sort everything out for you, so don't get yourself upset.'

That was a laugh, I thought to myself. Auntie Hilda or my father sort it all out for me? You would be talking about a miracle.

On arriving home with my twisted bike in my hands, I put it down in the front garden. Wondering what Uncle Alf and Auntie Iris would make of all this, I then crept into their flat and burst into tears again. 'What has happened, Georgie?' she asked.

I told her what had happened and described what my bike now looked like. Straight away, she assured me that all would be well and that I would get a new bike from the insurance company of the motorcyclist, and that it would not take very long and I would be back on the road in no time with a new and better bike. 'But the main thing is that you are not hurt,' she said. She then held me and cuddled me and kept saying, 'I am glad that you are not hurt, Georgie.'

Feeling reassured that all would be OK and that I would get a new bike, I went upstairs and waited for my father to come home from work, knowing that it would be useless trying to tell Auntie Hilda. She would say that it was my fault anyway, so I wanted to get my say in first. At least it could save me from another good hiding from my father. When my father arrived home, I told him the whole story from beginning to end. His only query was, 'Where is that bit of paper the copper gave you?'

As I was reaching in my pockets to find the piece of paper, Auntie Hilda said, 'He is lying again!'

'I am not,' I said.

'Don't answer me back!' she said. When I finally produced the piece of paper, she smirked and started her coughing again, trying desperately to get her breath back.

A few days later a police officer arrived at our home to talk to my father and me about the accident. All the time police were there in our home, my father sat picking his nose, then looking at the result and rolling it up with his fingers and flicking it around him. You could see that the policeman felt a bit sick and embarrassed by what he was doing by the look on his face. I too felt embarrassed at my father behaving this way in front of a stranger.

Just as the policeman was about to leave, he said, 'What's that lump and bruise on your head, son? Did it happen at the motorbike accident?'

'No, no,' I said, 'I fell over on the garden path.' The truth was that I had had a bloody good hiding the day before from my father, but I did not tell that to the copper or anyone else, because it would only lead to another good hiding.

A few weeks later my father got a cheque for a new bike and I got nothing – no new bike. He kept the lot. He stole my first ever gift from me; that's how I saw it. Later, when Auntie Iris and Uncle Alf asked about the insurance for the bike, I told them that the company did not pay out for the bike.

I started visiting Violet at the hospital again, making my way there by walking or bunking on the bus. I was not prepared to let her down. Going to see her was a big outlet for me. At least I had a blood relation who I knew was now getting closer to me. She could not understand what I was saying, but both our hearts were there as a brother and sister. Then there was Auntie Iris and Uncle Alf, who I could turn to and trust, so my free time was spent with them and Violet.

Peace had come to the country. The war had now officially finished with Germany, but my personal war with my family was still running on, with no sight of it ending, apart from a moment on Victory Day, with thoughts of seeing the talent that my father had. Wherever I had walked around the streets of where I lived or going to see Violet at the Fountain Hospital in Tooting Bec, I saw Union Jacks flying all over houses across the streets with V signs everywhere, celebrating our victory with the end of the World War Two.

Uncle Alf decorated our house with Union Jacks and helped decorate our road with flags across the street. Like almost every road in the country, ours was to have a party to celebrate the arrival of Victory Day. Our road was ablaze with Union Jacks, and long tables were set along the road laden with food and drink. With the tables there were long stools and chairs. One table was from the local church hall, supplied by Mr Crookshank. On either end of the street was a big bonfire that left a big hole in the road. The party had started with all the kids with their mums and dads sharing the excitement with them and making sure that they were getting their fair share of food. The food was provided by the good neighbours along our road.

Auntie Hilda and my sister, Joyce, turned up, with Joyce being treated well by Auntie Hilda; but I was left as usual on my own to get on with it. I could not share the party with Auntie Iris or Uncle Alf, as that would have caused problems with Auntie Hilda, as I wasn't supposed to be talking to them, let alone seeing them. So I was drifting from one end to the other to avoid eye contact with Auntie Hilda. But every party needs some music, which my father provided.

An upright piano was put on four wheels, and every now and then it was pushed down the road for my father to play – and what a player he really was! I don't think they needed to push the piano down the road for him, for he was playing so good, he made the piano talk and it seemed to dance with him as he played. Everyone was cheering him and clapping for the whole day. He played that piano like you had never heard a piano played before. I just felt proud of him. I wanted to shout out for everyone to hear, 'That's my dad playing that piano!' But I could not bring those words out; I was too afraid of him.

At the end of the party, which lasted late into the night, my father played 'God Save the King' like it had never been played before. He was the star of the road that day, and I was proud of him. Free beer was flowing, and that was what was needed to bring out the best in him.

With the party now over and everyone gone home to bed, I found myself alone again amongst the party rubbish that lay on the road. The tables and chairs were still there, with leftovers all over the place, and the piano that my father had been playing was still standing there alone, just as I was. I sat on the chair that he had sat on, playing the piano and with my finger making a quiet note. I cried not for me but my father. The great piano player who gave so much joy that day to so many children and parents could not make me a happy child in my life; and there I fell asleep, dreaming that perhaps one day he would make me happy, like he had today with all the other children and their parents.

Chapter Four

I am eight years old today but totally unaware of it. I didn't know that I had a birthday or how old I was because it was never celebrated and no one ever mentioned it until today. As a child I remember asking about how I was born, only to be told that I was not born but found under the gooseberry bush, whatever that may mean. I always felt that I was a reject, just a thing that was called Melsham, a name applied to me by Auntie Hilda.

I was made aware of birthdays mainly by noticing that when it was my sister's birthday, the day was always made extra special for her. Joyce always got packets of sweets or a small doll from Auntie Hilda. I think that the special effort made was purely to tease me and rub my nose in it. I always thought that birthdays were for posh kids or good ones like Joyce; that's what I always believed until today.

I woke this bright sunny spring day with the sound of birds tweeting as they laid their eggs to produce their chicks.

Auntie Iris and Uncle Alf had a lot of concern for me, and would seek out whatever information was needed from my father when he was drunk. Uncle Alf would wait until he had a few drinks to loosen his tongue then ask him whatever information he needed.

Auntie Iris and Uncle Alf must have often wondered about my birthday. Surely I must have a birthday like everyone else. Uncle Alf had made it his duty to ask my father, who told him. It was a surprise that he knew, really, as he had no time for me; but what may have helped to jog my father's memory was that he was born in the same month, and the date was only ten days apart. I suppose it must have taken about ten pints to come to that figure, and that's how Auntie Iris and Uncle Alf got their information about me. Later I learned to use the same technique.

I was learning, and learning fast. I had to in order to survive. I had heard about birthday parties but I had never been invited to any, maybe because I never looked smart like other kids, and that I could be an embarrassment. I had never been given a birthday card or present, so I had never been able to count how many days to my birthday. We had little or no money, so in our house birthdays were just another day. Auntie Hilda and my father knew when my birthday was but never bothered to tell me or celebrate it.

I must have mentioned about Joyce having birthdays to Auntie Iris at some point on one of my frequent visits to her, and that could be why she decided to make today special for me.

As I was leaving for school I saw Auntie Iris hiding downstairs by the side of the stairs. She waved to me and put her other hand over her lips. She had beckoned me to follow her into her living room and closed the door behind us. She looked at me with a big grin on her face and seemed excited. So that she was sure that I could hear her, she asked me to repeat very quietly what she had said to me; it seemed very important that I understand what she was saying and had to repeat what she had said. 'When you come home from school today you must come around the back door to see me, but don't let anyone know or see you. Now, do you understand, Georgie?'

'Yes, Auntie, I understand what you said, and I will see you when I come home from school,' I replied.

All day at school I was wondering why Auntie Iris wanted me to come back to her flat; it was bugging me all day. I know that I hadn't done anything wrong. Had it been Auntie Hilda who had given me those instructions, I would know for sure that something was definitely wrong.

At last my school day was over. It was time to put an end to the suspense and find out why it was so important to go straight to her flat. As instructed, I came round to her back door, leading from the garden, and made sure that no one could see me. It was obvious that she had meant Auntie Hilda or my father – or even Joyce, because she would tell Auntie Hilda. I knocked on the back door and opened it. 'I'm here, Auntie,' I said, popping my head around the door.

As I walked in, I saw Uncle Alf and their daughter, Deirdre, and all three of them had smiles on their faces. On the table were freshly cut sandwiches, jelly and a big cake in the middle of the table.

'Happy birthday, Georgie!' they all yelled. 'Georgie, it's your birthday!'

'How do you know?' I asked, and Auntie Iris put her finger to her lips and smiled.

Then they handed me a birthday card, the first birthday card that I have ever had. Uncle Alf read it to me, then they gave a present all wrapped up. I unwrapped my first ever birthday present to reveal a big comic book called *Desperate Dan*. I was overcome with emotion. I just could not believe this was happening to me. Cheekily, I asked, 'Have you become rich?'

'No, no, George, it's your birthday. Now, tuck in and fill your belly with food.'

I was so excited that I just could not eat as much as I would normally. Excitement seemed to put knots in my stomach, but what a swell party this was, and how lucky I felt.

Then Auntie Iris said, 'Now for the birthday cake.' It was covered with icing and had eight candles on the top. She then lit them with a match.

'Why are you doing that? Are you cooking it?' I asked.

'No,' she said, as they all laughed, 'all birthday cakes have candles, and each candle is for each year that you are, and you are now eight.'

Then they sang 'Happy birthday to you'. This was complete magic to me. It was my first birthday and birthday party. Auntie Iris took me by each hand to face her. 'Now, Georgie, when you have a birthday cake with candles on, you must try and blow them all out, and at the same time you have to make a wish.'

'Will my wish come true?' I asked.

'Yes, your wish will come true.'

'How many wishes can I make?'

'As many as you want!'

I thought about it for a few moments and then said, 'I am ready, Auntie.'

'Then try and blow them all out together, and make your wish, Georgie.'

So I blew with all the oxygen in my lungs then blew out all the candles – well, most of them, as I never had any practice before then. I made my wish out loud: 'Please make my sister Violet better, and I want my mum.'

At that, silence fell in the room and there was no more laughter. I thought for a moment that I had done something wrong.

'Georgie,' said Auntie Iris, 'let me give you a birthday cuddle!' I had noticed a teardrop running down her cheek but I could not understand why at the time.

'Come on, Georgie,' Uncle Alf said. 'I have got something for you – another surprise and a present for your birthday.'

He then led me to the side of the garden, with Auntie Iris between us holding on for support from both of us.

'Now close your eyes,' Auntie Iris said, as Uncle Alf got ready to remove a cover at the side of the fence. I closed my eyes, wondering what could be under that cover.

'Open your eyes,' Uncle Alf said. When I did, it was not a new bike but a go-kart. It wasn't something that I could travel to see Violet in, but I could use it to play with my mates.

I'd wondered what Uncle Alf was making in his shed of a weekend, and now I knew. He was very good at carpentry, and made most of his furnishing from timber at his building site. We used to call them 'soapboxes'. It had two big pram wheels on the back, with two little ones on the front. A piece of string was tied from the front axle to steer the kart, and there was a piece of wood on the side for a brake. When you have nothing and then out of the blue get something like my bike, then have it taken from you soon after, you want to hide it; that was my first thought. Here on my birthday, which I had never celebrated before, I was being given this second present. I just could not believe what was happening to me. I was so excited, and sat in the kart like any proud owner.

'Come on, Georgie, let's go on the outside pavement and let's show you how to really drive it for real,' said Uncle Alf. He took me around the corner, away from any peering looks from Auntie Hilda, and explained how to use the brake and steer the front. Having satisfied himself about my safety, he then left me to play and enjoy myself with it. Having gone around the back streets a couple of times, it didn't take long before I found other local kids to play with me and my soapbox. We all took turns in pushing the back of the driver rather than using our feet to make it move. I now felt like one of those lucky kids who seem to have everything round where they lived. I think I had one of the first soapboxes in the local streets.

I don't think I ever laughed so much with enjoyment. I was beginning to feel part of the local boys, all because Auntie Iris and Uncle Alf took a huge interest in my growing up; but for all they were doing for me, it had to be hidden from Auntie Hilda and my father, and even Joyce, who could tell them what I was doing.

A staircase kept our flats apart, but a mind of steel had been built between our good neighbours and me. I had to live in that house one life upstairs and a better one downstairs. My birthday seemed to have given me my longest day, playing with my new toy until darkness had taken over the street, with the gaslights burning a dull light. I was still out enjoying my first birthday. I took it to where it had first been covered to re-cover it in order to hide it from Auntie Hilda. I knew that if she saw it she would say that I had nicked it and say, 'Wait till your father gets home!' So I was taking no chances this time. I returned and took myself back upstairs to home, which I had left some twelve hours earlier to the sound of Auntie Hilda coughing her heart out, with her fag still on her bottom lip and the ash hanging on for life. After she got her breath back, she took one look at me with her cold staring eyes, but not once did she say 'Where have you been?' Because I knew, and she knew, that she did not care.

As usual I took myself to bed, and lay there feeling worn out and tired. I was thinking of this great wonderful day that I had with the full taste of my birthday cake in my mouth, and I fell asleep feeling lucky and happy, not knowing that the two wishes that I had made that day in Auntie Iris's flat downstairs would be changing the corners of my young life.

Joyce, my youngest, sister was very timid and afraid that the hidings I got would be directed at her if she were seen to be on my side. Hence she would side with Auntie Hilda, not really understanding the problems and the misery it gave me, and sometimes I hated her for it. Joyce was getting all the attention from her, and had the freedom of the house. She was dressed better and given the love that I was denied and wanted, so anything Joyce said to her was accepted as the truth about me, even if it was a lie. Consequently, unknown to Joyce, Auntie Hilda would use her to find out what I was up to, so that she could find another reason to tell my father some cock and bull story about what I had or had not done.

I was staying out of the house more, starting from the time I woke early in the morning to late at night. This was getting to Auntie Hilda, as she was running out of personal ideas on which to base her tales about me. No way was I prepared to give any clues or games away about my activities. I had to focus on widening the rift between me and Auntie Hilda. I was keeping secrets about what I had or was doing; the only loyalty and trust I felt was towards Auntie Iris and Uncle Alf. I was learning fast that keeping my distance helped to reduce the regular hidings and punishment.

After a few days of enjoying my new soapbox and making new friends with it, Joyce had seen me with my soapbox and one of my playmates. She asked me about it and I told her that it belonged to me; unfortunately she saw me put it in our back garden and when I arrived back home after covering up the soapbox Auntie Hilda was waiting for me. She said, 'Where did you nick that soapbox from?'

Straight away I knew it was Joyce. She had told her aunt about my new toy and where I had kept it. Auntie Hilda yelled again, 'Where did you nick that soapbox from?'

I had to think and think fast and find an excuse to use that would not get Auntie Iris or Uncle Fred into trouble. Telling the truth would be the worst thing I could possibly do. There was no way I could explain that it was my birthday present, given to me at my first birthday party. After all, I was not supposed to know I *had* a birthday…

I confessed, telling her what she wanted to hear, and I believe I blurted out, 'I nicked it from a boy!' She started firing questions about the boy. Knowing this was a lie that could spiral out of control, I just said that I could not remember. In my mind I was thinking to myself, Why prolong this? Because whatever I say or do I am going to be punished anyway.

I just waited for her to repeat her famous words that she'd repeated so many times… here we go: 'Wait till your father gets home!' She said it with great pleasure, knowing that she had something to tell my father that would lead to my suffering again. She had repeated those words – 'Wait till your father gets home' – so many times by now that it was beginning to become a habit of mine to confess to things that I had not done, to save the troubles of others. I think that when you are almost being brainwashed and told what you have or have not done, you start to begin to believe that you don't deserve anything, that you are a thief and a troublemaker, and then you begin to confess to a lie just to try and stop it.

When my father came home I was ready for anything, including dying to save my guardian angels Auntie Iris and Uncle Alf, given the trouble that they would find themselves in. But this time I did not get my usual good hiding. Instead, my father just left the house and returned within minutes with my soapbox in his hands, after listening to Auntie Hilda telling him where it was. This time she had hard evidence of my theft. Then, without a word spoken by either of them, my father broke the soapbox piece by piece into tiny bits of wood, and piece by piece put them on the open fire. Auntie Hilda stood there with that cruel smirk on her face, grinning more with every piece that was burning. This was the worst thing he could have done to me. I would have preferred to be given a good hiding rather than see my soapbox burn on the open fire, and just save my only first birthday present.

I slumped to the floor on my knees, hoping that this was a dream, but it wasn't. This was reality. As the smoke from my soapbox was rising up into the chimney, I was thinking of all the fun I had with it and the new mates that I had found because of it. The hardest bit was holding all the anger and the misery inside of me, because if I had made an attempt to tell the whole truth, Auntie Iris and Uncle Alf would most certainly be in big trouble for giving me a birthday present. I also had the fear that my father would confront Uncle Alf and possibly hit him. As I watched the burning continue on the fire, I could not help or stop the shouting and screaming inside of me. I so wished that I had been physically punished instead. At least a cut and bruising can heal, but you can't bring back a birthday present from the fire and heal it; that's gone for ever, and only memories remain. Even today, when a present is given to me for a birthday or at Christmas, that memory comes flooding back, and somehow in the back of my mind I sometimes think it is going to be taken from me as well. So I tend not to get as excited as one might expect when receiving a present.

Auntie Iris and Uncle Alf had noticed that my soapbox was not around and that I was not happily playing with it. When they asked after it I could not tell them that the birthday present that they gave me, which Uncle Alf had made, taking him hours to build, was now ashes, burned and destroyed by my evil father. Again I was in a position where I could not tell the truth. I had to tell another lie, saying that someone had nicked my soapbox. Doing that made me feel worse with myself. I was now having to lie to the very people who took care of me and who trusted and believed in me, and their friendship with me meant so much. I was not going to see that destroyed as well; but one thing that Auntie Hilda or my father could not destroy was my memory. They could take my soapbox and burn it but they couldn't take what was left in my mind. The memory of that great day remains for ever; it also gave me a new strength of mind to learn to lead a more independent life from them, to keep and hide what was mine, to learn to defend and look after myself. It was to start my ducking and diving strategy for survival. I kept asking myself, Why can't I have a normal life like any of my mates? They had a mum and dad who cared for them and never pushed them to one side. They never took from them but just gave them the security and love. They played with them, sharing the laughter and happiness. I was beginning to see this more clearly in my growing up, and now so wanted to be part of that circle. Why was I always classed as the bad egg, the unwanted one – dead or alive? Why can't I ever be seen doing the right thing? Must I always walk as a shadow that disappears in the darkness? What have I done wrong – am I to blame?

I needed to be reassured and my survival depended on it. My 'first birthday' had begun to open my eyes to a new outlook, a new life, and that new me would help me to help my sister, Violet, and give her what was taken from me. Auntie Iris and Uncle Alf had said the stepping stone for me to reach my goal now was to begin that survival. Pick yourself up, brush yourself down, and fight on: my life was about to prove that. Still feeling the hurt of losing my soapbox, I needed to get away, to shut myself away...

I was feeling even more rejected and took myself off to the lock-up garages around the corner to our road, where there were about thirty lock-up garages in blocks of ten. Behind them was an abandoned air-raid shelter that had been used during the war years. It was a place that became a playground for me and an imaginary home. I would often just go and sit in there and think that I was in a family home with my mum. Over time, I had cleaned it out and had started to furnish it with an old settee found on the local bomb site. There was a table and chairs and even some old carpet. The walls were decorated with old pictures to add colour and cheer up my hideout, and often I would go there and play in my imaginary home. I felt a bit of happiness in being there, enjoying my own company by myself in my own happy little home. It was not much, but at least I felt happy away from Auntie Hilda and my father; but this time, after what had happened, I just wanted to stay away from them. Before I would sometimes stay on my own for half a day, but now I was staying all day and some nights a week. It felt so peaceful just being away from all that misery of life at home.

I also thought it was a good opportunity for Auntie Hilda to realise that I was not a bad boy and begin to appreciate me, now that she had to go out and get her own John Players cigarettes every day, and had to do her own errands because I was not around. All kind of things like this were going through my mind in my decision to stay away from home. I had already had a lot of old curtains that I could use as blankets, and thankfully the weather at the time was warming up. I then made an inside lock so I could keep out any intruders, as there was a lot of types around in those days trying to find a place to rest their heads; but my lock to keep out the intruders had also locked in the intruders who were already sharing my home, unknown to me.

On my first night, when darkness had set in I fell asleep dreaming of playing in this field full of flowers with a big swing in the middle. I was running around with this beautiful woman, calling 'Mommy, Mommy,' as I gathered lots of flowers of all different colours in my hands and gave them to her. 'George, my darling boy,' she was saying, 'I love you!' She kept repeating the words, as we lay down amongst the flowers surrounding us. 'I love you, Mommy,' I was saying. Her warm hands were now stroking my body; her hands slid to my feet, and at that point I woke, but was half asleep, still thinking how real this dream was of mine. I no longer felt the hand of my mother, but something was moving from my feet up my leg. I froze! I was terrified. I dared not move. I held my breath, as this moving thing was still moving on me. Now and then it stopped, then it moved again. I was lying on my tummy. It had now passed my bottom and was moving up my back, and felt the wetness of my wee; it was still warm. My heart started to beat with a loud ticking and I was still frozen in fright. I thought my eight years of life was about to disappear as the movement was now on my neck. I opened my eyes, and I could see it was getting daylight. I dared not move as it moved over my head. I jumped up from the settee to see that the thing that had travelled up my back was a large rat! I screamed at it, and as the rat was trying to find an escape from my home I shouted at it saying, 'Leave me alone, I'm a good boy!' Then I ran from my home onto the streets. I was so thirsty with fright I had to have a drink. I then saw a milkman delivering the daily milk from his horse and cart. I needed something to stop my thirst, so I waited for the milkman to lead his horse and cart further up the road before going to the rear of the milk float to steal a half-pint of fresh milk to satisfy my thirst. Then I began to shiver – shivering at stealing the milk, and shivering at the cold early morning air.

I returned to my air-raid-shelter home with a big stick to make a loud noise by banging the side of the shelter in order to frighten away the rat, should it still be there, and to add courage to myself in order to remain in my home. I was unable to continue my sleep with the thought of the rat returning later that morning. Still holding the big stick in my hand, and smelling of my pee, which had now dried to my trousers and skin, I headed for the back alley of my road, to avoid being seen by Auntie Hilda or my father. I started to drag my stick along the fence to make a noise, and as I was doing this I found a loose panel fallen from the fence. As I picked it up, an idea stuck in my head. If I could chop it up I could sell it for firewood. Firewood was very popular then because almost everyone had a coal fire, and I was about to join in supplying this fast-selling item. I then sneaked into Auntie Iris's back garden to get myself a chopper. I had often helped Uncle Alf chop up his firewood so I had a good idea how to do it and knew where he kept his chopper.

Returning to the site where I had found my fence panel, I started to chop it up into firewood. A six-foot single fence panel makes a bundle of firewood. With my bundle of firewood, I went around the corner of my road and knocked on the first door, which was opened by a cheerful old lady.

'Do you want a bundle of firewood, miss?' She was my first customer… my first sale! I remembered all the patter I had learned from Rosy Lea at the market.

Almost all the houses around the local streets had back alleys, so, armed with my chopper, I started to take some panels from the fences and chop them up as firewood. I knew it was wrong, but I had to in order to buy food to satisfy my hungry belly. I then started to knock on the front doors of the houses to sell my firewood. At one old penny a bundle, my sales was taking off. Some of my customers could have been buying their own fences. My ducking and diving days had started! Well, they say that the streets of London are paved with gold: how true it was with me – including back alleys!

In my early days I had many ways of earning money; I had to, as you will find out. My firewood was selling well, and I was earning a lot of money. All the money that I was earning would give me an opportunity to help Violet. I could get the extra bits that she needed, like sweets, toys and colouring books with crayons, as she liked doing colouring with bright colours. I could also take her out to the cafés more, which was another thing that she liked doing.

My first working day over, I returned to my air-raid shelter with drinks and food. I also brought myself some candles so that I could see during the dark nights. I hoped that the rat would not return, with a candle glowing. At the time I thought that rats only came out when it was dark. I spent another three nights with the rats, after a tug of war with them over my food and being bitten by them on several occasions in all. I'd had enough, and I thought that I would rather put up with my home life and Auntie Hilda than share my food and get bitten by the rats. After five nights and days living in those conditions I made my way home. There was no home welcoming party for me. There had been no search party out looking for me, no concerns about where I had been. I could have been kidnapped for all they cared! I now felt even more rejected and unwanted. Instead, the only response I had from Auntie Hilda was, 'Look at the state of you – you look like a tramp!' She also said that I stank, and was a no-good-for-nothing. 'Now get yourself in the sink and wash yourself!'

What I was expecting was, 'Oh, poor Georgie, I have missed you, we were worried about you! You sit down while I do you a nice hot bath...' But no chance.

Having strip-washed from the running cold tap hanging from the wall, I began to wish that I had not come back. I would have gone back to the shelter but the thought of living with the rats again stopped me. Having cleaned myself, I then took to the streets again selling my firewood from fences that I had taken down. The money that I was earning was by now growing. It was all profit and it needed to be hidden. I could not hide it at home because my father would keep it for himself, or if Auntie Hilda found it she would say that I had stolen it from someone and that would lead to another good hiding. So I set out to hide my money, and tried to find an ideal spot. I decided to dig a hole by the side of the fence in the alley and bury it, and as I needed it would return to unearth it. It wasn't long before I had many holes that I had dug to hide my money. There must still be a lot of money there now that I had forgotten about.

I was still seeing Violet at the Fountain Hospital, but now I had money to buy her toys and colouring books. We would both sit down with one each and colour away. Unlike mine, her colouring looked like the scribbling of a little child, due to her mental health; but I enjoyed just being with her and enjoying each other's company. I was getting to know many of her friends. Amongst them were mongols and patients with a variety of different mental problems; they were now friends of mine as well. One of them in particular, Jean, still remains Violet's friend to this day. I used to make all of them laugh, and they made me laugh. Very few of them had visitors, so I took time to see them as well. They all called me 'Dorgie' as they always heard Violet calling me that. It was the only way that she could pronounce my name, but I understood. I can never understand what she says to me, and I have to rely on others to repeat it to me. This is not just due to my deafness, but I have to watch the speaker's lips. When Violet talks she rarely uses her lips, so I have to rely on her body language. That's how we got to understand each other. It was the warmth of our brother and sisterly love that expressed it all.

Then I would take her for quite a long walk to the café. Her walking was slow, so that I suppose made it seem even longer to me, but I was determined to keep seeing her. When she was walking with me, people would stop and stare at her and make funny noises. This used to upset me, and I would get annoyed with them when they were taking the piss. After all, she did not understand, but on several occasions I would lash out when some of the young kids followed us out of the café making funny noises behind us as we walked up the road. Sometimes I could take no more. I was already damaged goods, from being knocked around at home, so one or two boys were not going to make any difference to me. I would explode like a volcano and lash out at them, hitting them as hard as I could, trying to hurt them like I was hurt by my father. When you are fighting for your own, believe me, you do become a wild animal and gain strength that you never knew you had. I would fight for my sister, who was unable to fight for herself, and I did not care if I got killed. In fact, many times I got hurt myself, and Violet would cuddle me and try to protect me. So I had learned not only to survive a battered life but I also learned to defend myself and use my fists. I was becoming hard and fearless. Although I never looked for a fight I was more than willing to stand up for those who could not stand up for themselves.

All my life I have been fighting for other people's rights as well as my own. The fights over my sister were as regular as my ducking and diving. I have lost more fights than I have won, but I felt right afterwards. I knew that I had done the right thing in protecting my sister. Why shouldn't she be allowed to go in peace like anyone else, and walk down the road without some idiot stopping and taking the piss out on her? She had not asked to be the way she was born, no more than I wanted to be deaf.

From taking down fences, I started other scams. I had armed myself with a bucket and hand shovel borrowed from Auntie Iris. (Just what would I have done without her?)

I had already seen horse dung being collected by the householders so I guessed that there must be a demand for it among keen gardeners. In those days, from early morning to late at night we had all deliveries done by horse and cart. The coalman, baker, milkman and the greengrocer, the paraffin man... and so the list went on. It seemed that everyone had a horse, so you might think that the supply of horse dung would be plentiful; but there was competition, as everyone was doing the same. So I had to go that one better, and took myself to the local stables down the road. There was plenty of supply there. I used a potato bag – again from Auntie Iris, who had her potatoes delivered direct by a potato supplier in sacks via a local firm. So, being armed with my horse dung, I knocked on the doors, selling it at six old pennies a bag. It was a lot of hard work, but the rewards was good. I told Uncle Alf of my ideas selling items, and he said I should try the allotments, which I did. I set out with my horse dung carrying only two bags at a time, as they were heavy for me. First I went to the bigger houses that had large gardens. Then, as Uncle Alf suggested, I went to the allotments. These contained my best customers, who grew their vegetables, including my favourite carrots. My aim was to please, which I have always tried to do in life.

When the carrots had grown, I would pull them from the ground that had protected them. I'd bag them up and return to the stables and horses and then feed the horses with my carrots. I would wait for them to discharge their dung in my bucket, and while it was still fresh and steaming, put it into my sacks and travel back to the allotment to flog it, telling my customers that I had the freshest horse dung ever, and that the horse ate nothing but carrots! On one such occasion a customer had said to me that he had had a lot carrots nicked from his allotment, and had wondered if there was any connection. I may have been the first person to start recycling... but at least I had convinced my customers that I had the best horse dung in town, and that it would give them the best gardens and allotments. Often when I got home Auntie Hilda would complain that I stank of horse's dung. Then she followed it up by saying that that was all I was fit for.

I soon became a regular at the stables. I was amazed how a large horse could show its friendship to you, and I was getting very attached to them. Perhaps it was because all animals sensed your love for them, so they show their affection – something that I was not having at home. I think my 'first birthday' had set alarm bells ringing for me. I had felt cheated by Auntie Hilda and my father. How could they hide something from me that was part of every other child's upbringing? Well, I had taken revenge to prove that I was somebody and not some out-of-the-world boy, put out on the scrap heap. I was determined not to let anything hold me back, with the help of Rosy Lea, who had showed me the tricks of the trade in the markets, which I had not forgotten. So with all that behind me I started to increase my ducking and diving. After all, I had Violet to look after.

Another job that I did to raise money was collecting newspapers which, when sold to the rag and bone yard, would fetch 8/6 per cwt. Books and magazines sold for 7/- per cwt, and cardboard for 4/-, which I used to take to Warminster Road in South Norwood. I sometimes went to a log merchant to buy logs at 10/- for a hundred to resell them at 12/6 with Raymond on an old pram, going round peoples' houses knocking on doors.

I found another money-spinner. When I was young, kids would collect empty beer and lemonade bottles. When customers bought bottles of beer or lemonade they had to pay a deposit on the bottle, which was refundable upon return of the bottles. This was because there was a shortage of bottles due to the war. So if you had twelve empty bottles to return, you would get twelve old pennies back, which was one old shilling. Today it would be 2½ pence, but back then children could do a lot with those twelve old pennies. So I would go around searching and collecting as many empty bottles as possible. It was less hard work than dragging horse dung. Then I would go to the Bottle and Jug, which was like an off-licence bar, but for the children to go into. There I would take empty bottles to claim my prize money of one old penny a bottle.

I was finding it so easy to do this because my father was one of their best customers and Uncle Alf was using the pub, The Railway Telegraph. Normally a child who took too many bottles in was refused because the landlord knew that the kids were nicking them or collecting from door to door like me. Some children came back with their empty bottles still in their hands, unable to get the deposit. That is when I came to the rescue – by offering them a farthing for their bottles.

There were four farthings to one old penny, so I was making a good profit again. I would take them back to the Bottle and Jug, and having the cheek and patter, I was able to get away with it and claim my rewards on the bottles.

One day the landlord had said to me, on seeing dozens of empty bottles, 'Where have you got all them from? I don't think I should take them in.'

'Come on, governor,' I said, 'my father drinks it like tap water, and my Uncle Alf drinks here as well.

'Well, they must own the bloody brewery too, what with all the bottles you bring in!'

I still managed to get rid of them. Perhaps he had done it because of my bloody cheek. Again, learning the patter from Rosy Lea had paid off.

I was getting much bolder now, and I was now fighting back. I was digging holes all along the back alley in order to hide my money. No one was going to take from me again, that was my nest egg to be able to spend as I chose, and that was on my sister, Violet. She was my first port of call, and to see Violet's face when I had given her something made all the hard work worthwhile. Somehow I never got the same loving touch from Joyce. Maybe Auntie Hilda had built a barrier between us, but you just don't understand these things at the time.

Although Auntie Hilda was so cruel towards me, I still bought her presents from time to time from my profits. I would buy her twenty John Players to try and win her friendship, but the only response I got was, 'Where did you nick them from?' However, she never said, 'Wait till your father comes home!' Perhaps she felt guilty at taking them, but I did feel good about giving them presents. Somehow it gives me a surge of joy to be able to give, just as I felt on that first birthday of mine. I may have been buying love or attention, but whatever it was it made me feel good every day. My greatest pleasure is giving. The best part of my childhood was to learn from it, so everyone was getting something from me, including Auntie Iris and Uncle Alf, who had first given me my birthday, a birthday that I had never known of until I was eight years old. Then my angel Auntie Iris made sure that I would know and never forget.

In the high street of Thornton Heath there was an old cinema, which had a nickname 'The Fleapit'. It looked dirty, with torn seats and a wooden sloping floor, and showed black and white pictures. Saturday morning was my cinema day. I never was given money for it by Auntie Hilda or my father, instead I used to pay for myself. The other kids were getting their cinema money from their parents, and that's when I would make a deal with some of them.

They would pay me half the price to bunk them in, which was either through the toilet window or the side exit door, which had a heavy curtain in front of it. The money that they had saved either got them extra sweets or ice cream. The only loser would be the cinema so I would imagine that when they added up their takings they would have found that the number of kids did not add up to the money taken by them. But Saturday morning cinema was always my pet love; it would take you into a kinder life. We would watch a cowboy film, then *Tarzan*, with the lion on the screen, and subtitles that I was unable to read. Then us kids would get noisy when the projector went wrong – which often happened. We would shout, 'Turn it back on!' or whistle, and when the projector went back on we would cheer. Another of my favourites was Laurel and Hardy, but sometimes I would get my mates to read the subtitles for me. Mostly I would put up with it, and in most cases used my own imagination to figure out what the story was about – and finish up getting it completely wrong! This was to happen for the rest of my life – getting the wrong end of the stick.

Guy Fawkes Night was another winner for me. I would knock on people's doors for old men's clothing to make a guy. I even had some given to fit me, so I must have looked a bit of a state. I would then stuff the trousers with old rags and newspapers. After sticking two bits of wood in each leg, I would next stuff the jacket, which was being supported by the two bits of wood. Another piece of wood in the centre of the jacket would hold the head, made from an old football. Then I'd paint the face, trying to make it look like Auntie Hilda; even the guy looked prettier than her. I would take my guy to Thornton Heath station and give my patter, shouting 'Twenty brothers and sisters to support for their fireworks, so let's make them happy!' Or I'd shout anything that would come into my head; just the cheek can win people over, and I knew that from the experience at the market with Rosy Lea. The rest was from my nature and it paid off for me. I was getting more money than my mates put together. They were asking me how I did it, but I was not letting on to them, just in case they ended up earning more than me, maybe.

The kids were trying to copy me but getting nowhere. First, they didn't go where the people were gathered; they were on the side streets where few went. The ones who did had already given me money for my guy; anyway, as I had already caught them coming home from work at the station entrance they were not giving twice.

My mates did not seem to have that special something about them with their cheek. You either have it or you don't. So in the end I did a deal with my mates. I said to them that if I give them the patter and it worked for them, whatever they took I should get half, and so it was agreed. Now I had an army of Guy Fawkes collectors, and I would place them at each station: Thornton Heath, Selhurst Road, Norwood Junction and East Croydon. From there I was bunking on the trains to each station where my team was, and then giving the patter to the people, and also giving encouragement to the kids. Then I'd move on to the next station, and so on. My winnings were more than any boy could wish for. Now the holes in the alleys were fast expanding with all the money I was now earning. I had already seen my mates with their parents helping them to make their guys and do all the things that parents would normally do with their children, but I never had that opportunity. I had to do everything for myself.

Soon after Guy Fawkes Night, and with a bank full of money in my alley, I would wait for the snow to fall. In them days we seemed to have more snow than today. When the snow did fall, I would have my gang of workers armed with shovels to help to clear the snow from people's front paths and pavements. I was doing all the talking and patter to the householder and charging them for clearing the snow.

I must have been good at it because one of my local roads was completely cleared and free of snow. One of my offers was a free bundle of firewood, which would have meant a lot of broken fences again. I was still trying to practise my selling on someone, including a nightwatchman. Whenever there were road works, we used to have a nightwatchman. He would have a canvas hut that was sited at the beginning of the roadworks. His job was to be responsible for the red oil lamps that were placed around the roadworks, making sure they were kept lit and that there was no danger to the public.

Then he would sit there all night and keep watch. In the winter he would have a home-made brazier on metal legs with holes around the sides to keep warm. While out late at night, I would sit with him in the glow of the lamplight and talk with him.

I remember having this stray cat that followed me around. I used to pick her up for cuddles. One night I took the cat with me into the nightwatchman's hut and started to pretend to sell the cat to him and got carried away. The next thing I knew, he said he would buy it from me, much to my surprise! I explained that I was only kidding, but it did prove that I could sell at that young age.

Christmas was then upon us with the shops showing off their Christmas decorations and Christmas presents. No one ever forgot the good old dustman, who had lifted up the dustbins all the year through onto his back… no wheelies then! Then you'd watch them do their own recycling, putting newspapers to one side with the rags and woollens, then after flogging their recycled goods, sharing the money between them. So I started to collect old newspapers and rags to earn more money to buy food.

So there was no way that Auntie Hilda or my father could try to hide Christmas away from me. It was something I knew about, from watching others doing their preparations leading up to the excitement of the big day.

When my big day came, like all kids there was the excitement of pushing your little legs to feel for your Christmas stocking.

On opening mine I pulled out an apple and orange and a small packet of sweets. We had nothing, so really I expected nothing; but one thing I was *not* looking forward to was Christmas dinner cooked by Auntie Hilda! I already had problems with eating her food at the best of times; now I was to have the same problem with my Christmas dinner. I was already feeling sick just thinking about it before the dinner was even cooked. My morning had become a nightmare to me as dinnertime drew nearer. I was heavy in my stomach and was dreading the moment when the dinner was placed before me. When the time came, I gave an almighty heave and brought up my apple and orange to my throat. I rushed from the chair to the toilet, and did not return until dinner had finished. My first excuse was that I did not feel well, maybe because I was excited about Christmas day; and this saved me from another good hiding.

I then left to go out to play. I was unable to go to the café, as they were closed on Christmas Day, so there was nowhere for me to buy food for my hungry tummy. So I sneaked round to Auntie Iris, to see if I could have some food. She did not have to ask me because she knew that I was hungry. She dished me up a little Christmas dinner and a piece of Christmas pudding with custard. She said to me, 'Close your eyes, Georgie.' I knew then what to expect next, it was to give me another surprise. 'Open your eyes, Georgie,' she said, and gave me a Christmas present and wished me a Happy Christmas.

Chapter Five

I had got myself ready for school, as I normally did every day. I have never known at any time being woken up with a kiss and told, 'It's school time,' or being helped to get washed and dressed, given a nice breakfast before being taken to school, like all my other mates. That never happened – not if like me you live in Auntie Hilda's household. It was a 'help yourself' world, where you did all things yourself. As I came down our stairs, with no mention of a goodbye from either me or Auntie Hilda (which was how it was on a regular basis), as I reached the bottom of the stairs I felt a hand touch my shoulder. It was Auntie Iris with her finger firmly on her lips, indicating for me to follow her into her dining room. I knew more of the surroundings here than in my own home. She then faced me to make sure that I understood her and said, 'When you come home from school come straight to me and come around the back. It's very important that you do.' Then she asked, 'Now do you fully understand, Georgie? What did I say?'

So I repeated what she had said to me, and when she was sure that I had heard and understood she gave me a big kiss and a sandwich and adjusted my clothing and packed me off to school.

Throughout the entire day at school I sat and gazed out of the window, just wondering what Auntie Iris wanted to see me for. I knew that it must be important because of the way she had to be sure I had heard and understood her instruction to report to her after school. Different reasons kept going through my mind. Perhaps Rosy Lea had made contact with her, and wanted to take me back to the market; or perhaps Violet was now better, and she was coming home to live with me and Joyce; or my mother had been found and she was going to take me back on my return from school, and so I wouldn't have to live at Auntie Hilda's anymore. Perhaps I was thinking of all these things because that was what I wanted; but whatever it was I was now about to find out.

I rushed home from school as fast as my little legs could take me. As I reached Auntie Iris's back door, I gave it a little knock and then crept in. As I opened the door, in a breathless voice I called, 'Hello, Auntie, I'm back from school!' It was as if I was awarding myself points for getting back so quick.

She tapped her knees to beckon me to sit on them. I walked over, picking up a small stool on the way to place by the side of her legs in order to climb onto her knee. This lessened the pressure of my weight getting up to her knees. As I sat there, her face sprang into a gleam. She put her tiny arms around me and gave me a big squeeze. 'Georgie,' she said, 'do you remember that you had asked me about your mother?'

'Yes,' I said, 'have you found her?'

'No, not yet,' she said, 'but we have found out a lot about her that can help you towards the right road to finding her.'

Leaning over to the shelf beside her, she reached out for a photo and, holding it tight close to her as if she was holding the world close to her chest, she said, still holding the photo in one hand, 'Look!'

I glanced at it with a confused expression. I was looking at a picture of a pearly king standing behind a costermonger's barrow with handles that had been extended into shafts. There was a pony between the shafts. Sitting on the coster's barrow was a young girl aged about seven and a boy aged about nine. The barrow had been decorated as a carnival float. Around the barrow stood a further group of pearly kings. You could see that this was not a fancy-dress parade but a real group of pearly kings. The nine-year-old boy sitting on the barrow with the young girl had a pearly suit with fewer buttons being worn.

I looked at the picture for a few minutes. I had seen people dressed like this before; then it came to me. A group of them dressed like this had been shouting and arguing with my father, I said to Auntie Iris.

'Are you sure, Georgie?'

'Yes, I am sure. When my father was in his lorry delivering, he was arguing with people dressed like that, I know.'

'I believe you, Georgie. It all fits in now. Look,' she said, pointing to the pearly king behind the barrow, 'that, Georgie, is your grandfather! And that little boy in a pearly suit could be your uncle, and the little girl we believe is your mother.'

The little girl years later was used to compare my features with those of my mother. So this must be why my father had told me not to talk with people dressed like that – because my mother was the daughter of my grandfather, who happened to be a pearly king, and judging by the picture, an important one!

It gave me the impression that because he didn't see or love my mother anymore then I should not see or love them anymore, and I did not feel that it was right.

Auntie Iris carried on with what she knew. 'Your mother is alive, my Georgie, and she and your grandfather were last seen about sixteen months ago.'

'But I was always told that she was dead!'

'Who told you that, Georgie? She is alive and you must promise me that you will tell no one about what I said.'

'I promise,' I replied. Auntie Iris knew that I could keep a secret and a promise, as the only happiness that I had in life depended on it.

'I know how much that you like working on the markets, Georgie, so it will please you to know that your grandfather is a costermonger, and moves from market to market all over London, working.'

My mind was still racing back in time and I was wondering, Does he know Rosy Lea and her father? Has he ever worked at East Street market on Surrey Street, where I worked? Have I passed him or my mother but not known it?

Auntie Iris carried on her story. 'We are told that your mother is short – that's where you must get your short size from – and that she is pretty.'

I looked at the picture further, taking in every detail of that photo in my mind. Auntie Iris was now squeezing me harder. 'I am so proud of you, Georgie. Now you have something that your mates have – a mum. All we have got to do is find her.'

The shock was now setting in. So this must be the real reason why my father went mad at those pearlies when they started to talk to him. Maybe that's why he shouted at me when he knew that I had been at the market with Rosy Lea. This explained why my family had said that she was dead, and why they said nothing about my mother or her family. With this all running in my mind, Auntie Iris began telling me a bit about the pearlies' tradition, and how they made money for hospitals and charity. We will talk more about the full history later in the book, but so as to give some idea at this point, and help you understand part of the unfolding story, for now this is a brief outline.

The pearly kings' and queens' history started with the costermonger, known as the barrow boy, in the mid-1800s. Almost every main street in London had a marketplace where the costermongers sold their wares. They mainly sold food, such as fruit and vegetables, meat and fish, but they also sold many other essentials. The poor and needy relied on the markets because they were cheaper and friendlier. You could buy half a cabbage or half a cucumber, according to your need. So the working poor and needy relied on the costermonger, and they talked the same cockney tongue. The costermonger came mostly from a hereditary group of cockneys, and this is where the pearlies' history sprang from. The selected man who was the leader of each market was called a coster king, and he wore cockney traditional dress – a suit – partly covered in pearly buttons; there weren't as many in them days, just a few up the side of the trousers and jacket sleeve and around the seam of the jacket. Henry VIII made himself very popular with the working class in London and at archery contests by creating the strongest bowman in his bodyguards as the 'Earl of Hoxton', the 'Duke of Whitechapel' or the 'Count of Stepney' and so on. In many London boroughs all this was pure honorary. The cockneys loved it, and all this must have been in Samuel King's mind at the time. Why not start our own honours in the markets? Samuel King is thought to have been the first 'coster king' – coster from the 'costermonger', and 'king' from the surname of Samuel King. Thus the 'coster king' title sprang up all around London. There was a 'king' of Middlesex Street, Petticoat Lane, East Street, Roman Road and so on. All this was to start something that was to change the history of the cockneys. The kings had their queens, their children were to be princes and princesses in the same way as our royal family, which brought us the start of the working man's monarchy.

Auntie Iris went on with her story, and I sat on her knee when she was talking to me. I always thought that this was just affection, but thinking back about it as an adult, I realise that she wanted me to hear her words as well, because she knew that I was deaf. The coster kings were now operating fund-raising events for the poor, sick and needy as they saw it as important to care for them.

Then Auntie Iris said to me with a voice of a triumph, 'You, my Georgie, are part of that tradition from your mother's family!' Then I watched a tear drop down her soft cheek, a tear of pride and a tear of victory for me. I never forgot that story from her. The way she put it was so powerful to me. The mark was implanted into me; it gave me a strong sense of being with my mother – a link, if you like. There was nothing I could do to shake it off, even if I wanted to. A new beginning was to take place in my young life.

Auntie Iris made me some sandwiches and cakes, washed down with lemonade. 'Your first royal meal,' she said, and slowly but surely she was leading me up to wearing a pearly suit – 'like your granddad', she said. 'You could help your Violet at the hospital more.' She was putting all temptation in my path to wear a pearly suit. 'If I made a pearly suit for you to wear, would you do it, Georgie?'

'But your hands, Auntie…' I said.

'My hands are strong enough to do that, and anyway you are worth it.'

'Then let me help you, Auntie,' I said, feeling that I should.

'All right, Georgie, we have a deal. We will make it together!'

In no time at all, Auntie Iris had got a dark pair of short trousers, a short dark jacket and a cap. Then the knack of sewing on the buttons began. Starting with the jacket first, around the seams each shiny pearl button was sewn seven times then cast off. Then on to the next button; there were 2,000 to do to make the complete suit. I was still only a small boy, which meant less buttons than if I had been a normal size boy, so every day after school I would pop round to Auntie Iris to help make my new first pearly suit. I could not sew as fast as Auntie Iris, of course, even though she was slow.

I watched her place the needle into the small buttonhole, pushing the needle painfully with her hands to make a stitch. It was just as hard watching her face cringe with pain at each time she put the needle into the cloth, and if she had seen me look at that pain-filled face she would look up and smile to hide the pain from me. My heart cried for her when I saw that suffering. The suffering was for me too, and I pledged to myself from them days to not let her suffering be in vain. I'd go out in my pearls and do my best to return my thanks to her. After a few weeks, my new pearly suit was ready to wear. This would lead to millions of pounds for charity and leave a mark in people's lives to encourage others to do the same, and stories that could remain even more to many. Some of you will yourself share these with me as we travel in my world.

Auntie Iris said, 'Come on, Georgie, let's see you put your pearly suit on!'

Uncle Alf had by now come home to help me try it on. The last item to go on was the cap that Auntie Iris was holding. 'Come on, Georgie, let me crown you,' she said. As she placed my crown on my head I felt a sense of honour and pride. I felt I was no longer that little boy lost but somebody with a purpose in being. This was my destiny, my future – something for which I was going to care for ever and I felt a warm glow about it inside me. Now I belonged to something. I was no longer alone, and I knew why I felt so at home at the markets. It was in my blood, it was part of my heritage… it was my oyster shell!

Auntie Iris's plan for me was going well. She had got me to accept my title. She wanted me to help Violet and her hospital in my suit, and now there was one more part of the plan to do. 'Now listen very carefully to me,' she said, as I got on her lap. 'We are going to put this suit into this bag.' She picked up this old and worn dark brown cloth bag. 'I am hiding it until you go to Violet's hospital. You must take the bag with you and change at the hospital, and when you are finished, put the suit back in the bag and bring it back to me. No one must know – it's our secret,' she said, pointing her finger upstairs to Auntie Hilda. 'Or you will have it taken away from you.'

I certainly didn't want that. I think she had known about my bike and soapbox, but never let on. I took off my pearly suit very carefully. It had been the only suit that I had ever had, so it was like a Sunday suit to me. Then I gave it to Auntie Iris to replace in the bag until my next visit to Violet. This was my hidden 'whistle and flute' (suit) – something that was made for me in order to help others. Yes, it was my pride and joy, yet I had to keep it hidden from my family; and when you are proud of something it hurts to have to hide it. It was very hard having secrets that could not be shared with anyone. Had I shared them, I knew that the end result would be a beating or, worse still, to have much more taken from me. Had any of my father's family known that I had put on a pearly suit it would have reached the ears of my father, and then I would have been beaten until I could no longer walk.

The night before I was due to go to Violet's, I lay on my bed staring up at the ceiling in a half dream, thinking of the big day ahead of me and the added excitement about it. I had already met so many new challenges in this short life. This was to be an extra one on the list. How would I face up to it? What do I say when I meet anyone in my suit? Then I thought, I must tell them what Auntie Iris had said. Soon I fell asleep, dreaming of wearing my pearly suit, dancing and singing with Auntie Iris and Uncle Alf with Violet, all hand in hand and laughing.

The big day arrived. I had got up early to go down to get my pearly suit, hidden in Auntie Iris's flat. I gave a light tap on the door and opened it, seeing her drinking her early morning tea with that broad grin planted across her face.

'Good morning, Georgie. All ready for your big day?'

'Yes, Auntie, I can't wait!'

'Your bag is over there, George.' She pointed behind the chair.

I picked it up, and for the first time I realised how heavy it was for a small boy to wear. I put my arms around her, and with a tear in my eye said, 'Thank you, Auntie, for making me happy.'

She then gave me a big kiss and said, 'Now don't forget to come back here with that bag, so that I can hide it, and then you can tell me all about your first day in your pearly suit.'

Off I set with my bag over my shoulder, heading for the Fountain Hospital in Tooting to see my sister Violet, but this time armed with my pearly suit, which would be helping her and her hospital. As I walked into the hospital I felt like 'superboy' in my ordinary clothes, but now ready to turn into a superboy in my shining armour. I walked around looking for a suitable place to change and decided on changing in the toilet cubicle. Placing my ordinary clothes into the bag, I then hid it in the overhead toilet system and changed into my pearly suit.

As I walked around the hospital to find my sister, I noticed people staring at me and smiling. I started to feel like somebody. I was being noticed and I was beginning to see how friendly people were towards me. My heart was beating faster at the sheer joy of being noticed for the first time in my life by so many people I started responding by saying 'All right, ducks?' if it was a lady, or, 'All right, mate?' if it was a bloke. Then I found myself getting more cheeky: 'Lovely eyes, ducks,' or, 'What a beautiful face you have!' – all the kind of chat-up lines I had heard and learned at the markets. It seemed as if I had been doing this all before. My smile became a fixture on my face and I began to sing. It was like walking on air… the world was getting closer to me, and I was beginning to feel really loved by everyone for the first time in my life.

I opened the hall door to find my sister with her friends. She looked at me with the joy of seeing me again, as she always did and called out, 'Dorgie!' Her friends were advancing towards me as well, with all of them touching my suit of armour, not understanding what it meant. But they were all laughing, and if they were laughing it meant that my suit was bringing happiness to them; and if my suit was able to do that, then it had left a mark of happiness on their mind, giving them the freedom to express themselves. There were three blind people in that hospital as well, so I was able to let them feel the buttons in order to implant on their minds a picture of myself in my suit.

My next move was to take Violet to our usual café, and on our walk there arm in arm, I had calls from people, like, 'All right, Pearly?' There were smiles coming from everyone during our walk to the café. On arriving at the café I had ordered my drink and baked beans on toast, with a drink and egg and chips for Violet. 'How much?' I said. 'To you, Pearly it's on the house,' was the reply.

The owner then came over to where we were eating and wanted to know why I was dressed like this today. I explained what Auntie Iris had told me then said that I was helping my sister and her hospital. 'You give them this,' he said, giving me five old shillings – a lot of money then. Then he came back a little later with an old tea tin that he had put a slot in the top to put the money through, with a label around the tin.

'What's that for?' I asked.

'It's for the Fountain Hospital,' he said. Now people would put money in it for the hospital. So, putting his five shillings into the tin, he took it and with me collected from the café customers, including a couple of young boys who had took the mickey out of my sister a few weeks earlier. They were now more interested in what I was collecting for, and no longer taking the piss out of my sister. As we walked back to the hospital I felt as if I was wearing some magic suit, which brought a smile from their faces and money from their pockets.

On our way back I was shaking my tin, and more people had put money in it. When we got back I gave the tin to a nurse and asked her to empty the contents and to return the tin to me. She had not said what I was so used to hearing such as, 'Where did you nick that from?' Instead she said how pleased they were at receiving the money. The tin must have had three pounds at least, which was a lot of money in them days – a week's wages for some. Having completed my first day of charity work in my pearly suit, and after saying goodbye to Violet and her friends, I returned to the toilet and changed into my normal clothes. I then set off to Auntie Iris with the news of my first day as a pearly prince.

I opened her door and repeated all that I had done that day, about the happy faces, the café, the collecting tin – which I showed her – and how good I felt in myself.

'I knew that you could do it, Georgie, I knew it! God is working for us. I'm so proud of you!' She then gave me an enormous cuddle and kiss. She then put my pearly suit back into the bag, after checking that I had it all, and put it in her hiding place, in a cupboard which was next to her copper boiler, to be ready for its next trip to Violet's hospital – which to me could not come quick enough.

I made my way upstairs. I could hear Auntie Hilda choking on her usual John Players cigarettes, and in between choking and trying to catch her next breath, she said, 'Where have you been, Melsham?'

Without a care in the world on this occasion, I replied, 'Getting up to mischief again,' and waited for her to come back with, 'Wait till your father gets home!' Instead she said, 'How dare you give me cheek like that!'

But I'd had such an exciting day that nothing she said on this occasion bothered me. I just went to my bed thinking, So what? A good hiding is worth having for the happiest day in my life.

So every week I would repeat my trips to Violet's. My pearly suit was hidden in my bag, to be worn each time when I arrived. Then I'd return the suit into the bag and go back to Auntie Iris. On another of my trips, one weekend the helpers of the hospital asked if I would go on a carnival float to support the hospital funding, as the hospital was always looking for funding like any other hospital; but the Fountain found it harder because it was for people with mental health problems, so they must have thought that a little prince bouncing by the side of the float would be a big attraction and a chance of raising money! I didn't know at the time, but it was the costermongers who helped start the League of Friends at London Hospitals; so here I was, again unknowingly following my fate by helping out at the time.

The result was that I was collecting so much money at the carnival that I had started to drag the bucket along the road, and what made it heavier was the fact that in them days there were no plastic buckets, only heavy galvanised ones. If the Fountain had a fête, I would be there helping out in my pearly suit, helping to raise money for Violet's hospital.

At one of their fêtes I met a Mr and Mrs Gibson. He was a builder on South Norwood Hill, South Norwood around the corner from where I lived with Rosy Lea. They were both in the League of Friends at Violet's hospital and they themselves had a daughter with a condition just like

Violet's, so when they knew of the role I had with my sister, they showed a lot of interest in Violet, and over the years helped to get her into a nicer environment in Streatham Common in South London, which would be better for her. So my pearly suit had not only helped the hospital raise well-deserved funding, it also helped Violet get to a more suitable home.

In between my pearly work, I was still doing other jobs cutting down fences. There must have been more missing fences around those streets than the whole of London! I was also collecting horse dung and bottles, and there was my gardening job, which Joyce did with me a lot. It was on one of the gardening jobs that, with the excitement of knowing that Mr and Mrs Gibson were doing all they could for Violet, I felt that I had to tell Joyce. I don't know why it had to be Joyce who I decided to share this with, but I did – to my downfall!

When I got home much later, I was met by Auntie Hilda. With a look of hatred, she asked, 'So you been seeing that girl who is not right in the head?' (She had not said 'my sister'.) 'Why? Your father will give you the hiding of your life when I tell him this! Now get into your room until he gets home – you are nothing but trouble!'

I went to my room, petrified. Why did I have to tell Joyce? I should have known that she was Auntie Hilda's messenger. I thought, I am in for it now. I started to wet my trousers, a shiver went up my back and then I heard shouting. Auntie Hilda was telling my father what I had done. Then I wet myself again as the bedroom door was flung open and my father entered with his eyes ablaze. As far as he was concerned I had just committed the worst crime by going to see Violet. Was he ashamed? Was he scared that maybe I had bumped into my mother? Violet would, after all, be very easy to find, had my mother wanted to; or was he just trying to put Violet and his guilt as far away as possible? Whatever the reason, he was going to take that anger out on me. He grabbed hold of me, with my feet leaving the ground as he tugged at my hair from the scalp. His giant shovel hands came down on me like lumps of concrete. Of course I was not allowed to defend myself because this was my father, and I had to take it. I was rolling around trying to avoid the blows and the more I rolled the more exasperated he became and the more violent he got. Then he kicked me like a rag doll. The kick lifted me up in the air and threw me down the same stairs that I had been down many times before. Was this the final blow? Down and down the stairs I went, over and over. I then landed at the bottom of the stairs, which I had seen more than enough, catching my right knee on a bag of tools that had been left at the bottom. I felt the blood run out of my knee and then… silence. My father must have thought he had killed me, as I lay there frozen, feeling like I had broken every bone in my body. I was lucky that I was light and thin or maybe I could have broken every bone in my body. If my head had hit the tool bag, I may not have seen the next day. I just lay there still, unable to move, with no response from my father or Auntie Hilda. I was thinking that I was going to die, and felt what a relief that would be!

By now, Auntie Iris and Uncle Alf, who had heard all the commotion upstairs and then the thump at the bottom of the stairs, had come running out of their flat. When Uncle Alf saw the mess that I was in, he was filled with rage and shouted upstairs to Auntie Hilda and my father, 'What the fucking hell have you done to this boy now, you fucking bastards?' I had never heard Uncle Alf swear like that before, but could understand his reaction.

Slowly and carefully Uncle Alf picked up my limp body which just hung like a rag doll that had had half its stuffing removed. Carrying me to their bedroom, he gently laid me down. I was still too weak and battered to move. There they bathed every lump and bruise on my body. My knee had been bandaged up for possible further treatment. I lay there unable to move unable to speak; I just lay still, wishing that I was now dead, while Auntie Iris was bathing my head and assuring me that everything was going to be all right. She was repeating, 'You are safe now, Georgie,' but I was still wishing that I was dead. In her eyes, I could see that she wished that it was she who was suffering and not me.

I was still shying away from her love. I had found it very hard to accept love from anyone. To me it was a foreign word that I felt ashamed to say. In my upbringing it was an unknown word; so, for all they had done for me, for all the that they and Rosy Lea gave me, I still could not accept it. Maybe it was because of rejection from my father and Auntie Hilda, or because I felt I was betraying them if I showed love to others. But that night as I lay on their bed while they were just sitting on it, as if they were the intruders, and not a word being said, I felt a stronger bond coming between us. Now they were ready to defend me, neighbour or no neighbour, and this bond was to remain for many years yet.

The cut on my right knee was getting worse as the days drifted on. Auntie Hilda had not bothered to change the dressing that had been put on, and me being out on the streets for long periods of time did not help. Auntie Iris looked at it to change it but said it needed proper medical treatment. The wound itself looked really horrible, weeping yellow pus; the more that I walked on it the worse it was getting. One of the teachers on playground duty stopped me and told me to go and see the duty nurse in the school, as my knee needed urgent attention. The nurse took one look at it and called an ambulance to take me to hospital. I was sent to the local casualty department at the local Croydon General Hospital. I watched them with all the care in the world slowly clean the wound, trying their utmost not to put me in too much pain, and reassuring me their concern was for me. They then had my knee bandaged up and I felt back on the road to recovery. The doctor then gave me very careful written instruction on how to keep my knee clean and bathe it. I was then given some iodine to help it heal. Iodine was the stock treatment for helping wounds then, but it stung like mad! Within a few days I should have been up and running with the boys again, but it wasn't as simple as that in my household.

First, I had Auntie Hilda as my full-time nurse. Second, she had so much hatred towards me that anything could happen. So she was given the full medical instructions, and as I was to be her patient now, this gave her the pleasure of seeing me suffer and to take her hatred out on me. Twice a day the dressing on my knee had to be changed and the knee cleaned. When the nurse had done it at the hospital she was so gentle in treating me, talking to me so I felt far less pain because of it. But now it was Auntie Hilda's turn she rubbed it, played with it and tormented me with it. When she put the iodine in, instead of a small amount she poured it on. I was already screaming with pain with her cleaning it, and now I was in agony with the iodine. 'Wait till your father gets home!' she shouted, but even a good hiding from him would mean less pain to me. When my father got home, I was still in just as much pain. I was still weak, and felt that my life was on a thread… one more pull and it could break! I was now waiting for that one pull. He laid into me, but this time around the head. Auntie Hilda had told him some cock and bull story that I kicked her while she was dressing my wound. Well, that one more pull never arrived. Maybe by now my body had toughened so much I must have been made of hardened rubber! Following this, my knee took weeks to heal, and rather than have Auntie Hilda be my nurse and suffer twice I decided to steal the iodine from the cupboard where she kept it. That's when I had discovered just how much she had used on me the day before: for one dose she had used a half a bottle.

Each day I would go to my air-raid shelter with some water, unwrap my bandage and slowly clean my wound in the same manner as I had seen the nurse do it. Then, a bit at a time, I'd dab the iodine on, while crying in pain. I knew I had to do it, and when I needed new bandage I went round to Mr Crookshank at the church; he had a first-aid box. How I never got gangrene to my leg I don't know. What I do know is that it was all part of my survival. My thoughts were that life was given to me and that I had to just get on with it. I still carry the scar on my knee to this day.

I have always tried to find excuses or reasons for the treatment that I had. The main reason for Auntie Hilda's behaviour must have come from her childhood and upbringing. Like her sisters and her two brothers, she had lost her father and mother at a young age. Auntie Hilda was the youngest, so her upbringing was shared by her much older sisters, and she never seemed to have had any relationship with boys. Her one and only relationship with a man had finished in her late twenties. He died of TB, which was very common in them days, due mostly to the black smog. It was so thick that you could not see your hands in front of you and a white handkerchief would become black from wiping your nose on it. At the time she said that she would never look at another man again. I was part of that male group, which did not help, but she did carry on going to her boyfriend's church at the Elephant and Castle, where his mum and dad, Mr and Mrs Green, would pray every Sunday. She would take Joyce to that church, then on to a Sunday lunch at their home. Then, in the afternoon Joyce would go with Mr Green to the Sunday school attached to the church.

I was never ever taken to that church by her. When I asked if I could go one Sunday, she said to me that I was too bad and wicked to go inside a church of God. I could never understand that, as I really did feel that I was what she was brainwashing me to believe. I also tried to understand that here she was a young lady who'd just lost a loved one, now given the task of looking after two young children. She had no form of experience in raising any child, perhaps because she was helped by her sisters. Then she had to do the same for her brother; but for whatever reason it was not helping me.

I tried to avoid mealtimes at home, but not once did Auntie Hilda ever ask me if I was hungry. Perhaps she had got fed up with trying to force-feed me, or maybe my vomit was making her feel sick and guilty. Sometimes I thought that she saw me as a machine that no longer needed oiling; the only time I had fresh fruit at home was on Christmas Day. In my stocking there'd be an apple and an orange. Boys did not look forward to their regular wash, and I was no exception. Auntie Hilda's knew that this was another pet hate of mine. She would pour a kettle full of hot water into the sink and add the cold water from the only cold water tap hanging from the wall over the sink.

She would make me climb onto the draining board in our small kitchen, where my feet would paddle in the big butler sink. Then I would be left to wash myself all over – what you would call strip wash. You would often start to shiver, as most nights were cold; we had short summers then. But I had often had to wait when I had finished because she would be busy on her sewing machine. When she did arrive it was to inspect my neck. For boys this was bad. When she came to inspect my neck, whether it was clean or dirty it was always 'dirty', even though I would be sure to clean it, so that she wouldn't say, 'You are a useless dirty sod – what are you?' And, shivering, I would repeat, 'I am a useless dirty sod.'

She would put my neck under the cold-water tap, which took my breath away, and scrub my neck with the kitchen scrubbing brush. I didn't dare move, or I knew she would say, 'Wait till your father gets home!' This strip wash would take place twice a week, but when Joyce took her strip wash Auntie Hilda would check that her sink of water was very warm. In fact I could see the warm steam rising around Joyce's body and Auntie Hilda soaping her down and talking with her all the time. Then she would lift her out of the sink wrapped in a big towel and then she'd be dressed.

I always had to dry myself then clothe myself; like everything else, I had to do it myself. This used to make me feel more insecure. Then once a week I would watch my father take down the tin bath hanging on the hall wall. He would then take it into the back room, where he had our stove. On top of the stove would be four big cooking pots full of water being boiled, the fire throwing up the flames heating the water. This would go on for over an hour until my father thought that the water was nice and boiling. He then put the tin bath in front of the stove and poured in the boiling water, using the same cooking pots, then he'd go into the small kitchen and get the cold water. Adults could only sit in the bath, but Joyce and myself were able to stretch our legs out in the bath, me more so having tiny legs. But there was not a chance of having to lie out and relax. It was always Auntie Hilda's turn first. She took the longest, then my sister, and after her my father. He was always the quickest; I think he was too big to sit in the bath, so he had to bathe in a standing position.

Then came me, last in the queue. By then the water was dirty, with a thick scum floating on the top, making it look more like a swamp than a bath, but I had to step into that water. I had no choice unless I wanted a good hiding. With my teeth chattering, I would get into it with my back freezing. It was turned away from the heat of the fire. Then, after washing the front of my body, I'd turn around to get the heat onto my back. This I would do for about fifteen minutes, as I had to make sure that I was clean, or else… Joyce had already been helped by Auntie Hilda in her bath time, but I had to get on with it on my own, until it was time for Auntie Hilda to come and inspect me to make sure that I was clean enough by her standards. Regardless of how well I'd washed myself, she was never satisfied. She would come in, pointing to the grey scum that was floating on the top of the water, and say, 'See that? That's what you are – a dirty scum, a no-good-for-nothing. Now what are you?'

I knew that I had to repeat her words. Pointing to the scum on the water, I would repeat, 'See that? That's what I am – a dirty scum, a no-good-for-nothing.'

'Again!' she would shout. 'Repeat it!' as if she was enjoying hearing it.

Then, unexpectedly, she would put her hand on the back of my neck as I was kneeling over the bath and push my head into the scum floating on the water, and on many occasions because I wasn't expecting it I'd try to take a deep breath, and end up taking in mouthfuls of everyone's bath water and scum! As a result of this it would make me sick and cause me to vomit in the bath.

This happened hundreds of times during my time with Auntie Hilda. To this day that fear still haunts me. It would be unthinkable for me to get into a bath that had even the smallest of spot of dirt in it. I would have to wash it away before running my bath or getting into it.

When you have experienced torture like that, week in and week out, it does affect your way of thinking about yourself. It leads to you undervaluing yourself, and you begin to think that yes, you are scum, just like the scum that floats on the bath water…

I then fixed my gaze at the scum floating on the water and seemed to relate to it. I was being brainwashed. The only praise that I was getting was from our neighbours, whom I mostly knew, and Auntie Iris and Uncle Alf. Perhaps Auntie Hilda was right. I *am* a scum… I *am* a useless a no-good-for-nothing! She had told me so many times before it still preys on my mind even today. You can't seem to shake it off, it's like a growth. Auntie Hilda was making sure that any member of my father's family should feel the same way about me. If anyone made it known that I was a good boy, she would most certainly brainwash them to think differently. She wanted everyone to despise me like she did.

At home I lived in isolation, and had to stop my mates short when nearing my home, or what was supposed to be home. I could not invite them back to my home even if I had wanted to, anyway. If Auntie Hilda ever met them she would make sure that she turned them against me. Also, they were boys, and she did not like boys. Had I invited them back home she would brainwash them into believing that I was a no-good-for-nothing, a scum and not to be associated with. That might lead to them telling my other schoolmates, and as a result I could end up being singled out and bullied by them. My life was hard enough and I needed no extra aggravation. I was beginning to live my life day by day, careful about whom I should trust. At the same time I was an outgoing boy who would talk to anyone.

So as a nine-year-old it was very hard. The streets had not only been my battleground but my entertainment. I watched for hours, seeing our local roads being resurfaced, watching the brewery doing the local deliveries, and hopping on and off horse-drawn vehicles – of which there was plenty about then – doing all my different jobs: anything to keep away from home. The streets were my survival routes. I'd already known 'steal or starve' or 'work or starve', and I did have days of feeling very unwell, so survival was the name of the game. As I saw it, you had only one chance, and you had to take it. There were many kids in them days who had to live like me. There was nobody who cared about you. If you had told a copper about your troubles he in turn would have clipped you around the ear. But many of us was too scared to tell anyone. That's why in them days you had a lot of dirty men after you, if they knew that you had a broken home. A lot of kids did not survive in them days. Some got into more trouble and went into approved schools, borstal and then on to prison, and spent the rest of their lives in and out of prison.

We had no help or guidance, and no one to listen to us. It was a case of 'children should be seen but not heard'. I had mixed with many of them, and with my own suffering had wished that I could have taken some of their suffering as well. Most of us were orphaned babies. Many were in children's homes like Doctor Barnardo's, where they were not getting the love and care. Many children's homes were a cover-up for child abuse. There was the odd time when I was proud to be the son of my father, regardless of the beatings that I had, and that was when he played the piano. It was on a rare occasion at the local Railway Telegraph pub.

Many a Saturday night, mostly after taking the bottles back for my deposit, I would sit on the Railway Telegraph steps to listen to my father play the piano, and through the cracks of the public bar doors I could see Uncle Alf sitting with his mates and my father at the piano. The pub would be full of cigarette smoke, with everyone singing or dancing and enjoying themselves; but the main centre of attraction was in no doubt – it was my father. He was just an outstanding piano player – no music sheets – just hum a tune to him and he would play it. The best way to have described his playing was the sound of people like Winifred Atwell, Mrs Mills, Bobby Crush, who were famous in the 1960s and '70s. People would sit there amazed at how the piano would dance with him, with all his tunes. The pub was full of all sorts of people shouting and encouraging him to play. Had he made an effort he most probably would have become a famous piano player, but he never pushed himself into anything, only me. I had never seen a sheet of music on his pub piano ever. He just played by ear – a gift that he had, and he'd give it that extra beat to make it sound even better.

Every Saturday the bar was full to capacity, with everyone singing along to his tunes. You could see the faces of the people admiring his playing, and lined up on the piano top was glasses and glasses of beer, in rows of two, that people had bought him in appreciation of his excellent piano playing; and believe me, when it was time at 10.30 p.m., them glasses were truly empty. He could certainly drink. That was his main drinking night, and when he drank he became talkative and friendly, a real pleasant person. I had wished that every day had been a Saturday, and grateful that I would not be abused. After I'd spent that night outside the pub enjoying his playing, my father came staggering out of the pub pissed to his eyeballs. When my father drank he was a non-stop talker, and that would be the only time that I could talk to him without being afraid or frightened. If only he had always been drunk! It was at brief times like this that my beatings from him were truly forgotten. Now I was with a different father, a father that I wanted, a kind talkative one. From the pub I would support this six-foot giant from falling about from side to side on the pavement. I did not want harm to come to him, and people were shouting 'Goodnight!' to him as they were passing us, and I'd reply back to them, 'This is my dad!' I felt proud of him, half carrying my dad, the world's best piano player.

It was a short-lived moment of closeness between father and son that I wanted to carry on and on and not stop. That moment of pride had taken me over. Gone were the days of my beatings, and without any thought of fear, still struggling along the road with him, I said, 'Where is Rosy Lea?'

'She's gone back to Peckham to live,' he replied.

Now I was learning and learning fast, and to learn any other thing I should wait for a Saturday night when he got drunk. Holding this information in my head, I had something to work to find her, a clue. Finally, reaching home at last, we started to climb the stairs that I had been thrown down so many times. I was holding on to the banister with my shoulder trying to push and encourage him to climb up, and at the same time he was blowing off in my face, which stank.

Bit by bit I was pushing this dead weight up the stairs, slipping back now and then, but trying to save him from falling. Finally, after what seemed like hours, we clambered straight into the bedroom and onto the bed. I climbed in beside him, both of us still dressed. Then he rolled over in the bed and positioned himself on the side of the bed. As he turned in the bed it felt like the house was falling onto you! He stank of all the beer that he had drunk. The sweat of his beer was running onto me.

He had his usual bucket beside him. He gave one big long heave and brought up almost half his beer in the bucket. After several more blow-offs and a couple of more heaves and a few burps, my dad fell asleep, snoring; and for a few minutes I put my arms around him and gave him a cuddle – a cuddle that I so wanted from him, but was deprived of. With the piano still playing in my head, I just wanted to remain like this. I loved him. This was my dad – who could replace him at this moment? My two sisters and I may have been cute, and fun as babies to play with, but that seemed to have left him as the early months went by. Then he found that we were just a horrible mistake, or too much responsibility. Unfortunately, I was no longer that cuddly little baby but a young little boy.

The bedroom was now stinking of beer and sickness, and every now and then he would blow off again, and it smelt as if you were sleeping with a room full of cows. Who really cared, as I lay with my dad cuddling him? I was proud of him because he could play the piano like Winifred Atwell. Then I fell fast asleep with my arm around him, a chance that I rarely had. By morning he would have clean forgotten that his son had cuddled him. So slowly I was learning the good bits about my father, from experience of his talkative moods when drunk, to how he loved and adored babies, as with babies he was soft and caring for them.

Many children in those days seemed to work, in some cases to cut out boredom. Some children would often help their parents by working around the home and doing chores, and in some cases they took on a part-time job in order to help themselves and the family. They did jobs like milk rounds or delivering groceries.

We were still in the last years of child labour, so it was not unusual to see kids working all hours. I also think that we had less laziness in those days. We seemed to be born to work, whereas today children seem to be born to laze around. This could be due to having too much done for them and being wrapped in cotton wool.

In my case I worked in order to survive, and I found that working could hold the fear and misery inside you. I found that it was a way to cope on my own and deal with my problems and survival. Any job that I would take on, honest or not, I was always looking to work somewhere, regardless of how early the start was in the morning. I would be out searching or looking for something to do, especially if it meant that I could get out of going to school. I was not learning anything anyway.

I had known of Surrey Street market in Croydon, and that it was known to have the same character as East Street market had. I had often walked the two miles to reach the market to find work; after all, if Rosy

Lea thought I was good at the market work, others must form the same opinion.

As I arrived at the market I could see this wonderful mass of colour and could hear the sound of cries from the traders shouting out with their patter. I moved from stall to stall asking if they needed any help for the day. I just wanted to work in the freshness of the day absorbing the smell of the fruit and vegetables mixing in the air, which gave me the eighth wonder of the world. It wasn't easy finding extra work on the market due to the high demand by other children doing the same. Also, the majority of the market stall traders had either their own children or grandchildren helping out.

Every day I would run to Surrey Street to be the first in the early morning air, fuelled with eagerness to find work. After a few knock-backs my luck was in. As I yelled, 'Need any help?' a gentleman with the biggest grin you had ever seen and reddish face asked, 'What's your name, son?'

I politely answered, 'Georgie.'

'Oh, Georgie – not another Georgie!' he said. 'All the boys are called Georgie.'

'Well, when will I be called George then?'

He replied, 'When you can make your own living!'

Straight away I responded, 'I already do.'

'You're not work-shy, then.'

With a cheeky grin written across my face, I said, 'So can you call me George.'

He looked at me and then said, 'You've got the job, George.'

I liked Billy Cook. He was happy and cheerful without a care in the world. He was big-built with hands like my father's 'shovels', but he was too kind to use them against me. He had a grown-up son called Charlie, who had a stutter, and seemed to bring out all his personality with a fixed grin. All the traders that I have met always seem to have this fixed grin. Maybe as I saw them all, I did feel secure and happy with those who always took my attention.

The jobs that I had to do were more or less the same as I did while working with Rosy Lea and her father. I was given a chance to sell the odd market lines. This was not an everyday job, it was a case of trial and error, but if a job came along I knew I would get it first, as I got on very well with Billy Cook and his son. I had often asked around the market if anyone had heard or knew of Rosy Lea. Billy Cook came up with something better. He had met her and her father a couple of times, but not enough for an address, and that's really what I needed. At least she was known of, which could make it easier to find her. So she was near to my heart and mind while at the market. I also started to ask if anyone knew of my grandfather.

Apart from my job at the market, sometimes I would help Billy or Charlie on their greengrocer's round whenever they needed me. Part of their delivery round was down my road, and almost every neighbour brought their fruit and vegetables from Billy Cook. I would also help some of the older customers to carry their goods back to their doorstep. They would ask me how I was, as they all knew me and took a liking to me.

On one particular day Auntie Hilda came to the cart while I was helping to carry a customer's bag. 'Lovely boy, young George, isn't he?' said Billy to Auntie Hilda. With a look of disgust and resentment written on her face, she said, 'You wouldn't think the same if he lived with you! His sister Joyce could do a much better job.' Then she disappeared into the house and slammed the door behind her.

'Hang on, Billy,' I said, 'Auntie Iris has not got her shopping. I will just go and check to see what she needs.'

I came back with the shopping list for Billy to pack into her bag, and as he finished Auntie Iris came out to pay him. Her remarks to Billy were, 'Lovely boy, is our young Georgie,' to which he agreed. She said, 'He is the best boy in the whole world!'

'I thought that you might say that,' said Billy. Then I carried her bags into her flat and returned to help Billy again.

I know that Auntie Iris must have waited for Auntie Hilda to have gone back upstairs with her groceries before coming out, to avoid having to make eye contact or conversation with her. Somehow I felt responsible for the awkwardness between them. Looking back, I can understand the reasons why Auntie Iris and Uncle Alf took that stand. They were seeing injustice being handed out to a young innocent boy that they could do nothing about. All I wanted was for everyone to be friends and happy. I just felt uneasy and confused, and used to blame myself for all the problems. Auntie Iris and Uncle Alf were just trying to help me, but their hands were tied, so they had to do what they could in their own quiet way. By the same token, I had to live a double life in my pearly suit and my working life.

I was always looking for an excuse to work, and with a full list of jobs I was getting plenty of variety, from my firewood to my gardening, weeding people's gardens, cutting their lawns with shears (again borrowed from Auntie Iris) or cutting hedges. Being small, I was unable to reach the tops of the high hedges, so I would call on my sister, Joyce, to reach the tops and give her extra money for helping. I would also take her to the café, which was around the corner from the railway telegraph, for a treat with my earnings.

The café was run by two old girls who had lived and worked there for years. It was a double-fronted shop, and inside the floor was covered with dark brown lino. There were long tables that they used to scrub almost white, and long wooden seats with very high backs. The only way to talk to any one on the table in front or behind you was to stand up on the bench and look over. Each table had seating for twelve people. The counter was made of marble, with glass display cabinets displaying some of their pies, cakes and bread and dripping, and every time I went in the two old dears would say, 'Your usual bread and dripping, Georgie?' It was made from their Sunday lunch.

The café would get very busy with the workers from the railway. Joyce and myself would spend a lot of time in that café, me with my bread and dripping, and Joyce with her favourite jam pudding with custard. We were so hungry that we often crammed our food into our mouths, wolfing it all down; anyone watching must have thought that we had never seen food before. All that was part of my treat to her. I wanted to help her as much as I helped Violet. But I could never help Joyce in my pearly suit, any more than I could let her know of my secret life in my pearly suit; it was only Violet who I could help 'in my pearls', as I called it.

Chapter Six

Here I was sitting at the back of my new classroom – a position that I always placed myself in. Whether I was sat in the front, sides or at the back of the class, it still boiled down to one thing: I was unable to hear, so it made no difference. I was able to hear some teachers' voices, but only at a close range, but I could not pick out the words coming from their voice. My deafness was now taking a turn for the worse.

I had just started secondary school and was still unable to read or write. This was something else that existed outside my little quiet world, something else that I was excluded from. There was no help for my schooling. On top of my bad hearing, I had my own father knocking me around the head as if it was a football, then Auntie Hilda brainwashing me into not listening when other people were talking. With this sort of treatment, it's no wonder that my hearing is so bad, and will affect me until the day I die.

I would sit in my classroom feeling very much in a world of my own, and watch the other children as they raised their hands, eager and confident about knowing the answer to the teacher's questions. I had no idea of the questions that were being asked or what answer the teacher had got. I could see things written up on the blackboard that just looked like a mass of letters.

On a regular basis I sat and observed the other children when they were applauded for the good deeds they had done, or their achievements. I often dreamed and hoped that one day it would happen to me, but there was no chance of that. The only thing I received was bad reports; there was no room for change as no one recognised that I was deaf. So everyone just saw me as this naughty boy.

Still oblivious to being deaf, I assumed that everyone around me was experiencing the same hearing as myself. It wasn't like today. If a child is far behind like me, straight away a hearing test will be carried out to try and detect the problem. Whatever way you looked at it, I was on the losing end. I so wanted to be able to read and write like my mates, and be like them. I wished to experience recognition for some good I had done, to be on the receiving end of a compliment, just to know what it felt like. There was no chance of that ever happening, so as usual here I was at the back of the class, mucking about or daydreaming about my next scam. I was not getting attention at home, nor was I getting it at school. The only attention I received was in the way of punishment at home or, at school, for not paying attention to my schoolwork. I had more canings in my school than any other kid, so really I was being caned for just being deaf. I found it impossible to concentrate in class, which would get me in even more trouble. I did not know my problem, nor did the school. All the school could see was a mischievous little boy whose parents showed no concern for him. They had no time for me, the time waster who was always mucking about and also holding others back. I was the boy who was always at the bottom of the class with a big 'D' hat.

At school, I felt like I was in social isolation. My mates were all doing so well, and they were way ahead of me. I was not standing at their level anymore. I was bringing my fear of home to my learning. I just couldn't understand what the teachers were saying; they all just sounded like they were speaking a different language to me. Auntie Hilda had convinced me not to listen to others when they were talking, and so I would automatically switch off, for fear of another good hiding.

I really believed that the teachers saw me as this little scruffy kid who was only interested in making trouble, and based their opinion of me on my outward appearance. If only they just took the time to get to know me they would have realised that I just needed help to be able to understand what was going on around me; but no one there seemed interested in my welfare, my learning or me. Surely someone should be able to help me? I could not even help myself as I did not know the extent of my problem.

Early one afternoon when we returned from our dinner break, I noticed that the teacher was getting annoyed with me. I was trying very hard to do my work, but I began to get frustrated because the harder I tried the less I was able to grasp it. In the end my anger took its toll, and I pushed my schoolwork off the desk. Straight away this sent alarm bells to my teacher, who flew at me, and all hell let loose. I had got to breaking point. I'd had enough and that was it. All the pent-up frustration exploded.

With great urgency, the headmaster was called to the classroom. I was in a rage and out of control. The frustration that had built up inside of me exploded in a desperate plea for help, which I needed now more than ever. The classroom door was flung open, and standing there in the doorway was the headmaster, a man feared by all at the school. He was bigger than my father. When he came over to me, he grabbed me by the back of my coat and my feet seemed to leave the ground as he took me from the classroom along the corridor then up the stairs to his study.

As soon as he got me to his study he threw me down onto the floor. 'You, Major,' he said, 'are going to be taught a lesson. There is nothing in your school report that is good. You have no interest in learning in this school. You are a waste of time. You hold everyone back… you are just useless!' This was a word used so many times by Auntie Hilda.

'I am not useless!' I yelled, as I tried to defend my actions and my rights while being branded as useless, which must have inflamed the headmaster even more.

He had a reputation for being a cruel man, so it was no good me even trying to explain what the reasons were for my behaviour. Nor did I know them myself. Being a stern disciplinarian, he made it clear that he intended to punish me by caning me. But I was thinking to myself, You'll not, that's what others often used for my body. I am not a punishment block. I am just getting fed up with people bullying me and knocking me about like some old rag doll. At that point I ran towards the door for an escape route, but he was that much quicker than me and locked the door.

I was like a frightened rabbit as I ran around the room looking for another escape route. Then I headed for the open window, with the full intention of jumping out. Again the headmaster beat me to it. Then I dived under his desk, but he caught me by the legs. I was at last trapped by this powerful man and was at his mercy. Although I struggled to get free from his powerful arms I was defeated. I was so determined to escape from him, but he must have thought that I was his prey, and no way was he going to let me get away.

To my horror I was caught. He tied me over his chair like you would a wild animal, then he pulled down my short trousers to my ankles, leaving my bum bare as the day I was born. Then, taking a large bamboo cane in his right hand above his head, he whacked me with all the strength and anger that he had in his body. With me still struggling on the chair, again the cane landed in the same place as the first, so the pain was four times the strength; then the third time; then the fourth. I was now feeling drained and the pain was unbearable. Then the fifth time – weaker. I could tell when the sixth blow landed on me this powerful man was going to use all his anger on me until he was exhausted. By the time the seventh blow landed on me, I was exhausted and I knew I could take no more. After the cane landed for the eighth time, the headmaster untied me and pulled me up from the chair. All my energy had left my body. My legs had given out underneath me and I was in a collapsed state.

The headmaster then virtually carried my weakened body, as you would handle your prey, to the main school gates and told me to go home. I did not feel that I could take my body home or move anymore; but somehow, half crawling and half dragging myself, I took myself towards home. What would normally take five minutes to walk took me over an hour to crawl. As I moved each leg forward I could feel the pain of my skin moving and stretching on my bum, pushing my left foot forward and then slowly pulling my body forward with it. Each time the pain increased as I headed towards the alley, making a much shorter route home. Then I would rest. As the pain intensified, it was becoming unbearable. When I looked towards the back of my legs, I noticed blood running down the back from the open wounds. I had prepared myself for pain, like all the other pains; but this time I had to try extra hard to convince myself that I could defeat this agony.

Then a bloke came up to me and stupidly asked, 'Are you all right, son?' I had now lost all faith in grown-ups. I know I was taught you should respect your elders, but at this point, that was the last thing on my mind, and I just told him to piss off.

How could I put my trust in them anymore? What had they done for me but add more misery to my life? I travelled through the alleys to make my way home like a snail, each movement on my belly, dragging myself forward, each movement causing more pain. Somehow I managed to make it home and drag myself upstairs, but at the same time I felt that I was doing wrong by going home, knowing I couldn't expect any help or sympathy from Auntie Hilda or my father.

The best place for me to go would have been to my air-raid shelter, where I could take good care of myself until my wounds were healed, but I had no more energy to go on. I had to make my way to the bedroom and lay on my tummy. Before I could make it I was met on the top landing by Auntie Hilda with one of her fags hanging on her bottom lip and coughing in between her words. Without any concern or compassion, she asked, 'Melsham! Whatever happened to you?' Before I could begin to respond, she added with that evil smirk, 'Serves you right! I told you that you was useless and a no-good-for-nothing. Wait till your father gets home.'

I carried on crawling to my bedroom to get onto the bed and try and lie on my tummy.

I was to too exhausted to try to move or escape anymore. I just needed to rest and keep quiet and hope that the skin on my bum stayed perfectly still. The pain was increasing. Unknown to me, the cane marks were swelling, so stretching the open skin more and causing the excruciating pain. I could not sleep, so I just had to lie there and bear it, convincing myself to fight this pain.

Some five hours or so passed and not once did Auntie Hilda pop in to see how I was. To be honest, had she done so, I would most certainly have told her to piss off as well, and to hell with respect. I was alone and fighting my pain when my father walked in. I don't know what Auntie Hilda must have said to him but my father grabbed hold of me and dragged me down to the waiting tin bath. He had filled it with cold water and poured in loads of salt in the bath, and sat me in it. The salt was eating into my wounds. Then he stood me up and scrubbed me without any concern for the painful wounds that had been inflicted by the headmaster.

I screamed with pain and I watched the expression on my sister Joyce's face, as she cringed and looked like she had seen a ghost. The pain had got the better of me and I passed out. I will never know what was said to cause my father to react like that. The next morning, when I opened my eyes, my bum was still painful, and I was lying on my tummy feeling very sick and weak. I do remember Joyce coming into my bedroom looking very upset. I don't think she really understood the full suffering that I was experiencing, but somehow for the first time she was beginning to realise that something was wrong. I remember her stroking my hair with a tear in her eye, which made me think that maybe she was on my side. I needed all the encouragement I could get. Even the touch of her hand stroking my hair gave me a little reassurance. It meant someone cared for me, and meant a lot to me, with the suffering that I was undergoing.

Some weeks later my father took the headmaster to court. I don't know what the result was, but I do know that for my father to take him to court, it would not be out of concern for the way the headmaster had treated me, but for his possible financial gain from my suffering. He did not feel duty bound to protect his son. I never went back to that school again, for the reason of my punishment and my poor schooling. I was to await a new school that I should be sent to next; until then I had to remain at home.

What confused me about Auntie Hilda and my father was that every parent or guardian tried to work honestly to give their children the best upbringing they could, lavishing on love understanding and guidance to live a good honest life. It is all about respect, honour and loyalty. It takes a lot to strive and care for that goal. Each parent shares their love with their children and their friends, so giving their own children that security in their upbringing. Joyce and myself never shared games or normal discussions or laughter with Auntie Hilda, nor with my father. We were just there, simply in the way until money could be made out of suffering, like making money out of my bike or the headmaster who had almost beaten me to a pulp. As far as I was concerned, that's all I was there for. As far as Auntie Hilda and my father were concerned, it was all about disciplining me for imaginary and invented crimes, which I had supposedly committed. On the majority of occasions I didn't do anything to deserve the cruel punishments I received from my father, who would seem to use me as his swear box and punchbag.

The more the bruises rose on my body with the cuts I had, the more Auntie Hilda seemed to enjoy it. As my life was growing grimmer and more hurtful, I found my true life living with Auntie Iris and Uncle Alf. Whenever I was with them I felt safe, but I could not always be with them for fear that our friendship would be exposed, and that would be the end of the only thing I had left that encouraged me to keep going. I did not want them or anyone else feeling sorry for me because I did not know what sorry was, any more than I knew what love was. Auntie Iris and Uncle Alf knew of my suffering but never talked to me about it, and if they did they knew that I would deny it. They just had to sit, watch and listen to know my suffering as it took hold. They were too weak to help, anyway, and I just didn't want anyone, not even my sister, Joyce. This was to be something that I have only shared with myself until this day. It seems incredible, but I am glad that at last my mind is at peace and free from this evil past, after writing it down piece by piece.

I saw that caning as a final rejection. My trust in grown-ups was fast disappearing; after all, they were the only people who were misusing me. I had nothing to look forward to – only my visits to Violet, who as far as I was concerned still needed my help.

I had not been to school for almost a year, which pleased me. It gave me more time on the market and my own ducking and diving. As I was going around the back alleys to bury my money, I got attracted to this beautiful ginger cat. Its fur was well kept, and it had two lovely eyes. It always kept about four yards away, looking at me, and I seemed to think that it was either lost or wild. It would run away from everyone. So I went down to the local fish shop to get an old pennyworth of cat's fish, and took it back to the alley to find my hungry cat. Then he ran towards me, stopping at about four yards' distance; so a little piece at a time, I laid the fish on the floor, and each time the four-yard gap was closing. When the last piece was at my foot, I put out my hand to stroke him, and as I stroked him I could feel how soft his fur was. I could feel him purring by putting my hand under his throat. I knew he was enjoying me stroking him because by the time I had just reached his tail it would go up so that my hand did not slip off.

We cuddled each other in the alley for hours. Now I had my four-legged friend, and another mouth to feed. We became great friends and as I came back to the alley I would whistle, and from nowhere he was there rubbing against my legs. He would then start to follow me down the road. Wherever I went, he went. Whenever he was with me I felt happy and took him to my air-raid shelter, where I could talk and cuddle him, and he always seemed to be listening and understanding. Some of my mates used to say that he was like a dog walking with me. He even used to beg for food just in the same way a dog would. He was protecting me against the rats when I stayed out overnight in my air-raid shelter. I truly had a good friend.

It was now time for Auntie Hilda to disgrace me again. I had been given a new school, not an ordinary one, but as Auntie Hilda said to me, 'You are going to a dunce's school for boys who are thick in the head, for no-good-for-nothing boys – which you are!' It seemed as if she wanted to belittle me, but it was partly because of her I was so far behind in school anyway.

'Where is it?' I said.

'I am going to tell you once and once only,' she said, 'so let it sink in, and you start tomorrow.' She then gave me the directions. 'Turn left at the bottom of Boswell Road, past the fire station on your right, go to the end of the road that's called Brickstock Road. At the end you turn right, passing Thornton Heath pond on your left. Keep on walking for two miles and the school is on the right.'

Following the directions that Auntie Hilda said, with the address of the school, I arrived at this big school. To check that I had the right place, I asked a passing woman, showing her the address on my bit of paper. She read it out, 'St Christopher's School, London Road, Norbury SW16, South London… Yes,' she said, 'this is St Christopher's School. It says that on that board with the address.'

'Thank you,' I said, and walked back home. I had already timed myself on how long it would take to get to school, which the way I walk took a good hour. The following morning I took off to go to my new school. Auntie Hilda was right. It was a school for those with learning difficulties, but what I really needed before I could learn anything was a new pair of ears. But still no one knew about or cared about my hearing difficulties.

On arriving I saw all types of kids and somehow felt out of place with them. Many seemed to look silly, and I was thinking, Is this really St Christopher's School? On checking my piece of paper and matching it with the board that the woman pointed out to me the night before, I saw that this was indeed my school. It had high railings all around it and the school itself lay in between two playgrounds, one to the front of the school and one to the back. It was a very old Victorian building and stood on its own. It had two floors to it.

As I was standing outside I was watching all the kids having their final hugs from their mums and carrying their little lunch boxes, which I didn't have. I then followed the kids to wherever they were going. I did not know who to see or what I should do, but then I saw this teacher.

'Miss, my name is George Major. I am new here. What do I do?'

'Where is your mom?'

'Oh, she had to go straight away to work,' I said, wishing that my mother had brought me to school.

'Come with me,' she said, and took me to the headmistress's study. I was asked a lot of questions that I did not understand, and was taken to my new classroom. It was a bit more cheerful than the ones I had been used to, so that made me feel a bit settled. It was just that the children were strange. I was placed in my usual place, even at this school, at the back of the class. On my first day at school I did find that the teachers were very pleased and understanding with me. They were coming up to my desk and showing me things and spending one-to-one time with me, and I seemed to enjoy what I was doing at school for the first time in my life. At this rate I could even turn out doing better than Joyce, who could read and write! But like all good things for me, this was not going to last more than a year. There was to be yet another turn in my life.

Every day I happily went off on my own to my new school, full of excitement. Then each day after school my cat would be waiting for my return, perched on the top of the brick wall, under which ran a brook, which led to the rear of the houses of Boswell Road. My cat would jump off the wall to rub his body round my legs for his welcome cuddle; then he would follow me to the air-raid shelter where I would feed him and play with him. Sometimes I would buy a half-pint of milk and give him some and I would talk to him about the events of my day at school, or about what was troubling me. I knew that whatever I talked about would remain between us and go no further, so I was able to talk about absolutely anything without an ounce of fear. While I was out along the alleys in search of more firewood, my cat would follow me.

After being at my new school for a few months, news came home that my Uncle Jim, my father's younger brother, had died of TB. I had met him a few times. He was tall, like my father, but very slim. He had golden hair that I used to love. He was a very happy and jolly man. He was a part-time singer and dancer, and like my father if he had pushed himself he too could have been a top star. He was in the RAF for many years, and when he left he went to be a baker. He had left a wife and five young children – Jimmy, David, Brian, Phillip and Shirley, aged from four to twelve years of age.

We went off to the funeral at Rickmansworth in Hertfordshire, near Watford. Why I was taken I really don't know, as I was never included in this family. Perhaps it was because Auntie Hilda thought that I would rob the house; but whatever reason they had it would not have been in my interest.

The funeral was attended by all my father's family and the family of Auntie Vi, Uncle Jim's wife, with all my cousins – about twelve. Uncle

Jim's death was to be another turning point of my life – not for the better, but for the worse. I felt like the odd one out at this funeral and wished that I could have stayed at home with my cat. Everyone was holding everyone's hand, or had their arms around each other. No one was left alone except me. Even Joyce had Auntie Hilda's arm around her, so it did look as if Auntie Hilda had made a good job of brainwashing everyone against me. Joyce even had a new dress made for her to suit the funeral occasion. I was still in my old clothing with the toes of my boots hanging out. I had never had nice clothes where I could take pride in myself, but I did shed a tear for Uncle Jim. He was the only good one out of them all. He was a very good father to his children and a good husband to his wife. After the funeral we all went back to a reception at their home. Still having this sense of loneliness and the feeling of being in the way, I decided to slip out to my usual home on the streets in the hope of meeting some local kids to play with.

It did not take long before I was playing with the local kids, who seemed friendlier than where I came from. 'You don't live around here, do you?' they had asked.

'No,' I said, 'I am from London.'

'Cor!' they said. In them days if you came from London you was something special, as people did not travel like they do today, and Watford is only about thirty-four miles away, but to those kids London was like Hollywood, a place for gangsters like Jack Spot, who at the time was the king of the underworld. Then one of the kids said, 'Have you met any pearly kings and queens?' They were in the news a lot in them days.

'Yes,' I said, 'I have met pearly kings and queens,' but I stopped short of telling them that I was a pearly prince, in case they knew my cousins, and then I would get another good hiding. As I was playing with the kids I was becoming the local hero amongst them because I was from London. It was 'George this' and 'George that'. We played all kinds of games from hide-and-seek to cricket. By now I had forgotten why I was in Rickmansworth. Then a loud call came out. It was Auntie Hilda.

'Melsham! Come back here, we are leaving!'

'I thought that you said your name was George,' this boy said out of the blue, but I replied by saying, 'That's another story mate.'

Our journey home in my father's car, a Morris, was quiet. Not a word was spoken; just a sniffle now and then. When we got home

Auntie Hilda and my father were deeply upset at losing their younger brother. For the first time that day I wanted to comfort them and reassure them, but I was frightened to, as I knew what would happen. Even if I tried I would be pushed aside and told to mind my own business, and Auntie Hilda might even go as far as to say it was my fault that Uncle Jim was dead. So I could only watch and grieve for them in total silence. It was at times like this that I just wanted to help; I felt that it was my job to. I did have strong feelings.

I carried on doing my school run, and Uncle Jim's death had well passed me, but Joyce and myself had noticed that my father was going away in the car each weekend. This in a way pleased me, as I would not get as many good hidings. Because my father was away, I had decided to sleep in my air-raid shelter to get away from Auntie Hilda. On these weekends it was so peaceful for me, and I was still going to see Violet in my pearly suit, and returning it to Auntie Iris with my cat following me to Auntie Iris as well. When I did get to her flat, my cat would jump up on my lap and lick me, with Auntie Iris feeding him. Everyone knew I had a cat; no one could miss him with me. After a few weeks of my father going to Rickmansworth every weekend, I think Auntie Hilda had realised that he was not going there to give a helping hand but for other reasons.

She insisted on my father taking me, as I was in the way and caused trouble, and she could not handle me. Mind you, I was always away at the weekends myself, but that is Auntie Hilda for you. I did not want to go to Rickmansworth because I would end up missing my cat and would not be able to see Violet, and my life would then be empty. I tried to protest to my father, who as usual was not prepared to listen to me. After all, I was committed to wearing my pearly suit and collecting money for Violet's hospital. I had already agreed to go to their fête and help, and I never liked letting people down. So I knew I would be letting them down, and my sister. Nor could I go to the markets or do my other jobs. But my protest went unheard, and at Auntie Hilda's insistence I had to go with my father to Rickmansworth every weekend, praying that my father would give up on me and stop taking me. One comfort from all this was that I noticed how kind and fair he was getting towards me at the weekends, but I also noticed how much kinder he was to my cousins, and how he was giving them money and spoiling them, something he had never done to me.

The house was in Springwell Avenue, Mile End, Rickmansworth. It was a four-bedroom corner house, with a big drive and a very large garden to the rear, which was kept well clean and tidy. Auntie Vi's cooking was good. She was a good cook and always gave big portions to everyone. There was no chance of her boiling my father's handkerchief in her cooking pots! I could see the results of Uncle Jim's hard work: warm blankets, clean sheets, good furnishing and plenty of carpets – unlike at my home, dull and shabby with horrible food. I got on very well with my cousins, apart from our fights now and then, but we soon got over them. I also had the opportunity of getting plenty of country air, and my cousin, Jimmy, who was the eldest and looked like his father, would take me to see the jackdaws fly around the hilltops. It was so lovely watching them fly so freely. Shirley had her own room, and I would sleep with Jimmy. Brian, Phillip and David would sleep in their bedroom, leaving the fourth bedroom to Auntie Vi… and yes, my father.

It was obvious that they were having an affair, and I knew something had to happen to me. Auntie Vi had already made it known to me that I was not in her favour, right from day one, so I felt that my security was now slipping. I may have been having fun with my cousins, and I was away from Auntie Hilda's brainwashing, but up to a point I was quite contented with what little I had. At least I could get away and do my jobs and see Violet. Now all this was a threat to me. I had started to see my cousins getting a lot of things from my father. He was picking them up onto his lap and laughing with them, which he never did with me or my sister. I was being pushed out further and further; I could not understand what was going on. Perhaps my father was making up to them for the loss of their father, but I had never shared any of that with my father. So how does that fit in?

When I got home, Auntie Hilda would start on me. What is your father doing? Are they kissing? Do they sleep together? And a thousand other questions that I never gave answers to.

'Come on, Melsham, you know what is going on!'

'But I don't!' I would repeat. I just hated all this. By now Joyce was beginning to rebel and was getting told off by Auntie Hilda, due to my father being away more from home. Joyce must have felt a lack of security, with Auntie Hilda not helping with her and always saying, 'Your father thinks more of the children in Rickmansworth than his own kids.' Then she would blame me, saying it was all my fault. So now I was being accused of destroying the family, and I was to blame for everything. All this was scaring me. Just what was happening? Why couldn't Auntie Hilda or my father think of putting me first, instead of himself or herself? Why must I be put at the bottom all the time? My father had just proved he could be so nice to my cousins, so why not to Joyce and me – his own children? Now that I felt more settled in St Christopher's School I was doing better, but with my new added problems at home I was not able to cope at school, plus the fact that nobody was addressing my hearing problem, which was becoming a big issue to me.

There was a lot happening in my life and it was getting even more confusing. I would lie in my bed and cry, in desperate need of my mother. I was not seeing Violet, which was also affecting me, and also not wearing my pearly suit was adding to all this. I had felt useful and had a good sense of being while wearing it. It would help me to cope with the taunts and abuse I was getting from Auntie Hilda. After about five weeks of going to Rickmansworth for the weekends I was really getting very depressed. I was losing out on my visits to see Violet and missing working in my pearly suit, which had given me a new outlook on life and added to my confidence. Then there was my market work and other jobs; my cat was OK as I was giving him extra food before leaving him to go off to Rickmansworth.

On my sixth weekend on the Saturday morning my father called out for me to leave as he usually did. 'Come on!' he shouted. 'We are leaving now.' He held out the car door. I was standing by the brook wall where my cat was sitting on top as I was stroking him, and I could feel him purring.

'Come on, you bastard!' he shouted.

'No!' I said – the first time that I had defied my father. 'No!'

The next minute in a flash he had run over towards me. Then, without warning, he pushed my cat over the wall, and I shouted at my father, 'You bastard!'

I ran down to the side of the brook. The water was running at about six inches high with all kinds of rubbish in it: old prams, bricks, bottles, sticks and all sorts. When I arrived to look below the bridge, I could see my cat. He had landed on an open broken bottle. It had gone right through his body. He was just lying there, with just a movement now and then.

I jumped into the brook and picked up my cat. While I was sitting in the water blood was everywhere. My cat was looking at me and I started to cry. I was shouting, 'I love you! Don't leave me, don't leave me, I love you!' Then he gave his last breath. I yelled at my father, saying, 'You bastard, you bastard! You have killed him, you bastard!' By now half the street must have gathered by the brook side, as I sat in the running water holding my cat, still crying, 'Don't leave me, don't leave me!' to my cat.

Then I saw Mr Crookshank. He had jumped into the brook with me. 'He is dead, Georgie, he is dead,' he said. 'There is nothing you can do. Let go!'

But I still stayed there, sitting in the water. 'This was my best mate!' I was crying.

'I know, Georgie, but I can get you another mate,' he said.

'This is my mate!'

'Now look, Georgie, we have got to move from this water.'

By now, three other people had jumped into the brook to help. I looked up at all the people who had gathered and saw many of them sharing my tears; everyone just wanted to help.

Mr Crookshank and the three other men slowly lifted my soaking wet body from the water with the blood of my cat still running with the water. When they got me to the top of the bank people came forward to stroke my head and to share my loss, and all the time Mr Crookshank was holding me and comforting me.

Mr Crookshank asked, 'Shall we bury him, Georgie?'

'Yes,' I said, 'next to my air-raid shelter, where we had spent so many happy times together.'

So, still holding my cat in my arms, and still crying my eyes out, I led Mr Crookshank to my air-raid shelter. There he started to dig the grave for my cat, with tools handed to him by our neighbours. Finally I laid my cat to rest. Mr Crookshank who knew his prayers, prayed for my cat to go to heaven, and for us to remember the good times we had together.

That night I stayed at my air-raid shelter and lay next to the grave of my cat and cried, and there I stayed until morning, still in my damp clothes. During that day I made a cross for the grave, putting clean stones all around it and making it look like a grave that anyone could be proud of.

With my cat now gone, somehow I felt dead myself, and wished it were me that had been pushed into the brook. I would not have had any more suffering and if there was a God that loved children, like Auntie Iris always said to me, at least I would have had a second life where someone did love me. Now perhaps my cat is up there in heaven, rolling over on his back and having his tummy tickled, which he loved me doing. As I lay on his grave outside my air-raid shelter, I tried to sleep away the pain of losing him. The tears for him ran down on his grave. For all the tears that I had shed in my young life, more were now pouring from me. I felt stripped of everything I'd ever had, and over and over again the picture of my cat, who had shared my life, kept repeating itself. I was now left with just the memory of a four-legged friend who had given me so much love, love I did not have to fight for.

I may have said goodbye to my cat, but I've never forgotten him. He was yet another thing that was taken from me in my life by my father.

By Sunday late evening the next day I was still mourning the death of my cat. My father arrived home and came straight into my bedroom. 'Don't you *ever* defy me again!' he said.

'You killed my cat,' I protested. 'You killed my cat, and I shall never forget that.'

For the second time I was finding myself standing up for myself, as if my cat had left a defence mark on me, and if it got me a good hiding who cared? At that, my father pulled me from the bed and gave another good hiding, but this time I was taking it for the defence of my cat, who had no chance. I was beginning to hate my father even more for what he had done. I would have died for my cat; he never let me down.

As I again picked myself up after taking another full punishment for my cat, I felt the muscles in my body being torn apart by my father; he was flinging me around like a ball and then punching me as if I were his punch bag. I had a feeling that I wasn't actually on this planet and that I was somewhere else, but did not know where. I again dragged myself to my bedroom, trying to escape the blows, when something stopped me from going forward. I felt my legs leave the ground. My father had picked me up by my feet and flung me again, hitting my head on the coal bucket that stood by the fireplace. I felt the blood running down the side of my neck as I again tried to crawl to my bedroom, to safety. Inch by inch I tried to pick myself up so that I could escape quicker. I saw Auntie Hilda's legs and grabbed hold of them in order to pick myself up but she just moved her legs away. As I fell to the floor again, I felt my scalp leave my head as my father picked me up again to fling me yet again. But this time I landed at the top of the stairs, catching my shoulder against the banister, and lost my balance, falling down the stairs. Then I dragged myself, with almost all the strength left in me, back upstairs to my bedroom; I shut the door and lay on my bed. I felt my head bursting and became dizzy and passed out, for how long, I don't know.

Following my beating I crept downstairs to go to my air-raid shelter to nurse my cuts and bruises, and for the second night lay down next to my cat's grave, crying as I felt lost without my only friend. He lay beneath the earth. I again slept there for the night, cuddling my cat in my mind.

For the next few weeks I seemed to have won my battle, and there were no more visits to Rickmansworth. This was a good break for me, so it was back to seeing Violet, who had been very upset at my absence. After making excuses for not seeing her, I said that I would make it up to her and come one evening on a weekday after school, but I would not be able to wear my pearly suit, because I felt I might lose it, taking it to my school and leaving it all day. After all Violet was quite used to seeing me in my pearly suit. I was back on the markets with Billy Cook, and back doing my other jobs to support my two sisters and myself.

On one particular weekend, for the first time Auntie Hilda came up to me to ask me if I could go to Rickmansworth to help my father. I don't know if my father had asked her to ask me, or if my father really needed my help, but I did agree. Having helped my father put boxes in the car from our home, we set off for Rickmansworth, and on the way we popped into my Auntie Ethel's house in Peckham. I had been there a few times before with my father, and I liked going there, as Auntie Ethel was a happy-go-lucky person, always laughing and very talkative – the opposite to Auntie Hilda, even though you would have taken them to be twins, with Auntie Ethel being much shorter. She always wore a full dress apron with a belt to the waist. All her aprons were full of flowery patterns. It was a known fact that Auntie Ethel was a family mistake. My father's mother had an affair with some geezer and out popped Auntie Ethel. No one knew who the father was, so just like me she was the black sheep of the family – hated by them all except my father.

Her husband, Uncle Jack, was as bald as a baby's bum. He'd kept the eight long strands of hair that he used to brush over the top of his head

George in 1945

The Railway Telegraph.
Photo courtesy of Croydon Library.

Thornton Heath High Street, around the corner from where George started his childhood, 1942.
Photo courtesy of Croydon Library.

*William (George's grandfather) and George's mother, sitting next to her brother.
Photo courtesy of London Metropolitan Archives.*

*The front entrace of Mayford Approved School, 1952.
Photo courtesy of London Metropolitan Archives.*

The dining room at Mayford Approved School, 1952.
Photo courtesy of London Metropolitan Archives.

The dormitory at Mayford Approved School, 1952.
Photo courtesy of London Metropolitan Archives.

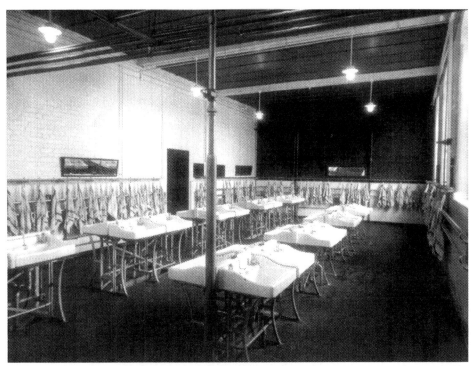

The washroom at Mayford Approved School, 1952. Note the hanging towels, all numbered. Photo courtesy of London Metropolitan Archives.

The schoolroom at Mayford Approved School, 1952. Photo courtesy of London Metropolitan Archives.

George revisits Mayford Approved School

*The World Turned Upside Down, 1948. Note the tramlines.
From the collection of Southwark Local History Library.*

Bill and Liz Cole, Pearly King and Queen of Islington

*Pearly Harvest Festival, Old Kent Road, 1949.
From the collection of Southwark Local History Library.*

Rose Matthew Smith

Pearlies in George's younger days

Pearly children

Henry Croft

Pearly Easter Queen

Beatrice Marriott

many times a day. They seemed to be his pride and joy. He was of medium build and stood at 5' 7" in height. He was very funny and used to make me laugh a lot. They had two boys; the youngest, Stuart, was about seven and John was about thirteen. I got on with all of them very well, better than the Rickmansworth lot. They lived in a row of terraced houses backing onto the railway lines in Kimberley Avenue. On this particular weekend my father was to pick up some more boxes to take to Rickmansworth. This got me thinking that he was moving, and I was hoping that I was not part of that plan, or that it was a planned easy trick to get me to Rickmansworth without any trouble. Over a cup of tea they were talking, when all of a sudden their voices were raised at the mention of Auntie Hilda, and they seem to slag off all the family as if they had been really hurt by them.

Then they started to praise my mother and say how she was misused and given the cold shoulder by all the family, and that they had seen her only a few months ago. My heart took a big leap; my father had already stopped them from talking any further because I was there. So my mother had been seen again! I knew it – and my heart was beating much faster. I was beginning to be more hopeful, a breakthrough, and maybe the start to finding her for real. All I needed was the help of Uncle Alf, so I set my plan straight away. First I must get this full address, so that I could come back with Uncle Alf. I had to know what else they knew about my mother, and I could not ask while my father was around.

I could not go outside to see the name of the road or even the district, as I could not read or write. Then I thought of John, my cousin. During all the shouting, I slipped out of the room to find John, who was playing upstairs in his bedroom. 'John,' I said, 'can you write down your full address for me?'

'What do you want it for, Georgie?'

'To send you something,' I said, having to think of a quick answer.

So John wrote down the full address: 99 Kimberley Avenue, Peckham, London SE15. Now I had the address, and slipped it in my back trouser pocket to keep safe. I could not afford to lose it. 'Thanks a lot, John,' I said, and I really did mean it.

My father and I set off to Rickmansworth. As we travelled in the car there were so many questions I needed to ask him. Why have my sister and I always been led to believe that my mother was dead? Why do you or the family never talk about her? What does my mother look like?

Why is she not with us? And hundreds or more questions that I wanted to know. But I didn't dare ever say the word 'mother' or I would get a good hiding, and I was still not happy with him about my cat, so our journey was taken in complete silence from leaving Auntie Ethel's.

On our arrival in Rickmansworth I helped my father unload all the boxes that we had brought, and all the time I was checking that I had my piece of paper with Auntie Ethel's address on it. I was now on my longest weekend ever waiting to return home, but while there and watching some of the boxes being unpacked, I got the feeling that my father was intending to stay at Rickmansworth; but I could not see anything that belong to me being unpacked, which pleased me. And all the time I was checking my back pocket to make sure I still had that address.

At long last, our journey back home took place. How relieved I was at not staying at Rickmansworth, and relieved that I was a short time away from seeing Uncle Alf with my piece of paper with the address on it and asking for help.

When we arrived home I went straight to the back alley to go to Auntie Iris's and Uncle Alf's flat. I knocked on the back door and slipped into her flat, as this door was always kept open until they went to bed. I think it was left open mostly for me to pop in at any time. Pulling out the address of Auntie Ethel's house, I said, 'Look, Uncle, can you help me?' Then I explained all that I had heard and seen about a chance of meeting with my mother. I said he must have felt the same as I was thinking, that if Auntie Ethel and Uncle Jack hated Auntie Hilda and the family so much, they would be willing to talk about my mother, and possibly lead us to where she lived.

Uncle Alf promised me the following Sunday he would take me to Peckham to meet Auntie Ethel and Uncle Jack, and get behind the mystery of my mother. I now had a full slow week in front of me, waiting to go to Auntie Ethel, but with my schooling each day and my jobs every night, except the night at Violet's, the week went quicker than expected. When the big day arrived I popped downstairs to Uncle Alf, who was just giving himself a final brush down. He always looked very smart in his suit, and his shoes were so well polished you could see the reflection of your face in them.

Off we set. First I went into the sweet shop to get John and Stuart some sweets, then we caught a number 68 bus at the top of the high street to Peckham. Then we had to change onto another bus to go to

Nunhead Lane, which Kimberly Avenue runs from. Then at last we arrived at 99 Kimberley Avenue. I gave one loud knock on the door knocker, and the door was opened by Auntie Ethel.

'Hello, Georgie!' she said. 'What a surprise!'

'This is Uncle Alf,' I said 'can we come in and talk?'

'Of course, Georgie.'

I think everyone called me Georgie because my father's name was George as well. We went into their sitting room, where Uncle Jack was having his cup of tea. Uncle Alf started the talking first, explaining that he and his wife were always willing to help me, and now wanted to help in finding my mother; they and I had always believed her to be dead, until last week. 'Then,' he said, 'you said that you had met her.'

'Yes,' Ethel said, 'it doesn't surprise me that they, the family, would make you think that she was dead. I did know Georgie's mother, a very nice woman. I liked her and I thought George – "my brother" – had treated her and her family badly. I don't know the real reasons how or why they split up, but it was a messy affair.'

'Do you know where she lives?' Uncle Alf said.

'No, love,' said Ethel, 'but the last time that I saw her was at Camberwell Green on the park bench feeding the birds and I was in a hurry and only had time to say hello; but I do know that her family live at the back of Camberwell Green, and are known to be pretty well off. That's really all I do know. But if I see her again I will get her address if I can.'

John and Stuart had come downstairs and I proudly gave them the present I had promised. After a very interesting two or more hours we left.

We then walked down the road with Uncle Alf holding my hand. I asked him if we could go to that park bench in Camberwell Green. 'Of cause we can, Georgie,' he said, and within a space of twenty minutes we were at Camberwell Green.

'There is the bench!' I said. I ran to the bench and sat in the middle with my arms stretched along the back with my legs outstretched. I sat there with open eyes and thoughts. My eyes wandered to the birds flying over the green, wondering if they had been fed by my mum. Then I watched every woman who passed, wondering if one of them was my mum. I sat on the bench that I knew my mother had sat on, maybe many times. In my mind I tried to leave a message for her to make contact with me and that I loved her.

'Come on, George, let's go home,' said Uncle Alf, holding out his hand. He knew that I was very disappointed and upset that not much progress had been made today.

We caught the 68 bus to go home, and sat in the front of the top deck of the bus, and all along our journey Uncle Alf was explaining about the different landmarks and cars on the road, explaining what this and that meant. This was something that my father had never ever done. To travel with my father was like travelling with a complete stranger; you felt isolated and cut off.

Arriving back at Auntie Iris's, I put my little stool up to her side to sit on her lap as I had done so many times and she then put her arms around me. Uncle Alf had already explained what had happened, and that we had been to the park bench that my mother had often sat on. 'At least you are nearer to your mother than you have ever been,' she said.

This really is what I had come to expect. I'd had so many disappointments in my life, but unknown to me there was worse to come and worse to face up to. I was still wishing that death would come to me early. I had no cat, no love and no security, just an empty unhappy life. I just did not have the courage to end it myself. I only hoped that a car would run into me and end my life and quickly.

Having succeeded in not going up to Rickmansworth each weekend, I was back to my normal everyday routine. After a few weeks settling down as I wanted I had come back from the market when I bumped into Joyce. We were both on our school holidays. She came running up to me and said, 'Georgie, Dad's leaving us to live in Rickmansworth and Auntie Vi is carrying his baby!'

I thought, How can he leave his own children, turn his back on them and go and raise five children belonging to another woman – plus one on the way? To me this was a final blow a final rejection, but what would happen to me? I know Auntie Hilda would not have me, and I would not be fitting into my father's arrangements as he did not want me; neither did Auntie Vi, as I was most certainly not the apple of her eye! Joyce would be all right, because Auntie Hilda loved her; but where did I now stand? What would happen to me? My next thought was about running away, maybe to Auntie Ethel's, or even to living on my own in my air-raid shelter. I had come to a crossroads. I told Joyce how I felt, and that this could mean the end of us even living together again. 'But is he going straight away?' I asked.

'No,' she said, 'so something may turn up.'

But hatred was now settling in my heart against Auntie Vi and my cousins, Jimmy, Brian, Shirley, David and Phillip, who as far as I was concerned had taken a father from me to replace their own, giving them a mother *and* a father, while I was to have none.

I know that it was not their fault, but they were getting everything as far as I was concerned, at my expense. They were getting things that I never had from my father: toys, pocket money, love and most of all security; and here I was standing there looking like a down-and-out tramp. What had Joyce or myself done to deserve all this? I can remember putting my arms around Joyce and kissing her and saying, 'Don't worry, we will somehow get by.' But really I knew that Joyce would get by, but the question that was troubling me was, would I?

I rushed back to Auntie Iris with the bad news and began to feel frightened. It was quite clear that I was being excluded from my father and his family for ever. This was the final curtain call.

Auntie Iris was in tears herself. I think that she knew that I would get the full brunt of this situation one way or the other, and that my life was to go in any direction but not for the best. That's why she was shedding tears, and there is nothing that she could do about it. I went upstairs to be met by Auntie Hilda, who was still choking on her fags. She said, 'So you have heard the latest news, then, Melsham?' I replied, 'Yes.'

'Well, I am not having you when he leaves, so get that idea out of your head. Your father is as bad as you, and had you not been such a troublemaker all this would never have happened. But Joyce will stay here. She is a good girl. But the last thing to happen is that you, Melsham, will not be here when your father leaves.'

She made it quite clear to me how I stood with her, but where would I go? I knew that Rickmansworth was out of the question for me. Within a few more weeks Joyce came up to me, beaming all over her face.

'We have a baby sister!' she said, but I was not impressed. Straight away I thought, This is the final nail in the coffin. This meant whatever small feeling my father had for me would be put out of the window, and I would be completely forgotten. This was the final whistle blown on my rocky relationship with my father; now I would be completely out of his life. After all, babies were the spice of his life. Even Joyce and my cousins in Rickmansworth would now be pushed to one side. So the final plan for Auntie Hilda and my father was to be rid of me, one way or the other. I was not in their plans for now or the future; to hell with what happened to me. It was a time that I could never forget. As I was seeing the last of our trams in Croydon in 1951, it felt like I was going the same way – onto the rubbish heap.

My father took me to see a Mr Hepworth in his office in Croydon. All I knew of Mr Hepworth was that he was to be a friend of mine. I must admit that when my father left me alone with him in his office I felt relaxed with him. He was a well-built man with a very kind face. He had ginger hair and was covered in freckles; perhaps the ginger hair stood them out more. Little did I know that he was some sort of probation officer! Over the following three weeks he slowly drew out of me how I felt at home and what I did in my spare time. He then put it to me that Auntie Hilda and my father said that I was always stealing money from them and other people. 'But I have not,' I said, 'I go out and earn my own money.' Now I was beginning to see behind the scenes. They were lying about me to get me into some sort of trouble… but why?

On one of my visits, in which Mr Hepworth was picking me up by prearrangement, he took me to his bungalow home in Sanderstead, south of Croydon. He asked me where I would like to live; in a tent in the middle of nowhere, I said. I wanted to shut myself away from this whole miserable world and stay on my own. Mr Hepworth must have thought, Why should a thirteen-year-old boy want to shut himself off from the whole world? I had not told him about my life at home, my beatings or being brainwashed, or how I had been supporting myself and my two sisters; but he must have seen deeper than I was telling him. I do know he liked me, by his taking me to his home to meet his family and being extra friendly with me. I was tired, worn out, confused and broken-hearted, and felt that very soon something was to happen to me… but why? What had I done to be put out on a rubbish tip? I knew, hand on heart, that I had done no wrong. I had never ever been involved with the police up to now. Perhaps I should have been, with stealing bread and milk to survive, or because of knocking down fences or nicking carrots. I, like many kids, had a lot of respect for the police. Many of us may have had a clip around the earhole from them in those days for being cheeky, but we did have a lot of respect for them.

It was September 1952. At the age of thirteen I left Boswell Road,

Thornton Heath, after living there about eight miserable years. Unknowingly, for the last time as a child I was walking in between Auntie Hilda and my father, being firmly held by their vice-like grip. I was being held so tight that the blood was unable to reach my fingertips. They didn't ever hold my hand, so to me it felt very strange, and I knew something was wrong; but had no idea what it was. No one ever told me anything. As we were about to turn out of Boswell Road, something made me want to look back into our street over my shoulder. Without knowing why, I took a last look. I was now on a journey to the unknown to start another chapter in my life. My life was to change drastically. Some of it would be worse than I had already had to endure at the time, but some of it would be better that I had before. Was I being thrown on the scrap heap, or was I being given a lifeline to a better life?

Chapter Seven

I was still being held firmly by my hands in a vice-like grip by my father and Auntie Hilda, whose nails were digging into the back of my hands. She was well aware of this but couldn't care less. It felt like I was being held by a pair of pincers. The more I moved my hand, the deeper her nails were digging in. Finally we arrived at our destination in Croydon, which my father and Auntie Hilda had planned. 'This is it,' my father said.

Looking up, I could see a very large building with a row of concrete steps outside that led to the large main doors, which were open.

Outside was this big printed notice board that I could not read or understand. With each step that I climbed I started to shake with fear. I did not have a clue about what was going on or where I was going or why I was here. No one had said anything to me. By the time I had reached the top step I was shaking in fear. I was still being held firmly by my father and Auntie Hilda. We entered an open hallway with seating on either side. There were lots of notices everywhere; again, I was unable to read them. We sat down and then my father went to a desk to announce our arrival. I suppose by now Auntie Hilda had held me by both hands until my father returned to take over my other hand. Off the hallway were doors leading to other rooms. The ceilings were high, and everything was so strange and so cold to me. I had a feeling that this was not a nice place to be in. Most of the other chairs were occupied by grown-ups sitting with their children and talking to them. Some were about my age, some younger and some older.

I noticed this boy coming out of this big room; he was frantically kicking and screaming and shouting, and he cried while he was being restrained by two men. They were also being followed by a lady, presumably his mother, who was also crying. They then took the boy into another room. It was very frightening. I had never seen anything like this before. Thoughts began to race through my mind. Was this a punishment block? I started to try and move my hands from my father and Auntie Hilda, with the intention to make a dash for it and run as far away as possible; but they must have sensed it and took a firmer grip of my hands. I had no chance against their firm grip. I was a small, thin and weak lad, with very little energy to put up any resistance.

Then I saw another boy come out of the same room. He was struggling and crying and being held by the same two men, but he had his mum and dad with him. After about two hours or more of waiting, and still unaware and puzzled as to where I was or why we were waiting, my name must have been called. It was now our turn. Although I did not hear my name being called out I was made aware of my turn, by being pulled from my seat by my father and Auntie Hilda and taken into the very room that I had seen the other boys coming from.

I entered this very large room with frosted windows and a very large polished table, the biggest that I had seen in my life. Behind the table were three large chairs. A man was sitting in the middle chair with a woman to his left and a further man to his right. Over to the right was another small table with three or four other people. Then on the left were two more smaller tables with about six other people, one of them being Mr Hepworth. By now my father and Auntie Hilda had let go of me and were sitting behind me. Little did I know at the time I was standing in a Juvenile Court.

I was told to sit down on a chair. Then I watched the first person stand up and talk, what about I just don't know; then a further person spoke again to him. Then Mr Hepworth stood up and gave a long talk, of which I did not understand a word. Then my father was asked this and that, and then he sat down. Next it was Auntie Hilda's turn. She seemed to have a hell of a lot more to say than anybody else, and then sat down. Then I was asked to stand up but had to be prompted to by another person, who had raised my arm. The man in the big middle chair started to talk to me, but unknown to him I was unable to hear his words. I just shook my head, meaning either yes or no, or shrugged my shoulders, as I do if I can't hear. Then I was told to sit down again. I was prompted to do so.

Then the three people left the room for some twenty minutes and later returned. The man in the middle chair again asked me to stand and started to talk to me. By now I was getting very tired with all the confusing events of the day and around me. I just stood there, none the wiser, from when I had first left Boswell Road to now after he had spoken to me for some time. Then I was told to sit down, and Mr Hepworth came over to take me out of the room into another room.

Mr Hepworth told me to sit down at a desk. 'George,' he said, 'do you know where you are?'

I said, 'No!'

'I thought as much,' he said. 'Well, George, you are in a Juvenile Court.'

'What's that?' I said. He then explained that if children get into trouble with the police they are brought here to be punished. I replied, 'But I have not been in any trouble with the police!'

'I know,' he said, 'but your father and Auntie Hilda have made a complaint about you and said that you were in great need of care and control.'

So, I thought, this was their plan for getting rid of me. It was them that was out of control; and as for care, it was me that was caring for myself. They did not know how to care for me.

'George,' he said, 'did you hear all that was said in that courtroom?' He sounded very concerned.

'Some of it,' I replied.

'Do you know what is going to happen to you now, George? The majority has said that you have got to go away to an approved school for a long time.'

My bottom lip dropped. I just could not believe that this was happening to me. I broke down and just sobbed; I was a cornered animal, trapped in a cage.

Mr Hepworth led me out to the passage, holding me tight as his prisoner. When we got to the top of the stairs, I saw my father, who put his hand on my head and said, 'Sorry son.' It was the first time that I had ever heard him say 'son'. Then Auntie Hilda came up to me, while I was still sobbing my eyes out, and said, 'I told you that you was a good-for-nothing! Now you are going to a children's prison, where you belong!' A big evil smirk was written across her face. At that point, for the first time in my life I took a big kick at her, landing my foot on her leg as hard as I could, inflicting just a fraction of the pain that I had endured thanks to her scheming lies, and it felt fantastic doing it. That was my farewell to her.

She shouted at Mr Hepworth, 'I told you he is out of control!'

I was then led to a waiting car to take me to the approved school, which was at Mayford Green, near Woking in Surrey. I was put into the four-door car in the back seat, followed by Mr Hepworth, who sat next to me. My first thought was to escape by opening the door next to me, but nothing happened. There must have been many kids who had tried the same, but something must have been done to the door to prevent any escape. Well, my father and Auntie Hilda had succeeded in getting rid of me out of their lives, so that my father could now move to Rickmansworth to raise another man's children at the expense of his own. Auntie Hilda now had my sister, Joyce as her own child. In those days a child had no say, it was all decided on their behalf without them having a say in the matter, or being able to try to defend themselves. My last words to my father, as I stood on those steps, were still ringing in my ears while I was crying out aloud. I was saying, 'Don't let them take me, Dad! Please, Dad, don't let them take me!' But all my words just fell on deaf ears.

My freedom was now being taken from me, like everything else had been taken from me: the freedom to see Auntie Iris and Uncle Alf, the freedom to see my sister Joyce and, most all, freedom to see Violet and wear my pearly suit that was helping her. The freedom to be just me. All these things had been taken from me by my father and Auntie Hilda to accomplish their own freedom and be rid of me.

As the car moved away, I kept on asking Mr Hepworth, 'What have I done wrong? Why am I being taken away like this? I have not harmed anyone.' I could see the sympathy within his eyes and I think he knew that I was telling the truth. I had never spoken out about my father or Auntie Hilda, any more than I had spoken out about Auntie Iris and our secrets, or about my sister, Violet. Had I done so, maybe all this would have been over, and maybe I'd have had a chance to live with Auntie Iris or even Auntie Ethel; but it was too late for all that now.

All through the journey I was trying to plan my escape. I did not want to be locked up for no reason. I was innocent. I had done nothing wrong. I planned in my head that when the car stopped at the traffic lights, I would jump over the front seat and get out of the passenger seat, which would hopefully not be locked. Then I could jump out to freedom. Mr Hepworth must have sensed this, and told me that none of the doors would open. They were all locked. He then tried to get me to settle down and reassure me by telling me all about the place that we were heading for. He explained that I would be well fed and given a chance of a good education, and when I got out I would be able to learn a trade and look after myself. He went on to say it was a good place if you kept your nose clean, and it gave boys like myself a sense of security and an opportunity to learn discipline. Again I tried to explain that I had done no wrong, so it therefore did not need to be like this.

I cried out, 'Why don't anybody listen to me?' Why did the court not ask me what I was feeling?

Mr Hepworth replied, 'But you were asked to say something, George, in that court but you just nodded.'

'No, I never heard that!' I protested, but again it was too late. If only I could hear, maybe I could have put my side of the story, and then a different decision could have been made. Then, instead of being on my way to a children's prison, maybe I could have been off to some loving foster-parents who would care for me.

Our journey took one and a half hours to Mayford Green, a very deserted part of Surrey. We then turned into this big driveway that took us around the biggest building that I had seen to the main front door. This was Mayford Approved School, my prison. Looking up at this Victorian building, it seemed quiet and still. You wondered if anyone would be living inside, it seemed so cold. The building had been constructed in the early 1800s. It stood on twenty-eight acres of farmland and woodland and it was an approved school for 165 boys from the age of thirteen to sixteen. All the boys sent there had been in trouble with the police for one thing or another. Some were really bad and violent, and some like myself were victims of family circumstances.

We walked towards this very imposing three-storey Victorian building with a lot of greenery all over the walls and headed to the massive wooden door with steel panels that lay in the centre of this building, which was big enough for thirty large houses. Mr Hepworth pulled the bell, and the door was opened by a very large man who had this frightening look about him. I was taken with Mr Hepworth to the headmaster's study to be formally booked in as prisoner George Major. I was introduced to the headmaster, Mr Wallet. You could see that he was a strict, firm man, and he ran his school on full military principles. He then read the Riot Act to me.

'George Major, you are here for punishment. Your stay here is what you make it. Misbehave, and you will be punished with the cane. You don't get any second chance in here. You will always be clean, neat and tidy while you are here. You will be taught at our school in this building. You will have pocket money each week only if you follow the rules, and work for it. You will live here, learn here and work here. After a period of three months, if you conduct yourself properly and abide by our rules, you will be allowed to go unescorted into Woking on a Saturday afternoon. Should at any time you try to escape you will be punished, with twelve strokes of the cane on your backside and your privileges suspended. Your number throughout your stay will be 101. Everyone has a number given to them until they are discharged. Now do you have anything to ask?'

'Pardon, sir?'

In a louder voice, Mr Wallet said, 'Do you have anything to ask?'

'Yes sir! How long am I here for?'

'Were you not told?'

'No, sir.'

'Three years. Take him to his accommodation.' He pointed to Mr Armstrong, who had been standing next to me with Mr Hepworth. I was then led out of the headmaster's study by Mr Armstrong into a long corridor.

The corridors had brickwork on either side leading towards a high ceiling. The brickwork had dark green paint going up halfway, then a lighter shade of green to the ceiling. The floor was a polished concrete floor and there was a cold feeling as I walked by the side of Mr Armstrong. Coming towards us along the corridor were about twenty boys on parade in rows of two, marching in time and swinging their arms. They were all dressed smartly in different coloured Harris Tweed jackets and grey short trousers. Not one had a smile; they were being followed by a teacher. As they passed me all their eyes were firmly set towards me. The only sound was their marching feet. I felt icy cold and frightened, I was just hoping that this was some bad dream and that I would wake up and all would be well; but the further I walked down that corridor the more I knew that this was for real, and I began to feel my knees giving way with the sudden shock of today's events. My young heart was feeling as if at any minute it would just split. I knew that I had done no wrong, and that I was wrongly sentenced to a crime that I had not committed, and that was making it harder for me. Had I done wrong I might have been able to come to terms with the punishment and accept it better. I was an innocent victim, and paying the price of three years for it.

Mr Armstrong then led me to a clothing room to be fitted out with some underwear, which I was not used to, then a grey shirt with a striped tie and then some grey socks. Again, I had not been used to them. Next came my shoes, a new pair, something that I have never had. Then came this reddish Harris Tweed jacket with grey trousers. The clothes that I had been wearing they must have put on the fire as being well past their sell-by date. So there I stood, the smartest boy that I had ever been, and for a moment I felt quite proud of myself. Then Mr Armstrong handed me another set of the same, together with a pair of pyjamas, something that I had never worn. I was then marched along the corridor again to go up a flight of concrete stairs carrying my new clothing into a large dormitory on the west wing of the building. The floor was so highly polished you could see your face into it, the walls were the same two-tone green, with the lower half being dark green and the top half a lighter green. The ceiling was the shape of the sloping tiled roof, with its big wooden oak beams spaced out every five feet, with crossbars supporting them. Had you been able to reach the beams only by a tall ladder, I would expect that you would not have found any dust. From the beams hung about twelve big metal lights with metal lampshades.

The dormitory was very long and narrow. There were four rows of iron beds with twelve beds in each row, a total of sixty beds. Not one bed was out of line. Each bed had three blankets folded up on top of each other with the white sheets folded around the blankets, just like the army. Nothing, just nothing, was out of place. There was a highly polished wooden floor. There was your own locker by your bed for your clothing and any personal possessions. I had nothing; after all I had not expected to be coming here.

Pointing to a bed in the corner, Mr Armstrong said, 'This will be your bed until you leave, and you will keep your space and bed clean at all times. Now put your things down and follow me.'

Back down the very wide concrete stairs we went to the ground floor, then along another short corridor to the dining-room door, which was open. I could hear the sound of many voices. We entered this very large dining hall, with its oak-panelled walls and tables laid out with seven chairs to each side of the table. The tables were laid out like the Savoy Hotel.

The whole dining hall seated at least 200 boys. Again, there was a highly polished wooden floor. As we had entered, Mr Armstrong had got this wooden hammer and struck the top desk that stood at the front of the dining hall with a heavy bang. Silence fell just as quick. You could see that when a teacher gave an instruction, it was obeyed straight away. Then Mr Armstrong said in a full commanding voice, 'This is our new inmate, number 101, George Major. Carry on!' Then the noise carried on as quick as it stopped.

I was then taken for a medical, for which Mayford School had its own doctor, nurses and a full hospital wing. I was asked to strip naked. I became worried and frightened as I had never been to a doctor's before, except when I had been injured with my knee. They looked all over me to see if I had any diseases, they even pulled at my willie and lifted my testicles and pulled open the crack of my bum, which really frightened me. Even more I was wondering what they were doing, and I had a tingling sensation running through me, which I had never experienced before. Then they took a stethoscope to my chest to check if I had TB, which was still prevalent in those days. I was then told to get dressed and go with Mr Armstrong, and what a relief that was! I had felt so embarrassed, as I had never stripped in front of anyone before, and felt as if my privacy had been taken from me.

Mr Armstrong then took me on a grand tour of the school and its grounds. He showed me the layout of the school, which was much bigger than I had first thought. That made it more frightening to me. He then showed me where and when to go on parade. There was drill up to six times a day, and you lined up in number order, again in the style of the army. I had noticed how many rules and regulations this place had, and it was most certainly run like a military barracks. You had to keep on your toes, and remember to always do what was expected of you, which wasn't easy, if like me you had been used to coming and going as you liked, with nobody to care if you were around or not. There was a west and east wing with the same layout. If you slept in the west wing you would go to the schoolroom in the west wing and eat in the west-wing dining room. In the dining room you were allocated a table and a chair; there was no chance of picking here.

Mr Armstrong then asked me if I would like to go and have an evening meal. I said, 'No, I am not hungry.' This was to be my next battle. I couldn't eat here. What would happen? Well, we will see.

I was then told to go to the playground with the rest of the boys who were already playing there. I took myself off to the playground and sat down on the floor. I was in such a daze I put my head into my hands to try to understand my very confusing day.

As I sat there with my head in my hands I heard a voice shouting at me, 'What you in for, mate?'

'What do you mean?' I asked.

'What have you done wrong to come here for?'

'I don't know!'

'Don't know? You must know why you was sent here! I know why I am here – breaking into houses – and I got myself three years… so why are you here?'

'I don't know,' I repeated.

'I'll find out,' he said.

The same thing happened a few times while I was sitting on that playground floor. Why was I here? And I still did not know why I was here, but I knew I should not be here. I had started to hope that someone would find out that a mistake had been made and that I would be able to leave. Then there was a call for my first parade call, and everyone rushed to the line-up in their place; but I was so confused I had forgotten where I should stand. All the other boys were telling me, 'Here!' or 'There!' As they were making a fool of me, so in the end I went up to a teacher and said, 'Please, sir –' we had to call all the teachers 'sir' – 'where do I stand?'

'What is your name and number?'

'George Major, number 101.'

'Over there,' he said.

It was about halfway across the parade ground and, just like the army we were told 'at ease', 'attention', 'about-turn', 'dismiss'… with everyone in time except me, as I was unable to hear. Yet another battle I had to face here. Did the school find out how deaf I am? Well, we shall see…

It was now time for bed after our parade, and we all had to make our way to our own dormitory, which I had no problem with at first. Like everyone else, I had to make my bed, then for the first in my life put on a pair of pyjamas, which seemed very strange to me at thirteen years old. I got into the bed, which felt so soft and comfy and warm to me. Then I lay on my back and my thoughts started to take over. The teacher then shouted, 'Lights out!' After this, silence fell, which seemed to disturb me more. I was unable to sleep, thinking of the day's events and thinking of the last chance of finding my own mother. I was thinking of my sister, Violet too, and that I would not be seeing her for a long time, and perhaps she would forget me. I thought of Auntie Iris and Uncle Alf, and wondered if they knew where I was and if they would visit me, and maybe take me home away from all this... The more I was thinking of them the more I was filling up and then burst out crying uncontrollably.

'Shut up!' yelled one of the boys. Then another shouted, then another, then it echoed throughout the dormitory. I tried to hold back the full blast of my crying into a sob with the pillow over my head, but it was making my chest hurt holding back all my emotions, and after a while I fell asleep sobbing.

The following morning it was a 6 a.m. rise like every morning. First you make your bed by folding the blankets in a pile; then your sheets, which would be inspected later. Then it's off downstairs to the washroom with rows of basins back to back. Hanging all around this washroom are rows of towels, each one owned by one of the boys with a number marked on it. Mine, of course, is 101. Everything is tidy and clean and you have to leave your basin clean, or else. In order to warm up in the cold mornings, you rest your hands in the hot water in the basin, and with the steam rising up towards you it gives you a warm feeling. After your wash, you then line up to get your breakfast, which offers a wide choice, including bacon and eggs. You then take your tray with your breakfast to your table and eat it.

In my case it was still left on my tray. I was unable to eat. At the time I did not know why the other boys on my table had said, 'Aren't you eating?' When I said, 'No,' they asked, 'Can we have it?' and within seconds it was all gone.

We are then let out onto the parade ground for another count to make sure all the numbers and names are accounted for. Then we are told to go to our dormitory for an inspection of our beds and bed space. If anything is out of order you are booked to appear before the headmaster, and given punishment, which could be loss of privileges. From your dormitory you are marched to your classroom. Wherever you go you are marched there, with no talking. The only time you get any noise from any of the boys is when it is their own free time, and there is not much of that.

When I got to my class I was allocated a desk; no choice here. I was placed halfway up the class. The room held about twenty-six boys. It was very small and compact with the standard polished wood floor, with a larger than normal deck, and the teacher had his class within good reach. There was no chance of not being seen in this classroom.

My teacher was a very dark-haired average-sized man. He wore long grey trousers, a white shirt and tie with a jumper and a Harris Tweed charcoal-coloured jacket. I never saw him wear anything else, but he was always perfectly clean and tidy. He was my main teacher. During the day we would move twice, to other classrooms for other subjects. We had a mid-morning and afternoon break of fifteen minutes in the playground. On the morning break we would be given half a pint of milk. At lunchtime we would line up for dinner with our tray and go to our table again. I would not eat mine and the other boys would share it amongst themselves. Then back for another parade and count for us in the playground. Again, other boys would come up to me to ask why I was in here, and again I'd tell them that I didn't know why. In the end I got so fed up at being asked why I was there that I said, 'For murder,' thinking of Auntie Hilda, who had really been responsible for me being in there. The word started to go around that I was a murderer, and so the other boys came up to me to ask who I had killed, and I said, 'My Auntie Hilda.' Others were asking how I killed her. Then it was back on parade again, and yet another count. Then we were marched back to our classroom. There were no holidays in this school. We were learning for almost fifty-two weeks a year, with long hours – apart from everyone having a job cleaning floors, toilets, walls, gardening and washing-up. I was still waiting to be given my job.

At the end of my afternoon's schooling, my teacher asked me to remain behind when all the boys had left. He told me that word had got out that I was a murderer, and asked why. I explained that I was fed up at being asked why I was here, and told him that I really did not know why. Then he gave me a smile of approval. 'One other point, Major. Do you have any problems with your ears?'

'No, sir.'

'Well, let me tell you something, Major, we don't miss anything in here. We are always watching each and every boy in this school. Now I'll take you to the dining room.'

There was no queue by now, so I was served with my last meal of the day on my tray, and sat at my table. Again there was a scramble for my food. That night, as always, it was bed by 9 p.m. and lights out at 9.30. As before, I started to get upset, and had the same call to 'shut up'. I put my pillow over my head to soften the sound. This is when your mind starts to think about it all again. It seemed to sink in that I was here for three years. My frightened mind started to take over again. Why am I here? Why can't I go home? I don't understand what is happening to me… and where will it all end? Despite everything I'd been through at my father's hands and the mental cruelty of Auntie Hilda at Boswell Road, it was still my home, still a place that was familiar to me. I felt that I was in the unknown, and my tears were still pouring out of me. Thirteen years of emotion were bottled up in me; thirteen years of unhappiness poured out of me uncontrollably. How I was missing my two sisters already, and Auntie Iris, Uncle Alf and everything…

'Shut up!' echoed around the dormitory, and that command was obeyed; but I silently sobbed for most of the night, waking up the next morning after a restless night to the sound of, 'Get up, all you lot!'

Everybody jumped out of bed. If you didn't you would be booked, then punished. We again had to make our beds, then go downstairs to wash. Next to me washing was a boy called Peter, who became a great helper and friend of mine. He helped me get through my hard moments. Peter was much taller than me, with black hair and the looks of a girl. In fact he was pretty, not a handsome type, but he was known to be able to handle himself in time of self-defence; you had to be able to in a place like this. Peter also slept a couple of beds away from me and sat at my meal table.

'We all heard you cry last night, George, but don't worry. You will get used to it all. We all go through that now and again.'

'How long have you been here?' I then said.

'Six months,' he said. 'I am used to it now. You will find time goes so quickly, and it will for you as well.'

We went back together to get our breakfast and take it to our table. My breakfast was a free-for-all. Peter leaned over and said, 'You got to eat something, George! Why can't you eat?' But I fell silent, as with anything that troubled me in life.

After breakfast it was off on parade again, and another count. That evening I was able to get to know Peter better. I started to ask him why he had come here. He had a long list of offences for stealing, mostly food. He was raised by a drunken mother who used what money she had on drink, and just like me he had to survive by himself. What made it worse for him was that he lost his temper with the copper who nicked him and had a fight with him. I saw we had something in common. We were both from broken homes, both insecure, both been let down by society. He admitted that this was a good place for him, where he felt secure and looked after, with three hot meals a day, which had never been part of his life. Just like me, he had never had new clothes, only the ones he stood in. He had no facility for washing properly, and he only ate when he could steal some food; but for all that he still felt frightened of the unknown, and still felt a sense of injustice for being here. No matter how good he felt about this place, it was the sense of injustice that would never go away. We both agreed we had been cruelly taken from a life that we had made ourselves, and that our freedom had been taken from us. Yes, I could relate to Peter, and at once felt relaxed in his company.

On this particular day Peter asked again, 'Why are you really here, George?' I told him it was because of my father and my Auntie Hilda. They just did not want me, so they had me put here. He said, 'So, just like me, you won't be getting visits from them!'

'You must be joking,' I said, and we both laughed it off.

By 9 p.m. it was to our dormitory ready for lights out. That night, deep in my sleep, my whole childhood started to reveal itself, picking out all the worst parts, including the killing of my cat. I was in a deep sweat and I was in panic, trying to kick my way out of this big nightmare. I woke up still struggling and shouting. Then I felt a hand stroking my hair, and this voice saying the same words as Auntie Iris used to say: 'You are all right now, George, you're safe.'

The words were still being repeated over and over again, but this time it was not Auntie Iris but Peter, who had come over to settle me. Peter afterwards often did the same thing, as my nightmares carried on for months.

The following morning, sitting down and watching my breakfast being swallowed up by my table mates, I was beginning to take in more of my surroundings. For the first time I noticed how each mealtime the table cloths were freshly laid out on the tables, with shining cutlery looking like a set-up in a top-class restaurant. I had never sat at such a posh table in my life. I had also seen this notice carved our in the oak panelling in front of us. I turned to Peter and asked him what the writing was carved in the oak panelling in large letters. 'Go forward,' he said. Every now and then the housemasters would point to that carving, telling us to follow the words in life: 'Go forward, don't go back or stand still, but strive to go forward in life.'

I tried to do so, since each day that you are here you are learning the rules and regulations. You learn to be quiet and only talk when spoken to, which was hard for me, as I was used to giving my patter to impress people. It was made quite clear to me that this was not allowed here, which was another blow for me – something else that had been taken away from me.

Around Mayford School there was a row of houses where all the teachers and housemasters lived with their families, like my teacher, who was married but had no children. The rumour amongst the boys in the school was that he had only one ball and could not have children. How any of the boys knew this I don't know! Two full weeks had gone by when we were called out on an extra parade, but this parade was not for a count, it was to stand there outside the gym to listen to a boy getting twelve strokes of the cane for escaping.

In the gym your trousers were dropped to your ankles. You were then placed over a bench while a housemaster held you down. Then usually the deputy headmaster, a very large man, stood at one end of the gym, and with his cane took a run as if he was going to bowl a cricket ball to where the boy is at the other end over the bench. When the cane landed on the boy's bare bum, each blow was heard on parade, with the boy's screams. The whole school was on parade to listen to this. Corporal punishment was dished out so that it was a lesson to anyone else who might misbehave; this was what would happen to you – and in front of everyone, making it a personal embarrassment. Then I saw the boy in question dragged out from the gym looking half dead. My mind went back to when I had my caning at Ecclesbourne School in Thornton Heath. Then I went into a swoon and fell to the ground. I awoke in the Mayford School hospital on the first floor, feeling very weak and drained, and not knowing what was wrong with me.

I was still refusing food, even in the hospital. The following day the doctor came to see me and have a chat with me. He said, 'Look, we have been told that you have not eaten since you have been here.' Peter my mate had told my teacher – why I don't know. 'Look,' he said, 'I am here to help you. I want to help you. There is a very good reason why you are not eating.'

For over an hour that doctor was out to get the truth from me. Then gradually for the first time I told him about Auntie Hilda and my food problem. You could see in his eyes how upset he was getting, as slowly word by word I told him, in between breaking down and crying. I felt relieved at last I was able to tell someone for the first time. I wondered at the time if he ever asked himself, What is this boy doing here?

'I am going to help you,' he said, 'and we are going to do this together.'

The following day I was asked to get dressed and with a housemaster and the doctor we went by car to Woking and parked up. 'Now,' the doctor said, 'here is half a crown. I want you to pretend that you are at home again on your own and looking to buy food. Forget that we are behind you, just buy what you want and where.'

So off I set. First I stopped at a café, popped in, looked around and then came out again.

'Why did you not buy in the café?' he said.

'The counter was greasy and dirty, and the saucepan was dirty on the outside.'

The doctor made notes. Then it was off to a fish and chip shop. I stopped outside and looked inside and came away.

'What was wrong there?' he said. I explained that the glass cabinet was dirty and there were lots of flies.

Then we went on to a baker's shop, then out again.

'What was wrong there?' the doctor asked.

'The people behind the counter – I could not bear them to touch my food,' I said. He made more notes, then we went to the second baker's, where I brought a small crusty home-made bread, a jam doughnut and a cream cake.

'Now, why did you buy in there?' he asked.

'I felt that everything looked different. All the trays were clean, and people behind the counter looked right.'

More notes were made. 'Now you eat what you have bought,' he said, which I did in no time. I was starving.

I was taken back to the hospital wing. I was in that hospital for one month. In this time the doctor did so much to help me with my food, showing me the kitchen and how clean it was, how the food was cooked, and leaving instructions that if I just wanted meat on my plate or whatever, then that's how it should be. So slowly I was encouraged to eat. The problem was never solved as such, but at least I was eating small and often. Had it not been for that doctor, who knows? Finally, while I was in the hospital wing, my deafness was discovered. They had arranged a hearing test for me, and found that I was very deaf in both ears, and the right ear was worse than the left. At last my body was being slowly repaired; at least I had no more hidings to worry about, or being told how useless I was, and being told that I must not listen to others talking. No longer was my body hurting with all the beating that I was having at home. This was my home now, and school, and my welfare was of concern to them.

I was now living with boys and being taught by men. It was just a man's world. Now I had an opportunity to learn to read and write. I knew I wanted to read and write. I just knew I wanted to. I did not want to ask people for the rest of my life to read something to me. To start with I felt shy, lonely and sad, but with the help of Peter and the doctor and my teacher, I was beginning to adjust to my new life.

Every boy received weekly pocket money which he would be allowed to spend in any way he liked. The amount that he received depended on his grouping under a marks system. As a new inmate you were placed in Group 0 which meant you would receive 6d; those in Group 1 had pocket money of 9d; in Group 2 you got 11d; Group 3 got 1s 2d; and finally, in the dizzy heights of Group 4 you received 1s 6d. You could move up and down groups by gaining or losing marks depending on behaviour and good or bad work in schoolrooms and domestic work which shared between the boys. The marks system was also in operation during boys' leisure hours.

It was easiest to move from Group 0 to Group 1 but very hard to move from Group 3 to Group 4. The purpose of this was to encourage the newer boys and to direct the older boys to increasingly greater effort. Once you were in a group you had to go on earning positive points in any one month in order to stay there.

Increased points did not only mean more pocket money. It also meant further privileges. There were various houses which competed against each other for the number of points earned, and these were often gained when the whole school was assembled and on parade. The house which earned the most points in any one month was rewarded with the privilege of an escorted visit to a cinema and every member of that house was given a shilling, with the exception of such boys as had failed to obtain a positive total of marks or had absconded during the month.

It was therefore very much a team effort as well as a personal one. I never lost points, but those who lost points continuously would be punished not only by moving down a group but by being deprived of the week's feature or instruction film or having the privilege of the Saturday outing withdrawn. Normally, all boys were allowed to go out on their own from 12.30 p.m. until 5.30 p.m. on this day and this time was particularly valued by the boys. Corporal punishment was a last resort which everyone tried to steer clear of.

By this time I had also learnt about home leave – not that it would affect me as my family did not want me. But for those that did have a family to go to, unless circumstances made it undesirable, home leave was granted to every boy, with certain restrictions under the Approved School Rules. Leave was twenty-four days per year, with sixteen days at any one time. There were also seven days at Easter, eight days in August and nine days at Christmas. As with anything else, leave could be lost through serious moral delinquency, absconding or repeated breaches of the school rules.

Boys were allowed to receive parcels and cards, although their content was monitored by housemasters. If items contained money the boy in question was notified of the amount and this was added to their account. If, as a result, the account contained more money than was felt to be desirable, the boy was encouraged to put some money in a Post Office account. Any food received was to be shared with friends and any unsuitable literature confiscated. On occasion, when it was felt that letters contained unsuitable material, the housemaster would read selected sections out to a boy. News of the death of a near relative would be communicated verbally beforehand. On occasion, letters were confiscated entirely if felt to be from undesirable acquaintances.

We were also encouraged to write home at least once a month, and were given free stamps for this purpose, but of course I could not and never wanted to. All outgoing mail was also monitored for content and to get a feel for each boy's state of mind. If I *had* ever written, they would have been more than able to grasp the state of my confused and unhappy mind.

Parents and family were allowed to visit once a month, when they could take their son out to Guildford or Woking until 6 p.m. These visits were permitted for all boys except in exceptional circumstances where it was felt that the parents' presence may be harmful to the child.

This would have been the case for me had my family wanted to visit. As it was, they did not come to see me, never wrote to me or sent me anything. They had cut me out of their lives.

I was beginning to get to know all the rules and the types of boys that I was living with. When I was sent to Mayford Approved School, I found that it was populated by hardcore young criminals. Some were violent by nature, others were just thieves by nature, and would even rob their own mother. Some were actually born with a criminal mind, and regardless of any punishment would die with the same mind. I had learned from Peter that every boy is given three years, but if you behave yourself and prove to be an ideal candidate, you can be released for good behaviour after a year under the points system. I was determined to do just that. After all, I had my sister to help, and Auntie Iris and Uncle Fred to see and share my life with.

I was missing my market life and my odd jobs, so whatever happened I would work hard to be released in a year, and not do the full three years. I was also learning other things in life that I had never experienced before. At a school for boys you learn to play together, work together, learn together, wash together and shower together. Sex was on many boys' minds – not mine, because at thirteen I didn't know anything about sex. I was not taught it, or had it explained to me, so I was still unaware of sex and did not understand it; but I had noticed some boys in the showers rubbing up to each other and seeing this would embarrass me. I looked at them out of the corner of my eye, afraid they might see me looking and try to include me. On one occasion, one of these boys came up to me and said, 'You have a nice big cock, George, let me rub it for you.'

I knew that this was not right and grabbed my towel and walked away, saying, 'I don't want my cock rubbed.'

Then he and another boy pulled me to the ground to try and rub my cock. Peter, who was always near me, came over to save me. So now I was beginning to see life in a different way, learning to live with others with a more surprising insight and, just like that carved notice in the dining room, I was learning to go forward. Don't look backwards or even remember your past; just bury it and look to the future and behave yourself and go forward. So I did take notice of those two simple carved words saying, 'Go forward.' As the weeks went by, my friendship with Peter was growing. We had looked out for each other and he confided his feelings to me, but I was unable to confide mine. Perhaps it was because I was determined to put my past suffering behind me, as I was ashamed of it.

Peter and I decided to sit on the hot-water pipe that ran all around the corridors hanging from the wall about six inches from the floor level. As we sat there, Peter said, 'I heard you crying again last night.'

With all this bottled up inside of me, I now felt that I desperately needed someone to talk to. I felt that I was in a world where no one wanted to talk or listen to any of my concerns, so I pretended that I had a cousin who had gone through what I had suffered, and that his father was always beating him, and the mental agony he had from his Auntie Hilda. Now everything he had was taken from him and destroyed. I described how he was made to eat his own vomit by his Auntie Hilda, and how hungry he was.

Then Peter said, 'Did he have pain here?' rubbing his own tummy.

'Yes,' I said. Then I told him of his hidden suit, and how he missed going to his handicapped sister because he was wrongly put away. I was going on and on pouring it all out. The emotion and the agony of it all were building up inside of me. The release from hurt was what I was bringing out.

Then, out of the blue, Peter said, 'Are you trying to lock it all away, George?'

'Yes,' I said, and in that split second I realised that he knew I was not talking about my cousin but in fact about myself. Then he said, 'I've been there and back,' putting his arm around me. 'Sometimes, George, it is best to talk about it in the open.'

I wished I'd taken his advice all them years ago, but I have hidden it all these years until today.

My reading and schooling were still not making any progress. My education was the lowest mark you could get: zero. I could not read or write, so I was unable to express myself properly. Even though my teacher had me sitting at the front of the class I had not yet mastered the art of lip-reading. I was so far below average that my teacher was getting very concerned for me. I had already had my hearing test and I was to have fitted a hearing aid. The mould had been made of my ears for the sound to enter my ears. It was just a matter of waiting for my new hearing aid. Finally it arrived. First the hospital at the school gave me two big, quite heavy batteries, with the cases strapped over my shoulder, one for each side. Then, attached to the batteries was my microphone, with a strap over my neck so that the microphone lay at the centre of my chest. From the microphone I had two wires going to my two ear moulds when they were switched it on. The sounds that I was hearing were frightening. For the first time in my quiet world, I could hear noises that I had never heard before. People's voices were so different. The doctor and the nurse had asked me to walk up and down the stairs – why, I don't know – but I could hear my own footsteps and my own heartbeat. This was not the best improvement for my type of hearing, but it did help me. It could never have happened to me at home; hearing aids at the time were new and they were massive things and they were very heavy to wear, so I was the only deaf boy at Mayford School who had a hearing aid, and it stood out like a sore thumb.

At school I was getting more attention and being told to watch the teacher's lips more. All the school staff were aware of my problem, and now they kept a very close eye on me. Somehow I often wondered, from the way they spoke to me and had watched me, whether they were thinking to themselves, Did this boy really go for fourteen years without being able to hear? No wonder he is here, and no wonder he didn't know why he was here!

The worst part of wearing the hearing aid is when you take it out to go to sleep. The best way to ever describe it is like turning off a radio. It becomes quiet and very frightening, and that's when it really hits you just how deaf you are. The shock alone devastates you. I never felt sorry for myself about my hearing. I had learned to get on with what I had.

I was now getting the understanding that I always needed from the staff, but it did have its drawbacks with the boys in the playground. As in all schools, you can open up to bullying, and with my hearing aid sticking out like a sore thumb I was being teased. Normally I would ignore it, but on one particular day this bully, who was known to throw his weight about, started shouting, 'Deafy, deafy, big ears!' Then he pushed me. He was quite a big boy, probably fifteen or sixteen, and well built for his age. He then pulled my hearing-aid wires from my ears, leaving me in silence and feeling very frightened.

'What did you do that for?' I said.

'Deafy, deafy!' he kept shouting, as he grew more vindictive towards me. I was an easy target for him, a little titch and deaf.

'Cut it out!' I said to him, trying to restore my loss of hearing, but still he came back. 'Deafy, deafy!' he was shouting. Then he said the words I had heard and hated to hear from Auntie Hilda. 'You are stupid and useless!'

I was now in a rage, and by now Peter had come over to my side. He could see all the anger building up inside of me. He said, 'Leave it, George, you will get the cane.' But his words fell silent on me as my anger had come to boiling point. Everyone in the playground was now turning up and shouting, 'Fight, fight!' They were all shouting, knowing that something was going to happen, and did not want to miss the excitement. They were dead keen to see what was going to happen next.

By now I'd lost all control of myself. Cane or not, I was not going to be told again that I was stupid and useless. Very bad memories of hundreds of times in the past when I had been told that I was stupid and useless came flooding back. Now I had lost all my control and I could feel my fists tightening and my muscles tightening. Then, with all the strength and power of my right hand and arm, I aimed a blow to his jaw. Down he went – a direct hit! He did not move. I stood there ready to aim a second blow should he get up. After a few moments I recovered myself and picked up my fallen hearing aid. As I replaced my hearing mould back into my ears I heard clapping. I had just knocked out one of the head bullies of the school!

Then the bully staggered to his feet, just as my teacher came on the scene. 'He just came up to me and hit me,' the bully said to my teacher.

'No, he did not,' said my teacher. 'I saw all that happened from that window. Now you are on a report!' For this, the bully received four strokes of the cane.

At last someone was defending me, but I was warned not to take the law into my own hands. I listened and nodded to my teacher. I had learned to respect him, because if it had not been for him and his first-class professionalism as a teacher with a caring eye, I would not be standing there with a new pair of ears now.

I was the most talked about boy of the school and made many friends, but I had no more fights or bullying about my ears. Here, I had lots of friends, respect and understanding, and a new pair of ears. I had good meals, which I was now eating, a warm bed and good schooling – everything I had been short of while living at home. At Mayford I was secure and well cared for, and never afraid of being punched like a rag doll or humiliated by Auntie Hilda. I was clean and smart with a tie, like every other boy at the school. It was now becoming part of a normal life, but even with all that you know that your freedom has been taken from you – your freedom to do as you wish and when you wish. Really, the hardest bit was knowing that I was in this boys' prison as an innocent party, all down to the wickedness of my father and Auntie Hilda, and I was determined to prove them wrong and get out of there with good behaviour. I had already won my rights to a Saturday afternoon outing to Woking, which I was having every Saturday. Peter often missed his rights due to his behaviour not being at its best, but when he was allowed into Woking we always went together. We would walk to the town, which took us about one hour depending on how we walked. It took us through open country. We loved walking down the country road towards Woking with the pride of freedom, even though it was just for the Saturday afternoon, dressed up looking like a dog's dinner and not a care in the world. When we arrived in Woking we would wander around the shops with our pocket money and spend it on sweets – or in Peter's case on tobacco. I was never one for smoking, and of course Peter was, and got the cane or loss of privileges for smoking many a time. I would give Peter some of my pocket money, as he was always short due to smoking, and at Mayford smoking was strictly not allowed.

It was during Saturday afternoons and Sundays that most of the boys had visits from their mums and dads, but a few of us never had visits. Peter was one of them. I did not expect visits, anyway, but it does hurt when you see the mums and dads coming to visit their sons, and see the warm, loving feeling between them, and then watch the parents cry as they leave. I did so wish that I had visits, and I know that if Auntie Iris and Uncle Alf knew that I was here I would be getting visits from them. After I was put away, Uncle Alf could not get any information out of my father. As my father had moved to Rickmansworth to start his new life, he no longer drank at the Railway Telegraph so much and Alf lost all contact and information about me.

I had been at Mayford Green Approved School for fifteen months and it was Christmas. We had our usual Christmas dinner, but no presents. After all it was a boys' prison, and we were there to be punished, not to be spoilt. So no Christmas decorations, no Christmas tree… Most of the boys were having their usual visits from parents, and I could see them with their Christmas cards by their beds. I had not seen or heard from anyone – no letters no cards no memories from home, just an empty shelf and shut away. Peter and I would find things to do rather than watch the happy families enjoy their short Christmas visits together. Just like me, Peter had no visits, so we were able to understand how we each felt. Our parents had deserted us, and so we did not want to be reminded of this, even after fifteen months.

I was still having nightmares, and they sometimes took control of me. They used to haunt me, and I was unable to stop the horror. I had visions of Auntie Hilda's face coming closer and closer to me, and I was backing away, but still she kept getting closer. She was surrounded by smoke and her eyes were getting bigger; the sound of her voice echoed in the distance, talking to me and frightening me by saying, 'Useless, useless… die, die!' Then someone's fist was hitting me. I saw lots of blood and there was laughing. 'Go away!' I would be shouting. 'Go away!' Then I'd be awake. It was Peter saying, 'You're safe now, George… you are safe!'

I am in a sweat. I am frightened and Peter's still saying as he sits on my bed, 'You are safe now, you are safe now.' He had been doing this regularly for fifteen months. I looked at him in a daze, trying to adjust to where I was. Then I realised that I was still at Mayford Approved School, and I started repeating Peter's words in my head: 'You are safe now, you are safe now, you are safe now.' No other words were said by Peter, only that I was safe now, and as those words drifted into my head I always seemed to drift into sleep again.

Peter must have had the same sort of dreams. He had talked about his own childhood. Perhaps he felt like me and did not want to share them. If he had bad dreams like I had, I would have been unable to help due to being deaf, as I would be unable to hear him. We shared our thoughts between us, as well as our nightmares and dreams. I had dreams, and some happy ones. One dream that kept popping up was about my mother. She always looked pretty in my dreams, and came over as very gentle. My dreams would take us to an open field full of long grass and flowers. We would be picking flowers, running in this endless field that was full of love and full of laughter. 'Mommy, Mommy, I love you!' I would cry. 'I love you too!' she would call out. Then we would roll in the long grass, arm in arm, kissing and laughing… and then the dream would fade away. I had many dreams like that, including some about my two sisters, and each one I wanted to keep; but like all dreams they went.

My education was becoming a success story. I was getting into the art of reading – not to a high standard, but on the ladder to attaining that goal. My teacher was impressed, and in his report had said that I had got guts, determination and courage, and that if my deafness had been discovered many years earlier I could have reached very high standards; but that was not to be. This was another missed opportunity. Had I had the care and security that I should have had, then who knows? My teacher understood my hearing problem more than anyone; perhaps he had someone close to him with the same problem. He used to tell me to watch his lips, so I began the art of studying people's faces and their lips. I hadn't realised at the time, but Auntie Iris had taught me to lip-read a long time ago. Whenever she wanted to make me hear she would always put me on her knee and turn my head around so that I could see her lips, and always asked me if I understood everything she said to me. She knew that I was deaf, but could do nothing about it. Again, Peter was there to help me in my lip-reading. Peter would stand a few yards away from me, then I would watch his lips and repeat what he said.

I was getting a lot of other help with my lip-reading as well. Each month after breakfast while still in the dining hall, we would all be brought to attention by one of our housemasters striking the wooden hammer on the desk in the front of the hall. Behind him was the carved out motto, 'Go forward.' He would then read out on average eight names that had been successful for an early release, so everyone, including me and Peter, would be listening while biting our nails.

I had already started to pay more attention when I had finished my first twelve months. That's when we were eligible for release on good behaviour. I had not had my name called on my twelfth, thirteenth, fourteenth and now my fifteenth months, but I knew that I had behaved myself and always received top marks in my grouping. I'd been on no reports, had no bad complaints, and had no caning – so why was my name not being called? We will find out later. After sixteen, seventeen, eighteen and nineteen months, my name was still not called. Peter had never expected his name to be called, due to his attempt to escape and odd troubles that he was in. He had served two years and one month so far, and expected to do his full three years, but he was listening for me. He did not want to lose a mate, but felt that I deserved to leave and restart my life.

On the twentieth month, which was May 1954, we were as usual waiting for our names to be called. Then Peter said, 'Did you hear that,

George? They have called your name!' Yes, I had done it! I was going to be free at last. I could not hold my excitement in. Now I would be seeing my sisters, Auntie Iris and Uncle Alf. What would I say to them? How could I explain where I had been? All kind of thoughts entered my mind. Then it dawned on me... What about my mate, Peter? He would still be here, still doing his parade, still listening to boys being called, still marching on the double and still doing all the things that we hated? I felt sad for him, which took part of my excitement away, and I was even annoyed that I was to leave my mate here – a mate who'd helped me come through the last twenty months.

Peter turned to me with tears in his eyes and said, 'George, you have made it! Boy, you have made it – and you deserve it!'

Unknown to me at the time, but many years later looking back at some of my records from Mayford Approved School, I came across a note for my first release date at thirteen months: 'George Major – Auntie Hilda refused to have him back home and it is not a suitable place for Major at present and his father is not interested in him.' Had Auntie Hilda agreed to have me back, I would have been out at thirteen months, so because other arrangements had to be made for my welfare, it took another seven months for them to be made and meant another seven months of being locked in a children's prison through no fault of my own. But the other arrangements the approved school made for me I did not like, as you will see. When you are released before your three years are up you are placed on licence for the rest of your sentence, and have to do what they tell you to do. If not, you will be recalled back to the approved school to finish your sentence; your family or home circumstances decide what happens to you on your early release. In my case, now at fifteen years of age, I had no family or home, and because of this the school decided what was going to happen to me, where I went and what I did. All this was prearranged for me, and I would only find out what they had planned for me on the morning of my release.

Peter and I spent our last evening together, both upset. He said, 'Now, George, you take care of yourself. The world is out there waiting for you. Grab it with both hands – don't look back, but *go forward*! Show people what you are made of, and that you will not be beaten.' He pulled me towards him and kissed me and I then said to him, 'Are you queer?' and we laughed it off together.

That night, for the last time at Mayford Approved School, I lay in my bed shedding no more tears, but thinking of home. I was thinking how it had been a long time since I had my cuts and bruises, and they'd long since disappeared from me, but the memory of my past will always remain at the back of mind. My bitterness about them has faded away and I am thinking perhaps they had really done me a favour when they took me to that court house, and had they known that it would do me a lot of good it would be them that would now be sick and bruised. I had better hearing and I could understand people better by lip-reading. I was beginning to read and write, and most of all I had self-respect. On the morning of my release I was marched to the headmaster's study to be formally discharged and told what they had decided to do for me.

'You will not be going back to your Auntie Hilda, and we advise you not to go and see her or your father. You are going to be taken under escort to Woking station, then given a rail warrant to Kentish Town in North London, to a hostel where you will be then taken to be fitted up with new clothes. Then tomorrow, with another rail warrant, you will be going to Cambridge, where you will stay at a hostel for boys in your position. You will then be offered the chance to learn a trade and become a useful member of society. Best of luck for your future.' He then rose from his seat and shook me by the hand, like so many before me. I was then taken to the very door that Mr Hepworth had brought me through twenty months earlier, out to my waiting car and escort. I got into the back seat and we slowly drove off. As the car moved away, I turned my head to look up at the dormitory window where I had slept and had so many nightmares, to see Peter at the window looking out to see me. He was waving, his face full of sorrow, and a lump came to my throat as I waved back. I was wishing that he was coming with me, as he looked so lonely. I was still waving and watching Peter as the car turned right onto the main road. Then Peter and the school disappeared; that was the last time I ever saw Peter, but a few years later learned that he had done his full three years, then went on to borstal and then finally to prison for robbery.

He, like many others, never made it – all because his mother never cared and society turned its backs on him. So Peter, if you are reading this, just like you said, *don't look back but go forward*. Today I still believe in approved schools and borstal. It made most boys into men; it gave them self-respect and a future. I have met many former approved school boys, and have found that most had a trade and became useful citizens of society.

Some fifty-five years later I returned to Mayford Approved School to try and recapture those moments with Peter and try and find his and my names carved onto the brickwork around the school building. There were hundreds of names still there, and each one with a story behind it. Some of those boys were forced into a life of crime, like Peter, or else forgotten and unloved and institutionalised for the rest of their lives and prevented from 'going forward'. But there were also some who went on to become useful citizens to society.

As I walked around the building I remembered the sound of marching boots echoing through the corridors and the cries of sadness of many of the unwanted boys like myself who were there. It is now a Business Centre owned by Surrey County Council where people are given a chance to start and run their own businesses, unaware of the many boys who once lived there who were left to defend for themselves and were never given such an opportunity.

Chapter Eight

As I took my journey to Kentish Town, the excitement that had built up inside me soon disappeared.

I most certainly did not want to go to Cambridge, as that was taking me further away from Auntie Iris, Uncle Alf and my sisters, and not forgetting the markets.

I just wanted things to go back to how they used to be. Cambridge to me felt like it was a lifetime away from home. My excitement had turned to disappointment at this thought. I arrived at the hostel in Kentish Town and felt strange at meeting new people all over again, and in a way began to miss Mayford Approved School, maybe because I felt so frightened and alone. However, what caught my attention on the way to Kentish Town was the fact that there were a lot of black people about. The only time I had ever seen black people before was in Tarzan films where they were portrayed as boiling and eating white people so this new aspect of the outside world became a source of fear for me. Furthermore, so much had changed while I was away that now there were many more cars on the roads and I nearly got knocked down by one of them.

When I arrived at the hostel I mentioned both these things to the people there. I was told that the people I had seen had come to Britain to start a new life and we were to help them with this fresh start. My first reaction was one of indignation and confusion as I felt that I had been deprived of such a fresh start. How could we help others from other countries when there were people already living here who needed help with starting their lives over again?

I was then taken off to be fitted out with my new clothing and working overalls. I was given a two-piece light blue suit, which had long trousers. This was the first time in my life I was given long trousers to wear, which made me feel quite special and grown-up. Then, after that, to my surprise I was given money to tide me over. 'Wow!' I couldn't believe my luck, because no one had ever given George money before. It made my day.

After living at the hostel for a week I was given my rail warrant to enable me to travel to Cambridge. Having found the right train, I sat myself down as we travelled across open country, every now and then the steam from the train blocking out my view. It was a journey that seemed to take for ever. I felt like I was being torn away from my roots. I was getting further and further away from what I could call 'home' all the time, and I was feeling the loss. I also knew that I would not find my own mother while being based in Cambridge, so right from the start I had planned to make my stay there as short as possible while still focusing on making sure that I kept within licence rules.

I arrived at Cambridge station, where a warden from the hostel where I was to stay met me. We drove from the station for about ten minutes until we arrived at Brooklands Avenue and a very large house with an enormous drive in pleasant surroundings. It looked immaculate from the outside. I was taken to the office and told all about the rules of the home. One of the rules was that you were free to come and go as you pleased, but must be back home by 9.30 p.m. There was no chance of popping down to London. There were four large bedrooms, which accommodated four boys in each room. All the boys had come from approved schools, but none from Mayford, where I came from.

All the boys had jobs where they were able to learn a trade. In my case I was to be an apprentice plumber. How it worked was that the firm that you worked for would make an arrangement with the hostel to make sure that when you got your wages – which wasn't much, about thirty shillings – you had to pay back twenty shillings for your keep. The disadvantage was that most of the firm's staff knew that you were from an approved school, which did not work in your favour, as they would just assume that you were trouble or a thief.

I made friends with all of the boys at the hostel and we used to go into Cambridge quite a lot. There wasn't much for us to do as it was a fairly posh area, and bikes… well, there were more bikes in Cambridge than the whole country put together. Just about everyone had a bike, all wearing their college gowns. I just was not happy at Cambridge. For a start there were no markets as such, and basically I just hated being so far from home.

Unlike my other mates I did not smoke, so I had more money to save. Quite often some members of staff at work would accuse me of nicking or reading crime stories, which was not possible as I could not read properly; but they were always trying to blacken my name or get me into trouble so you could get the sack. This treatment was not only directed at me but also at the other boys from the hostel. As I was used to being accused of things that I was not guilty of by Auntie Hilda I was not prepared to tolerate it any further and would defend myself.

After about nine months I went to see my sister, Violet, for the first time in over two years. I found the meeting very emotional and upsetting. Violet was so thrilled to see me. Repeatedly, she asked in her own way about how soon we would be able to meet again. This made me even more determined to move back to London, so I decided to go and see Auntie Ethel and find out if she could put me up for about seven months. Shortly after my meeting with Auntie Ethel, I managed to find an apprentice plumber's job around the corner from where she lived. The firm was in Nunhead Lane in Peckham. Now I had to try and get sacked in order to start my new job to keep within the licence rules, so I admitted to reading crime stories and they said that I would always be a criminal, which was what they often accused me of, so I told them what they wanted to hear, to my advantage.

Just as I had planned it, I managed to get sacked, and also maintain my clean licence condition, exactly as I wanted. Also, Auntie Ethel gave me a letter to confirm that I could live with her. The new firm that I was to start working for also gave me a letter about my new job. These letters would help to justify my move from the hostel in Cambridge and make my way back to London.

Soon I was back in London where I truly belonged. Living with Auntie Ethel and Uncle Jack there was never a dull moment. They made me part of the family and treated me the same as their two boys, John and Stuart. I was also nearer to my mother at Camberwell Green, and I still went to that park bench and sat there, hoping and praying that she would come along to feed the birds and that we could meet. I was not going to give up the fight to find my mother, no matter how long it took. My visits to Violet were getting back to a normal routine, just like old times, but without my pearly suit. Violet was always asking me when I'd be wearing my pearly suit again, and I was not going to let her down. I was now looking towards starting my fight back to rebuild my life, as I wanted. Just after I was 16½, I arrived at work bright and early as always by 7 a.m. only to find that the doors to the firm were locked.

There was a large notice on the door saying that the firm was in liquidation. This was like a nightmare, because I needed to be able to pay my way. 'How can I get my wages?' I asked openly. We waited in the café opposite our firm while the plumbers made phone calls to find out how we could get our wages, only to be told that it could take months before we got anything – if we were lucky. I had been at the job for seven months. But I could not wait all that time to pay Auntie Ethel for my keep. I had to see her to explain that I had no housekeeping money due to my firm going into liquidation, but I promised her that I would have another job by next week. She was very sympathetic and said that she would wait, and even offered me money to tide me over, but I refused. Later, John offered me a loan to tide me over, which I accepted. John was always a one for having a few bob.

The weekend was upon us so I decided to go and pay a surprise visit to Auntie Iris and Uncle Alf. Taking the same route by the back door, hoping that I would catch them both in, I gave my usual little tap on the back door and then turned the handle. It was locked. Then all of a sudden the door opened. It was Uncle Alf, and without uttering a single word, he flung his arms around me, calling, 'Georgie!' I could feel the tears from his eyes running down my neck. We stayed locked in that tight embrace for a few moments, just taking in the lost years. By now Auntie Iris came up to us with her walking stick, as she was getting more frail, and flung her arms around me. Soon we were all in tears with the emotion coming over us. Now I found myself as tall as her – and I only stood at 5 ' at the time.

After a long emotional and pleasant greeting, we started to chat about the missing years. They explained that they did not know where I had disappeared to and presumed that I was living with my father at Rickmansworth. They told me that Auntie Hilda was still not talking to them, so they had no way of finding out about my whereabouts; also my sister, Joyce, knew nothing about me. I explained in great detail about what had happened to me over the years, and where I had been. They explained that they knew that one day I would come walking through their back door. You could also see that they knew of all the suffering that I had been going through, but were powerless to do anything.

We spent a good three hours chatting and talking about old times. Then Auntie Iris said, 'I have got something for you.' She slid away to return with the brown bag that held my pearly suit.

I placed it against my grown body and said, 'I've outgrown this, Auntie!'

She replied, 'Then you must make another one, Georgie. I know that you have had a rough time and that you have been punished so much through no fault of your own, but you have got to fight back, Georgie, and prove that you can do it, and at the same time help others. You did have a hard life, but remember how you helped your sister and others like her. Look how you changed their lives. You are a young man now, and believe me there are thousands more out there who need help. Don't let others suffer like you did. You can relate to them now, and because of that you could be a good pair of hands.'

But I knew in myself that I was not ready for my pearly suit yet. I needed more time to sort out my own life, and when I felt ready for it I would wear it. Auntie Iris continued to tell me to make that suit, for the love of others. 'You can do it, Georgie. You can do it for your mom, your granddad… and who knows, by going out there in your pearly suit you may even find the real you!'

So I did promise that I would make my pearly suit and try to help others. It was time to leave the two people who had done so much for me. Having hugged and kissed each other goodbye, I said to Auntie Iris and Uncle Alf that I would go out the front way in order to see Joyce and Auntie Hilda. Given all the water that had gone under the bridge, I thought it only right to say hello to Auntie Hilda, and hopefully let her know that I was not the bad egg she made me out to be. Auntie Iris and Uncle Alf agreed. After all I was coming up to seventeen now, and did have a mind of my own.

I made my way up the stairs that I had been thrown down so many times and called out above the noise of Auntie Hilda coughing choking on her John Players cigarettes. 'Auntie!' I called out while still climbing the stairs, 'it's Georgie! Can I come up?'

Still choking on her fag, she nodded yes, to my complete surprise. 'Is Joyce in?' I asked, still choking on that fag, she again nodded. 'No.'

I went to the front room of the house, which was now the lounge and sitting room, and sat down to try and talk with her, to explain what had happened to me, and that I was learning plumbing. Not one bit of encouragement did she show, or interest, apart from asking me if I could get her sixty John Players. You could see that cigarettes were getting the better of her; you could see that she was getting very ill, and I was beginning to take pity on her.

I took the route that I had walked so many time before to get Auntie Hilda her fags. A lot had changed since I last came down this route. Her old tobacconist's shop had changed hands, so I did not meet anyone I knew. Having got her sixty John Players cigarettes, I made my way back to Auntie Hilda and handed her the cigarettes. Then she said, 'Look, you are old enough to smoke now. Take twenty of these and start to smoke.'

Now, I had never even smoked a fag in my life, but like a fool I took up her offer. Whether it was to impress her or please her or both I don't know; but what I do know is that I smoked two fags while I was there and was choking myself to death. But from that day on I became a full-time smoker. As I left Auntie Hilda's to go down the stairs I could hear her coughing and trying to catch her breath, so that at that next moment I thought the next fag might kill her; but that was a long way off yet.

I closed the front door to go back to Peckham to plan my future. The most important thing now was to get a job and earn some money, and as for my pearly suit that would be on hold at the moment. My mind was still ablaze with my past, and I did not yet have the full confidence I needed, but that was not too far away now.

Once again my life was to take a turn for the better. I started to walk the streets of Peckham looking for work; any job would do that could keep me afloat, so that I could pay Auntie Ethel and John what I owed. Each day I took off to begin trudging the streets again to try and find a job. I tried the biggest laundry in Peckham, which I'd passed so many times in Peckham Hill Street off the Old Kent Road. It was called 'The Dutch Boy' and was laid out like a Chinese laundry. I also popped into a store called Jones and Higgins, a very large department store known to everyone, which had been going strong since 1867. After all, I could sell. Another refusal: just no one could give me a job. Then I thought perhaps my hearing aid was holding me back. In fact I did have many complaints that my hearing aid was always whistling, and I was getting jibes about it, apart from the fact that it was heavy to carry around. Perhaps this was stopping me getting a job. So I decided to put the hearing aid away, and depend on lip-reading, which I had plenty of practice in, with the help of Peter. Taking my aids off seemed to give me more confidence in myself. I think I was getting embarrassed to be wearing them.

By the following weekend, still with no job and down to my last edge,

I made my way down to Rye Lane, the main shopping street of Peckham, with the full intention of trying my luck to get a job in the indoor market next to Rye Lane station. As I walked down Rye Lane, I was passing Sainsbury's food shop, and standing outside I noticed this old bloke. He was unshaven and was just a bit taller than me and he had a ruddy complexion with a twinkle in his eyes. He was wearing an old army overcoat that almost reached his ankles with a pair of old army boots. He also wore this large broad grin across his face. He was standing on the small forecourt of Sainsbury's shopfront. On the ground at his feet was a box full of lemons, and in his hand he was holding three lemons. 'Three for sixpence!' he was shouting, 'don't forget your lemons!'

It was the month of February, the pancake month. I stood there and watched his style. I was impressed; you could see that he had been doing this for many years, and as he was shouting his sales patter he was almost putting the lemons in the customer's basket. Before she could say 'No', he'd be getting his sixpence at the same time – almost a blackmail style of selling, but it was his style and marker that made him get his sale. The forecourt on which he was selling was private property owned by Sainsbury's and providing Sainsbury's did not object to him selling his lemons he was within the law. But as soon as he stood on the public path or road he was breaking the law, and would be charged for selling without a licence or obstruction or both. That was the law then, so really it was a cat and mouse game with the police.

I stood and watched him, and memories of my little experience in the markets came flooding back to me. I was looking at a man who was to lead me to a Delboy way of life long before Delboy was even conceived. His name was Freddy Floyd and he was an old hand at fly-pitching, and a market trader. 'Hello, Granddad!' I called out to him. Well, he looked like a granddad, perhaps the overcoat made him look older but really he was in his early sixties but still had the body and energy of a thirty-year-old.

'What do you want, son? I'm younger than you anyway!' he said, making the point that he would never get old.

The first thing that entered my head was Rosy Lea. 'Do you know Rosy Lea?' I enquired.

'I might do,' he replied.

'Well, I used to work with her and her father at East Street market. I've already made enquires about her in East Street, and nobody has seen them for a long time. Do you know them?'

'I haven't seen them for a few years,' he replied. 'Did you say that you worked with them?'

'Yes,' I said, and told him of my full market experience over the years.

'My name is Freddy Floyd,' he said. 'What is your name?'

I replied, 'George Major.'

'How much readies do you have?' ('Readies' meant money to Granddad Fred.)

'Not enough to buy any of your lemons,' I admitted.

Handing me a shilling, he said, 'Get me a cup of rosy lea [tea] over there.' He pointed to Lyon's tearooms across the road. I then went to get his rosy lea while he was shouting out, 'Get your lemons here! Three for sixpence!' I then returned with Granddad's rosy lea and gave him his change.

'Tell you what, Granddad Fred, let me have a go at flogging your lemons while you drink your rosy lea.'

'All right, Granddad George,' he said.

'Come on, you beautiful girls, don't be late, for Christ's sake – I bloody close at eight! Bright juicy yellow lemons, three for sixpence!' I was flogging them well and moving them faster than Granddad Fred, and with the last full box of lemons almost empty, Granddad Fred said, 'Look, George, are you working?'

'No,' I said, 'I can't find work.'

'Would you like to work with me?'

'I was hoping that you would ask me that,' I said.

After the last lemons were sold, Granddad Fred took me over to Lyon's tearoom and we got to know each other even better. I asked Granddad Fred why he had given me a shilling when he had plenty of pennies in his pocket. 'To see if I could trust you,' he said. 'Mind you, I was watching you like a hawk to make sure that you didn't do a runner! I've been looking for someone like you for a long time, and if you stick with me I will teach you all you need to know about street trading. I'll show you how to buy your stock, and the art of the game.' So our friendship and partnership was about to begin.

There was another person yet to join us. This was the start of Delboy and my best years, doing what I always loved: working on the markets. Was this meant to be? Was I on my way to start my new life – the kind of life that I had dreamed of all those years ago when I was working with

Rosy Lea? I could now see how that dream could be realised with Granddad Fred. Working in the markets meant my dream was now almost a reality. Even though my childhood had its problems, fighting for my next meal, getting beaten up and blamed for everything, and being made to feel useless, now I could finally break away from all this. Now I could do what I wanted to do. I was keen to get on with my life, despite my being deaf and my poor education. All that was to be part of my fight now that I was with Granddad Fred. I could learn from his advice, his knowledge and his art of market life. I also had other plans to find my mother and hopefully my grandfather, in order to carry on with my family tradition as a pearly king. But I knew I had to jump one hurdle at a time, or I would knock all the hurdles over. I always remembered that Auntie Iris once said to me to be a good charity worker and pearly king you must first get to know the problems. Well I already knew some of the problems: poverty, hardship and cruelty.

I had arranged to meet Granddad Fred on the Monday morning outside the Sainsbury's food shop where I had first met him on the Saturday last. When I arrived there, he was wearing the same old army overcoat with turned-up collar, selling his lemons. As the following day was Pancake Day, you had until Tuesday evening to get rid of all your lemons. 'Three for sixpence!' Granddad Fred was calling out. As I approached him I said, 'Let me give you a break with them lemons, Granddad.'

'You cheeky sod,' he said, 'I outrun you anytime!'

I picked up two lemons and then started to call out, 'Two for sixpence!' Nice and juicy... two for sixpence!'

'Hold on, Granddad George, we are flogging them at three for sixpence, not two for sixpence – remember, Granddad George?'

'I know,' I said, 'but Granddad, we have two mouths to feed now, remember, Granddad Fred?'

Things just got better between us, and our friendship was growing by the day. He understood about my deafness, as he was a bit deaf himself. He also knew about my poor reading and writing, and started to spend much more time at his own flat in Peckham teaching me to write and read. I had made my start at Mayford Approved School, and now Granddad Fred was to help me even more. Sometimes I would arrive home at midnight at Auntie Ethel's after a full evening learning how to read at Granddad Fred's flat. He must have been very clever at school, as his own knowledge was just unbelievable. He would go to the library and get me children's books to read to him, but he never spoke of his past to me. Our age gap never crossed our minds. But I did find out one thing about him, and that was he was a very good boxer in his younger day; so he was used to putting up a good fight, mentally and physically, which was what he had to do get a good pitch.

I had already told him about my handicapped sister, Violet, and about my pearly king tradition, and I remember him saying to me once that if he had not known that I was a pearly king then I would have made a good candidate. He did know of many pearly kings and queens, and one of his best mates was Fred Tinsley, the Pearly King of Southwark. After a few weeks I was learning and learning fast. I even felt that I was looking like a true professional market trader; the passion was just running in my veins. I could not wait for the next day's market work to come soon enough. I found out that some geezer was selling his two-wheel barrow, as he was packing up the market work. I told Granddad Fred how I felt that we could sell more if we had a barrow, and both would be winners; but he was not sure, because he said it would be more difficult to run away from Old Bill if we got caught. Then I made a joke, saying that he might be getting old; to which he replied, while laughing, that he wasn't, and that he could outrun me any day! We made a joint decision that I would run with the barrow, if caught illegally trading. Up to that day we would use a box or a suitcase to flog our goods from. If you saw a copper coming, you would pick up your box or suitcase quickly and try to run as fast as you could until the coast was clear to return. Perhaps that's why street traders are slimmer, with the exercise of running from Old Bill.

Anyway, I won the day and we brought our first investment, a two-wheeled barrow, which we would be making good use of from the days of selling lemons in February. You had strawberries in June, new spuds in the summer to Christmas, lines at Christmas then Easter, and in between times it was pick and mix. Never a dull moment, with the added joy of dressing a barrow. The more you dressed your barrow like a dog's dinner, the more you could flog. I learned how to trim the fruit and veg, how to show off the items that you were flogging. We were not making a fortune but we were living day by day and beating the taxman. Market life is not easy; sometimes you have your good days and you have your bad days. You tend to have more bad ones than good. Winter was the worst, or if there was a lot of rain or a lot of snow. After all, who wants to come out to buy when the weather is bad. Not many people do! We could stand there for hours in all sorts of bad weather with few people out, without a penny being taken. It's a hard life, but on the whole we had plenty of fun. You either enjoyed your market life or hated it, and those who hated it did not last long. As in every business there are what you call 'tricks of the trade', and the market life is no exception. So that you can follow the lead-up to some of my ducking and diving, I shall tell you some of the tricks, and how we as street traders stand as far as the law is concerned.

In the market world, to be legal you have to have a street licence in order to trade legally. That licence entitles you to trade on a certain pitch on the road. It is given by the local council, and most pitches are handed down from family to family. So there are few good pitches to hand out. You could go on a waiting list, and if there is a pitch spare on a market it would turn out more times than not to be a shitty site where you don't get the crowds. Hence people like Granddad Fred and myself were forced to 'fly the pitch' – which means giving yourself a licence and pitching up where you want. It puts you against the law, and if you get caught you'll be frogmarched to the local magistrates to be fined for illegal trading or causing an obstruction.

This often happened to us, and any readies you made dwindled away in fines. In fact we have been up to Tower Bridge Magistrates Court enough times to warrant ourselves a free parking bay outside the court. Some courts can be sympathetic to you and others hard on you, and you could be fined anything from £2 to £10, depending on which magistrate you came up against. There were some magistrates who believed that we should be locked up and the key thrown away. Some business people who had shops were always complaining about street traders. Their complaint was that they had to pay rates, wages and overheads, so why should we pay nothing? We wanted to pay; at least it would be cheaper than paying fines or going to prison if you could not pay. One such group of shop owners were in Leather Lane. Because of their complaining many years ago they managed to convince the local council to close down the market with stalls outside their shops. But after a few weeks they begged the market traders to return, as no crowds of people bothered to go down the lane, as there was no market; so it proved we can attract the crowds. So that's how we stood, with no street licence, but pitched up where we could get the business.

When I first met Granddad Fred he was standing on a small forecourt outside Sainsbury's, and because he was standing on that private patch he could sell within the law. But if Sainsbury's got the hump with him, they could have him removed by law. Thus, if you did not become a nuisance you would be all right. We knew of a few small sites like that. There was one across the road from Sainsbury's. There was a corner pub, and on the pavement outside the pub was a wooden trapdoor for the beer barrels to be rolled down a slide into the cellar below ground. We used to pitch up on them trap doors, which covered a 4' by 4' area – not much space for the stuff that you were flogging, plus the two of you within that space. Then further down Rye Lane just before Lyon's tearooms, was a set of concrete steps between two shops about three foot wide, leading from the pavement to the private flats above the shops. Here we used to also pitch up, in order to be within the law, but it would always depend on what you were flogging. Then, with our barrow we had the side-street corners leading from Rye Lane now you do take a risk with the law; it is on the side corners of Rye Lane. We would set up our two-wheel barrow, from which we sold mostly fruit and vegetables; then one of us would take it in turns to look out for Old Bill. Granddad Fred would do most of the looking out. This was what was called 'the copper's nark'. He would stand further up 'the frog and toad' – road – and look out for Old Bill. If he saw Old Bill, he'd run up to me and shout, 'Old Bill!' Then I would pick up the barrow and do a runner with all our stock on, including the scales, which is not easy from a standing position. The easiest way was to push down on the back end of the barrow, the other end to the handles, as you can build up more speed quicker; but it kept you fit and strong. Sometimes part of your stock would fly all over the frog and toad, and if the Old Bill was determined to catch you to get his pound of flesh, he only needed to follow a trail of carrots or cauliflower or whatever had fallen off the barrow, and you were nicked.

When the coast was clear I would push the barrow back to where I was flogging and start all over again. Some of our more loyal customers would sometimes wait for our return, for as I was flogging to them I would be chatting them up as well, either telling them that with their looks they should be in Hollywood playing the leading lady with Clark Gable, or that their hands were like velvet. Running from the Old Bill could happen four or five times a day, because if the Old Bill had a complaint, they would return time after time, determined to catch you at it. That's why I kept the wheels of my barrow fully oiled, to make it easier to push and cut out the squeaky noise so that Old Bill could not even hear us. Sometimes, to be sure Old Bill was well out of sight we would leave our barrow up the road, and while Granddad Fred looked after the barrow I would take a walk down to the side corner of Rye Lane to be sure Old Bill was gone. Sometimes he would be standing in a shop doorway trying to hide until I found him. Then he would eye me up and down as if to say, 'I know your game!' I would look him back straight in the eye as if to say, 'Who, me, guv? I've done nothing wrong.'

On another day Old Bill did the same thing and hid from us when he decided to change his walking pattern. Instead of coming up and down Rye Lane, as they always did, he decided to come down the side street from behind us – something they never did. But he was the worst of all the Old Bill; he was the most hated Old Bill who ever walked Rye Lane, hated by all the streets traders. We gave him a nickname and called him 'Paleface'. Well, he did have the whitest face you would ever see. He was a big overweight copper in Peckham. Today he was out for his pound of flesh; maybe he'd had a row with his trouble and strife (wife) that morning or she was demanding more bees and honey (money); but whatever, he was out to get me one way or the other. Granddad Fred had missed him, as even he did not expect Paleface to come behind us; so I was caught red-handed and nicked. He knew none of us liked him, and we always felt that he was nicking us for the sake of it. Yet after all, we were earning an honest living. Because of him, the next morning I had to go before the garden gate (magistrate). Granddad Fred and myself arrived at Tower Bridge Court at 10 a.m. Us street traders always went in first, as we always pleaded guilty, so the court must think, Get rid of them first and leave room for the more serious cases. So we were waiting for my name to be called so that we could get back on the market again to work extra hard to pay for the fine.

'George Major!' a voice shouted.

'That's you, George,' Granddad Fred said. So in we walk, with Granddad Fred going to the public benches, and me to the accused box. I had looked up to see who was on the bench and it was Mother Campbell, who always had a soft spot for me and seemed to always listen to whatever I had to say. When she fined me it was never as much. She had seen me there so many times she could be taken to be my dancing partner. As I am standing in the accused box, the garden gate's clerk to the court stands up to read out the charge.

'Are you George Major of such and such address...?'

'Yes, that's all of me.'

'You are charged on such and such a date with selling goods on the street without having a licence, and that you wilfully caused an obstruction to the highway.'

Well, I thought, two bloody charges on one offence... Paleface must have had a row with his carving knife [wife]! I then said to myself, Come on, George, fight this and make Paleface into a Red Indian. 'Not guilty!' I cried out.

Mother Campbell, who was resting her head on her hand, almost let her head slip off her hand, and Granddad Fred started to bury his head in his hands. Sod it, I thought, Paleface wanted his pound of flesh, so let me try and get mine and fight for my rights and the rights of other street traders.

The clerk of the court sat down. This had taken everyone by surprise, including me, so I had to make up my case as I went along. Mother Campbell had enquired what was my defence, to which I replied, 'Well, Your Honour, my case is that Paleface – sorry, slip of the tongue – has nicked me so many bloody times that he seems to think of charging me in his sleep, when in fact I was on my greengrocery round and just passing by, and that I was not flogging on the said day.' You are free of the law if you are taking your barrow around the streets or on a greengrocery round, and that I knew, so I played on this point. 'Now, Your Honour, can I question Paleface – *oops*, slip of the tongue – again?'

'Yes, you may question the police officer. Go ahead.'

They then called Paleface to the witness box so that I could ask him my questions. Mother Campbell had a hidden smile on her face and I could see that she was enjoying this show. I don't think she was a lover of Paleface either. I started my defence by asking Paleface, 'Now, you say that you had caught me flogging yesterday?'

'Yes,' he said.

'Then you must know what was on my barrow. Can you name the items that I was flogging?'

He just could not make up all the stuff that I was flogging. 'What was the colour of my barrow?' – 'I don't know.' – 'What type of scales was I using?' – 'I don't know.' – 'Did I have any price tickets?' – 'I can't remember.' – 'Is it true that you have nicked me a lot of times?' – 'Yes.' – 'So many times that if you see me on the street with my barrow you just assume that I am flogging?' – 'No!' – 'I put it to you that I was pushing my barrow down the road, minding my own business going about my greengrocery round, and you decided to nick me.' – 'No!' – 'I put it to you that you have nicked me so many times that when you see me you assume that I am flogging something illegally, even though I was just passing by… That, Your Honour, is my case.'

The whole court seemed to all of a sudden wake up. Mother Campbell said she would retire to consider her verdict, and with that the court adjourned.

Granddad Fred came over to me and said, 'George you'll get life for this! None of the street traders has done this before. We usually say, "OK, it's a fair cop," and pay up.' Granddad Fred was wetting himself. 'Look, George, if you don't get life, and if you are lucky you might get away with ten years, I have to admire your guts and charm, and Paleface looks as if he's had kittens and dogs all together.'

'All rise!' Mother Campbell was coming back with her verdict. I was summoned to go back into the dock. I was very apprehensive, but felt good about defending myself. Mother Campbell, as we all called her, addressed the court.

'I have listened to what has been said, that of the police and that of George Major, and because there are some doubts in this case I dismiss it.'

The courtroom was full of cheers. Many street traders had sat through the hearing with interest and you could see and feel the excitement. I looked over to where Paleface was standing, and his face was red with rage. I said I would make him a Red Indian man, and I had. He was not a happy man… As we left the court we was punching the air with excitement. I thought, You have bloody done it, George! You have just beaten the system.

On a personal level, this to me was a big lesson. I was now capable of standing up for myself for once. Never again would I let things happen to me without defending myself. I was leaving those dark days of my childhood behind. It was time Granddad Fred and myself got back to Peckham. I was already the talk of Peckham – the very person who had showed Paleface what all us street traders were made of and that we can give the Old Bill as much aggro as they give us. After a few days, and still punching the air, we were still as proud at winning our battle with Paleface, even though it was a one-off.

However, it was not to last. We had set up our barrow for another day's work with all our fruit and vegetables, and Granddad Fred was again the copper's nark. Trade was good, the sun was out, and I was so engrossed in my flogging that I did not notice or hear Granddad Fred running up to me and shouting, 'George, Paleface is coming!'

Perhaps I had let my guard down because of my success in court a couple of days earlier. Then at the last minute I saw Granddad Fred waving his arms about in order to get me to move on.

I picked up my barrow and did a runner, as I have always done. 'All right, George, he has gone,' I was told. So back to my flogging. That Paleface was playing a cat and mouse game, and I was the mouse. With about forty-five minutes gone by, and a large queue of people wanting to buy off our barrow, whom I was happily serving, I felt a hand rested on my shoulder and a voice saying, 'Got you, you bastard!'

Standing there hanging over me was Paleface. He had already gone back to having a white face. He had crept up on me without his helmet. 'I'm nicking you for wilful obstruction and selling without a licence, and anything you say will be written down and may be used against you. Have you got anything to say?'

Well, I just stood there speechless. Then, getting out his notebook, he said, 'The colour of your barrow is green, it has two wheels, you are using Avery scales, and you are selling potatoes at three pennies a pound and cauliflower at six pennies, carrots at two lbs for five pennies and cabbage at five pennies each…' The list went on. Not a thing did he miss. 'And I suppose that you are on your greengrocery round, are you?' he said.

That was the end of my defence; it was a fair cop. For the rest of the day we carried on flogging. We had to sell out to cover the fine that we would be paying the next day. That evening, having flogged everything, we went round to the corner of Peckham Hill Street and Peckham High Street to our favourite café, which we went to every day. It was run by a Greek Cypriot called Leon, whose wife did the cooking. They always gave up a slap-up meal. The café was known as the Blue Café, we mostly had egg, bacon, sausage and fried tomatoes with our doorstep bread and butter, and washed down with a cup of rosy lea. Leo was short, like me, and loved us street traders, and sometimes if we were broke he put our meal on the slate for when we were earning more. Peckham in them days was full of the likes of me. In the café there was a big jukebox, which also encouraged a lot of teenagers like me. It never bothered Granddad Fred, as he was always young at heart.

The jukebox would take centre stage belting out all the latest pop songs of the year: Frankie Lane – 'I believe' – Johnny Ray, Pat Boone and many more. The café had that homely atmosphere with the same old faces day in and day out, including the local villains, the Richardsons mob, and the Carters, with the café staying open until almost midnight. Cyril, an old mate of mine, came into the café and put his shilling into the jukebox to play one of the latest pop songs. He shouted out, 'All right, George! You really showed Old Bill what us cockneys are made of the other day!'

It was hard for me to follow all that he was saying due to the jukebox belting out the pop songs and the noise of everyone talking at once, but because I was having trouble in following what he was saying like all my mates he came over to me so that I could hear better. Cyril sat next to me and brought his mate over as well, who sat opposite me. His mate was a tall chap, six foot with blond hair, who looked a bit dim until he started to talk. He often went around helping out street traders, either as a copper's nark or helping to flog.

He was known to be a good all-rounder on the market. He was also on the rock and roll (dole), so he always had a steady weekly income and being a non-smoker he could make his bees and honey last, so for the street trader he was cheap labour. I and Granddad Fred knew of him but today we had the chance to meet him properly. His name was Brian Smith, a very likable bloke when you get to know him. So at my first meeting with him I was impressed with him. He had this everlasting curling hair with blue eyes to match.

'So you are the famous George,' Brian said, 'the one that got away!'

'Well, he is still here,' Granddad Fred said.

'I'll have mine over here, Leon,' Brian said, and Leon put his dinner in front of him. The dinner was piled high plus four slices of doorstep bread and butter, and we watched him stuff the lot.

'You don't like food then, Brian,' I said after watching him scrape the last bit of gravy off the plate with his bread.

Then he said, 'It seems that you need a good copper's nark.'

'I don't like the sound of that,' Granddad Fred said, who always spoke whatever was on his mind. 'Oh no!'

Brian explained how much he'd like to work for us both, and could save us a lot of fines. 'With my height and clear eyes I can see Old Bill leaving the nick.'

Cyril said, 'He is right. Brian is the best copper's nark in the business; it is very rare that any trader gets his collar felt with him narking.'

'I would love to work for you two I am told that you are a good team and I'm not looking for a big wage as I am on the rock and roll, so it is a bonus whatever I earn.'

I turned to Granddad Fred and said, 'Shall we give him a try?'

'It's the readies,' he said. 'We don't earn enough now but he could pay his own keep by what he saves us in fines.'

I said, 'And after all we are both five foot nothing and can't even see Old Bill's belt around his trousers! At least Brian can see over their helmets.'

'All right, George, we will give him a try, but if he gets us nicked he's out.'

So now there were three of us: Granddad Fred, Brian, the tall skinny one, and me. Delboy days was about to start… I turned to Granddad Fred and said out loud, 'This time next year we could be millionaires!' I really said it and somehow I could feel that it could be a reality.

The full excitement of my market life just seemed to run much thicker into my veins, and was drawing out something that I never thought was in me, bringing out more of the cheeky cockney chappie. Working with Granddad Fred was most certainly feeding me that new blood and sense of direction and bringing out of me that character that was hidden in me, but dying to get out. He was teaching me everything, to read and write, to flog and buy goods, and also the good and bad aspects of market life. I would forever be in his debt; but now we had an extra mouth to feed, and that didn't mean I was going to flog one lemon for six pence.

After having another rosy lea and agreeing that we work together, we got up from the table, and as big Brian was standing next to us, I said to Granddad Fred, 'Have you got a phone at home?' To which he replied, 'Why is that, George?'

'Well,' I said, 'with the height of Brian we will bloody need one to talk with him, with his head in the clouds!'

Brian soon proved that he was a good investment. We were going to court less often, so making us more readies, but the weather was a factor as well. If the weather is really bad there are very few people about so can't flog as much and a lot of our stock that we bought was already past its sell-by-date. So by the time the next day came along, we could be dumping what we had, and that meant that you was dumping your profit. This in turn meant less stock money to buy more goods, with few readies to buy anything decent. That's when you get desperate, and have to hunt further for a deal to make your next day's living – which we had to do on quite a few occasions.

On one particular day, having woken up at 4 a.m. in the morning with a big shortfall of stock money, the three of us set off to Borough Wholesale Market. It lies at the foot of London Bridge on the south side of the River Thames. We had pushed our barrow from Peckham – an hour's with a heavy load – hoping to buy anything that was cheap and could earn a day's wages for the three of us. When we arrived at the market it was already full of life, buzzing with street traders like ourselves, and the retail greengrocers and other traders all looking to purchase a deal from the wholesaler. While most was looking for quality and class, some like us who had little stock money, were searching for anything that could make us a few bob, whatever it might be. Within the market, each wholesaler had a compound with his wooden sales office within the compound. On the floor would be whatever he was flogging, with no price ticket. You would then ask what he was asking as a price. In your head you'd work out if the price he was asking suited the price that you were prepared to pay. The wholesaler would try to get the best price that he could get from you. Yet you could go to another wholesaler within the market who was flogging the same product at a cheaper rate, so we travelled around the market trying to find something within our small budget, and it was proving very hard to find something.

We had already tried a few wholesalers and done a bit of bidding, without success. It was just one of them days where we were out of luck, and we couldn't go back to Peckham empty-handed, so we were desperate to get something – in fact, anything within our budget. As we passed this wholesaler he called out, 'Can I help you boys out with anything?' – trying to get a sale from us. Then we started to ask, 'How much for them bananas a box?' He gave a price. 'No, too dear. How much the tomatoes?'… 'No, they are too dear.' Going from one item to another, we found them all too dear for our budget.

Then I noticed in the corner of his compound some open-neck string bags. You could see that they contained cauliflowers. 'How much are them?' I said.

'Porter's money,' he said. We all knew what porter's money meant.

If there is something on the turn or going off, rather then dump it you could have it at 'porter's money' for almost nothing. 'Half a crown a bag,' he said. There were eight bags, and each bag had twenty-five cauliflowers inside, some of them going very much off colour, with one or two not in bad nick.

'I'll have the lot at two bob a bag,' I said.

'You got a deal, boy,' said the wholesaler, who wanted to be shot of them.

'You are bloody mad, George!' said Granddad Fred, and Brian said, 'How the bloody hell are you going to flog them? They're all ready for the knacker's yard – even pigs would put their noses up at them!'

'I have an idea,' I said, 'trust me. If you don't try you don't earn.'

So, after parting with sixteen shillings, we loaded up our eight bags of cauliflower on our barrow and set off back to Peckham. I then told them about my idea. I said that good cauliflowers were getting six pennies each at the time, so we could sell ours at threepence each, so twenty-five in a bag at threepence each would fetch seventy-five pennies – over six bob.

'We bought each bag for twenty-four pennies. We have eight bags at seventy-five pennies, which comes to six quid. It cost us sixteen shillings, with a profit of four pound and four shillings if we flog them all.'

'And who is going to buy cauliflowers that are turning colour?' Brian said.

'We give them a bit of colour,' I said.

'What – are you going to spit and polish them?'

Then Granddad Fred said, 'We can bloody whitewash them.'

I said, 'I've heard it all now!'

Brian said, 'Anyone could see that they were whitewashed.'

'Not if you use your loaf they won't!'

'And how do you suppose you can stop the customer from seeing them whitewashed?' Brian asked.

Looking a bit puzzled by it all, I said, 'Well, that long empty shop doorway down Rye Lane… Granddad Fred can be at the back showing the white of the cauliflower while I am holding up the good ones that we have, and as I'm flogging them he wraps them up in newspaper, brings them to the front, and you put them in the customer's shopping bag and flog the lot before anyone becomes the wiser.'

So off we went to my mate's garage, where we kept our barrow and where he had some whitewash. We set out to make our cauliflowers white. In them days there was a soap powder to make your clothes 'Omo white', so from the empty shop doorway I'm shouting out, 'Best cauliflowers at three pennies, each fresh in today, each one is Omo white!'

At least I was shouting the truth. We did flog the lot that morning, but we kept clear of Rye Lane for a couple of weeks after. Like they say, he who dares wins, so I earned one pound and seventy-five shillings, Granddad earned one pound and seventy-five shillings and Brian earned nine shillings. After all, he was drawing on the rock and roll.

It was not just fruit and vegetables that we were flogging. We would travel around Houndsditch, Commercial Street and Whitechapel and around the East End where there was warehouse after warehouse of general wholesalers; but even there you could get the occasional bargain and could earn well if you were short of stock money. When you are short you are inclined to look further for that extra bargain, including rejects like watches whose minute hand did not move unless you shook it. Brian would often complain that his arm was dropping of at shaking our watches so that the customer could see the minute hand going round for a few seconds…

On another occasion we went into a wholesaler's in Whitechapel and saw a lot of caps losing their colour. At the time Norman Wisdom was very much talked about, and famous for his cap, which gave us an idea. It was a known thing that I was the image of Norman Wisdom, even more so when wearing his style of cap. Joking about, Granddad Fred put one of the caps on my head. 'What a double!' he said, which instantly gave us an idea, and we bought all the caps in the box. There were about a hundred, and we did a deal with the wholesaler and bought them for pennies. At the time we had no idea how we would flog them, but it was a price not to be missed. The least we could get was our money back, even if we flogged them for rags. But we had them, and that's when your thinking cap starts to come in with ideas! The plan was to dye them to make them look new, then flog them as Norman Wisdom caps, as worn in his films. We took them down Petticoat Lane, flogging them, and put a notice by our suitcase – *Trouble in Store* – the title of one of his famous films then. 'Buy the Norman Wisdom cap as used in his films.'

We almost flogged them all; the only problem was when you wore them the bleeding dye was left around your head after wearing the cap. We had asked Brian where he got the dye, but all he kept on about was that after we had dyed them we put them out on the grass to dry, and the grass must have made the rim damp, leaving the dye mark on the head. From that day on I kept on wearing my cap, but not a dyed one, for a few years. I even went to bed in it, at least it was a head warmer. And after that I got a new nickname – 'Norman'.

Life was not always easy on the markets. We had some good runs at earning our readies, and then on the other hand some very bad times. Trying to earn enough to even live on was hard work, and you may well ask, why work on a job that shows poor earnings? Why not get a job that pays well all the time? The honest answer is that all three of us had a passion for market life. It was in our blood, and we were determined to give it our best shot.

Being unable to find my full keep at Auntie Ethel's, every week my debt to her was growing bigger and finally she said, 'Look, George, you shall have to leave. I just can't afford to keep you.'

I understood that I could not go on like this. It was not fair to her, so I left Kimberly Avenue on the best of terms. But I was homeless once again, and had to find somewhere to live. Heading down Rye Lane with my suitcase in my hand, I saw Granddad Fred's brother, Joe. He was a little older than Granddad Fred, with white hair, and bigger than Fred in height and weight. You would not believe that they were brothers. Joe had a paper pitch on the corner of Rye Lane and Peckham High Road, and day in day out in all weather, you would find Joe flogging his newspapers. As I approached Joe he said, 'Leaving home then, George?'

I said, 'I can't afford to pay my way.'

'Well, go and see old Fred then,' he said. 'I'm sure that he would put you up in his two-bedroom council flat. After all, he does think the sun shines out of your backside, and if anyone would help you old Fred would.'

Putting Joe and Fred together you'd ask who was the eldest, seeing Joe was much bigger and fat, and Fred small and slim. Only his old army coat made him more full. So off I went to swallow my pride and took Joe's advice to see if Fred could help me out.

I knocked at Granddad's first-floor council flat, and he opened up the door and said, 'I know it is Sunday, George, but I hope you ain't got a suitcase of Bibles to preach the Gospel to me!'

'No, nothing like that,' I said, 'but Joe said that you might help me out. I'm homeless.'

'I thought that you got on all right with your Auntie.'

'I do,' I said, 'but because we don't always earn enough readies I am unable to pay my way, and I am getting into debt with her, so it is unfair to her.'

'George,' he said, 'you should have told me sooner! Of course I can put you up, but you have to help me with my rent, because just like you I struggle as well.'

'You got yourself a deal,' I said.

'But no birds here,' he said. He knew that I had an eye for the girls. I was happy again having got myself a roof over my head so quickly. I considered myself lucky, really, as at the time there was a lot of my age group on the rock and roll, and many living rough on the streets.

England as we knew it had been changing fast since the war had ended. It had affected many people's lives. Some had made a fortune as a result of it, while other had lost everything. There was a growing sense of pride when you saw signs on the billboards: 'Britain leads in ship-building, Britain leads in radar, Britain leads in this and that... The Union Jack was flying almost everywhere. On hearing how great the British Empire was, I like millions was proud to be part of that British Empire.

Immigration was now starting to take place with thousands of black people arriving by boat and mostly heading for London. People were feeling pushed out and bitterness was setting in, and people were complaining that immigrants were getting our jobs and houses, and being treated better than us. Then we started to see notices on house windows offering rooms to let for 'whites only'. We were beginning to see signs of racial intolerance, which was totally against my principles; and then on the other hand thousands of Londoners were taking up the offer of a £10 bribe to go and live in Australia to start a new life, including some of my friends.

Electricity was now found in almost every home and TVs in almost every home. Trams and trolleybuses had become a thing of the past, and wartime rationing had now been well forgotten. Now more people were taking their keys off the string that used to be in the letter box, and replacing it with an extra lock. Rock and roll had started, with Bill Haley and the Comets, and the Teddy boys, together with the Vicky boys, were with us. More people owned cars, creating congestion on our roads, and we were heading for the days of 'You've never had it so good'. Although Granddad Fred and myself were still struggling to make things meet, we were both still enjoying our hard times and fun. My pearly inheritance was coming to the forefront of my mind, with Granddad Fred and Brian encouraging me to start making my new pearly suit and wearing it. They felt that it was part of me, and that I looked lost without it; but I was not yet ready for it, even though I was still seeing Violet. However, I had my whole life in front of me, and soon my kingdom was to start, with the first buttons going on my suit.

Chapter Nine

The effects of my childhood were scarring my life, even after living away for almost five years from Auntie Hilda. I am still unable to eat just anywhere, thanks to memories of my father's handkerchiefs being boiled in the cooking saucepans that were also used to cook our meals, and Auntie Hilda's unhygienic standards and cooking methods. The memories have left me with a phobia towards food, and I tend to relate food to her.

I also still feel very insecure in myself due to the brainwashing from Auntie Hilda. Growing up in a home where I was not shown love or taught the values of love, meant I was unable to recognise it when directed at me. It is only when you are an infant and have attention and love bestowed on you that you can begin to learn the value of love and be able to pass it on. My upbringing has had a tremendous effect on my life.

I was now of the age to have it put to the test without any training or guidance. I was meeting and going out with girls on a one-night-stand basis, which would end in us having sex; but, not having any knowledge, I assumed that having sex was what being in love was all about. I knew nothing about showing love and affection and getting to know all the little things about a person. As I was working on the market stalls, there was no problem in finding a girl for the night's fun.

I served this most beautiful young bird, and as I eyed her up I thought, What a cracker you are, my darling! Well, I wasted no time in chatting her up. The first thing that I said to her was, 'You are the best-looking bird that I've seen today!' She returned my compliments with a lovely big smile. I had never met such a stunner, and I took an instant fancy to her. She had long jet-black hair down to her bum. Her skin was like velvet and she had a figure that any woman would give the world for. I carried on using my chat-up lines, which were working well in my favour. I had a result, and we made a date for that evening at the Tower Cinema, which lies in Rye Lane, Peckham. Her name was Eileen Chase, and we were to become the best of friends for the rest of her short life.

We met as arranged outside the cinema, with her paying, as she insisted. Then made our way to our seats among the other couples in the back row. I don't recall seeing the film, as I was too busy kissing her throughout the film. There was no chance of going any further, not with Eileen. She had her head on her shoulders, and was most certainly no one-night-stand sort of girl, which I really admired her for. After the film had finished I took her to her home, which was located in the more desirable part of Dulwich in South London. She was an only child living with her parents. Over the next few weeks I met her parents, who were well-to-do. You could tell that they loved their daughter dearly and thought the world of her. They would never see her go without; she had parents to be proud of. Eileen had it all: looks, money, parents who loved her and lived in a lovely home. I found myself shielding her from my mates. I was not shielding her out of jealousy, as I am not of a jealous nature, but because I knew that I didn't know how to show her true love like my mates. I did not want to lose her because of my lack of experience, but I was concerned. My mates had a lot of love to offer, as love had been embedded in them from childhood.

Eileen was now about to find out how much I lacked the art of showing and giving love in return. On one particular occasion it was raining cats and dogs as I was on my way to pick up Eileen. Her parents had gone away on holiday and left her on her own. As I walked towards her home I noticed a garden full of a beautiful display of flowers, and thought how nice it would be if I could give her a bunch of them to impress her even more. Off I went into this garden and helped myself to a bunch of flowers, hoping that I didn't get caught. For some reason I panicked and tripped over onto the muddy garden, full face, still clenching the flowers that I had helped myself to! I managed to pick myself up and carried on to Eileen house. Had anyone seen me and been asked me to describe what I looked like, they would have said that I looked like a garden covered in mud and flowers.

On arriving at Eileen's home I rang on the doorbell, still holding on to the bunch of flowers. She opened the door and burst out laughing. 'George, you look like a flower pot, what on earth happened to you?'

I explained what had happened, and how after all that I still managed to save the flowers, picked especially for her.

She was impressed and said, 'Ahh, George, thank you.' Then she suggested that I go and clean myself up. She showed me to the bathroom, where I had a good wash, and I had almost finished drying myself off, using the softest and fluffy bath towel I'd ever seen or used before, when I noticed the bathroom door opening. There was Eileen, standing naked as the day she was born, revealing her full figure. She gently closed the door behind her and walked towards me, then slid her arms around my neck while pulling me closer towards her beautiful naked body, and began kissing me on the lips. This felt so good it left me totally speechless.

It was amazing. Nothing like this had happened to me before. I was overwhelmed, and she whispered passionately, 'I love you.'

For the first time in my life here I was in the arms of someone who loved me and was about to learn just how it feels to be shown love by someone who loves you in a genuine way.

I felt like I was walking on air. My body became relaxed for the first time ever and my penis stood out like it was ready to accept proper, sincere love. For the first time, I was about to use it for what it was intended for. For a moment, time stood still as we writhed around madly on the floor, exploring and enjoying the intensity of passion. Suddenly it felt like there was an explosion within me, but not knowing what was happening to me I did not understand that this was what making love was all about. I was now in a world of love, a love that I wanted to last for ever. How did Eileen know that I did not know the true meaning of love? She had said to me, 'George, you need a real lot of loving and caring.' To her it was natural for her to express love, as she had been loved all her life right from the cradle; it remained with her and so it was easy. She needed no further training. It did not take much for her to realise that I was an empty shell who'd been brought up without an ounce of nurturing and love.

So here we were, two young people from completely different backgrounds. There was Eileen, who had all the love in the world, and then there was me, who was never taught or understood the true meaning of love. At this point I felt rejected and alone. I also felt like I was cheating her out of what she rightly deserved. She needed to be told and reassured that I loved her, but I just could not tell her. I loved her dearly, but just did not know how to express how I felt about her in words, and this was all because of my upbringing. What I do know is that love starts growing in you from the first time you cry as a baby. From there, every day it grows within you. If you are fed it daily, by your mum and dad, it gets stronger in you, making it a natural part of you.

If you are treated like me and that does not happen, instead of your body being fed love it is fed rejection. Love cannot be taught overnight, for as much as Eileen loved me and I loved her she could not teach me the real meaning of love, any more than I could learn it. The mind had already rejected it when I was born. We had a good sexual relationship, but I am told love is more than that. If you put a seed in an empty pot without earth or water, it will never grow; it goes the same with love.

I always thought that pleasing her through sexual intercourse was love. I had no idea that she needed more from me, yet she would do anything for me just to please me; but she had often complained of my lack of love and that I only thought of sex. Our relationship was fading due to the lack of love and understanding on my part. It was being replaced with a very strong friendship. For once in my life I was beginning to realise that the meaning of real love was letting me down, and there was nothing that I could do about it. I felt ashamed of myself, knowing that my lack of loving care had destroyed that courtship between Eileen and myself. Had I been brought up differently, like normal boys with loving parents, maybe Eileen and myself might have settled down and had a family. My upbringing had destroyed that; also it may have prevented Eileen from getting part of her future life in a mess, which I felt that I was responsible for.

Even though we were the best of friends, it was some eighteen months later that she had met this chap who introduced her to drink and drugs and she became fixed on it. She rejected her lovely parents, and to feed her drink and drug habit would sell her body, resulting in prostitution. Had I given her the real love she so desperately wanted, maybe she would not have gone down that road and ended up on a scrap heap.

I have always blamed myself for being partly responsible for her downfall, regardless what anyone may say, simply because I am the only person who knows what we had and also what we could have had. I would still see her parents from time to time, and they would tell me how disappointed they were with the way things had turned out, and how she had also rejected them because of their disapproval and concern about what she was doing to herself. All they wanted was for her to be the Eileen they knew and loved.

How could I explain to them that my upbringing may have contributed to her destroying her life? I had nobody that I could talk to about how I was feeling and all that had happened, so again it was all bottled up inside of me, and it was destroying my life and other people's. At times like this my childhood comes back to the surface in my mind and I hate myself for it. I felt that my childhood had given me my eating problems, and robbed me of my desire to love and be loved. It is when you are really growing up and finding your way in life that you find yourself tripping over the past. For me it was making it that much harder to settle in life. It was a long and bumpy ride, but I was prepared to face the problems full on.

Then I was to face another challenge, this time involving a girl called Pat. Like me she had a father who beat her. I did not know how I could face it or how I would react to it. I had met Pat in the Blue Café. She was much taller than me. She was a nice girl, outgoing and pretty, with sparkling eyes. We had been going out with each other whenever she was free, and we did not have a relationship as such, just company. One evening I had arranged to meet her at the flats backing onto the Blue Café. When she turned up her face was cut and badly bruised, her face was so puffy she looked a real state. I asked what had happened to her. In between her sobbing and crying, she explained in a roundabout way that her father for no apparent reason had given her another beating, and how her life was a nightmare. She had had enough, and no longer wanted to be there anymore, and wanted me to help her. Straight away my mind began doing summersaults, and memories of my past, with all the beatings that I had also encountered, went swimming around in my mind. I became dazed and confused. I was beginning to go through all that pain again inside of me, which was terrifying me, and I felt that I was going to get caught up in that lifestyle again. No way could I risk that. I wanted to help her in some way, but I had been down that road before, and I was not prepared to risk going there again.

As cruel as it may seem, I said, 'Sorry, Pat,' and took off like lightning. Part of me wanted to stay and comfort her, as she so rightly deserved. I just could not show her that understanding or love that she needed at that important time. Every time I think of her I often wonder why I left her to suffer the misery that I had experienced. Was it because I did not want to be reminded of my own childhood? Or perhaps I was afraid there could be another Auntie Hilda somewhere behind closed doors. Or was I just being selfish? For whatever reason, that girl needed my help, and I had refused to help, so she may have suffered even more. I so wished that I had the courage to help her. I have always helped others before, but why did I refuse to help Pat? Even to this day it still preys on my mind. I never saw Pat again. I was gradually beginning to find out how my past childhood was now affecting me.

My market work was the only thing that was taking my mind off my past, and the fact that there was plenty of community spirit in London meant everyone helped each other. There was no shortness of friendship, and I was becoming a well-known character. Wherever I went, people would shout, 'George!' or 'Norman!' as I was still wearing one of our Norman Wisdom hats. So it was a combination of things that was helping me to forget where I had come from, or even who I was.

Brian was next to find himself out on the streets with no home, for the same reasons as I found myself in. It was Granddad Fred who had helped him out and gave him a roof over his head and a bed to sleep in, in my room. My eating disorder was still with me and I was unable to eat in the flat. Granddad Fred and Brian could not understand why I would not eat at the flat, and it was embarrassing for me. They had no idea that I had a hidden past that I was not sharing with anyone.

This was the year 1955, the year that Winston Churchill resigned. I don't think that there was one person, young or old, who did not admire him for what he had done for us during the war years. Then Anthony Eden took his place as prime minister, and we saw the first polio vaccine introduced in this country. Then there was Ruth Ellis, who was the last woman to be hanged, and ITV, the first commercial TV broadcasting channel, was launched. The days of good, down-to-earth TV viewing were upon us. How it has all changed! It's got boring since then. In the same year a man of the future was born – Bill Gates – but most of us were still struggling day by day.

In late 1955 and early 1956 I was hearing a lot of talk in my age group about doing national service, which meant when you was eighteen you had to join the forces and do your national service for two years. The only way that you could avoid it was by having an apprenticeship or a special job or an illness or disability. Apart from that you had to join, and most people went into the army. You heard of all kind of scams that were thought up in order to avoid joining the army. The only trouble was to think of a good scam. Very few teenagers were willing to do their two years' national service. They were either happy enjoying their lives as teenagers or were busy making money and wearing their teddy-boy suits. I, like many in my age group, had my call-up papers to join the army, and came across a lot of mates who were getting their call-up papers against their wishes, and joined up under protest, complaining that their freedom was being taken away from them. But in reality they went in as boys and came out as men. It gave them a sense of responsibility and self-respect. It's a pity really that the national-service system was later stopped. Perhaps we could be living in a better country today.

With my experience of being at Mayford Approved School, and having learned to mix with others as a team, I thought it exciting to be able to wear an army uniform, and a chance to venture out into the unknown appealed to me. The only problem I had was it would be almost impossible for me to join because I was deaf. Like every teenager of my age, I had my call-up papers – in my case for the army – and I knew that I did not have a chance due to my being deaf. It ruled me out straight away. Let's face it, how can you have a deaf soldier in the British army? The enemy would walk past me without me knowing, and I wouldn't hear any orders barking at me, so any chance of fighting for queen and country was over before I started – or was it?

We were all used to seeing the billboards saying 'Your country needs you', with a sergeant major pointing at you. So here I am making it quite clear that I was one of those teenagers who wanted to join the British army but couldn't because of my deafness. Of course, in Peckham in them days word travelled fast. I was in the Blue Café eating my meal with Brian and Granddad Fred, feeling very disappointed at knowing that I would not be able to join the army. In my call-up papers it gave me the date and time when I was to go for my medical, to see if I was fit and able to join the British army. Had I not wanted to join, all I needed to do was see my doctor who would have filled in a form confirming that I was deaf, and that would excuse me from my army days; but I wanted to join, and everyone who knew me knew that.

I had finished my dinner when Bruce came along. He was a mate of mine, and the same age, same size and same build, but loaded with bees and honey (money). He shared a second-hand car business with his dad. He was dressed as a spiv, with gold chain around his neck and gold rings on his fingers. In fact he had so much gold on his hands it's a wonder that he could even lift them! In his car business, mates of mine were paying a £10 deposit for a Jaguar on HP that Bruce had fiddled with the HP company, never seeing their payments made. There was more fiddling in Peckham than all the rest of London! Bruce sat himself next to Brian, who was sitting opposite me, and said, 'I hear that you want to join the army, George.'

'That's right,' I said.

'But you bloody can't, can you, because you are deaf.'

'So why are you telling me something that I already know? Want to flog me a jam jar [car] that's so noisy so I can hear it?'

'No, George, I might be able to help you get into the army.'

'And how do you think you can do that?' I said.

'I have a scam that's worth a try – all legal, mind you – but a bonus if you join me in it.'

Bruce then explained his scam to me. He had his call-up papers as well on the same date as mine. Without giving too much away, basically I would take his hearing test and he would take mine; a very complicated scam, but a clever one, and Bruce did know his stuff, as many of my mates did.

My reward would be £250, and £250 in 1956 could buy you a new car, so it was worth being deaf for. It was a big temptation to me, and Bruce was a man whom I could trust more than his cars. Granddad Fred and Brian were against it. For starters, they would be losing their right-hand man and a friend; but I pointed out to them two years is nothing, and anyway I might find some scams in the army that we could earn out of. Besides, I would be getting leave to come back and see them a lot. I told Bruce that I would think about his offer and let him know my decision.

The next evening at the Blue Café, all that time Granddad Fred and Brian were still against me joining the army, but I told them it was something that I really wanted to do. Fred said, 'If you go ahead with this scam it could land you in trouble.'

'Well,' I said, 'it's a chance worth taking to get my hands on £250, and a chance to join the army; and anyway it's Bruce who would be more in trouble than me. At least I could say I wanted to join to fight for queen and country.'

The following evening, as arranged, I met Bruce and agreed to work with him on his scam. Part of the scam was that I was to use Bruce's name and he was to use my name. We both have to have nerves of steel and our wits about us. Our medical appointment had arrived to attend the army medical centre at Blackheath in South London. He reminded me to use my best patter and that he would do likewise. 'But remember,' I said, 'if we don't get away with it, and you go in the army, I will be left £250 short, so do your best and I'll do mine.'

We assured each other that we could make it work. Bruce reminded me, 'Don't bloody call me Bruce.'

I said, 'It's now George, and I am Bruce, because I so much want a taste of the British army.' I was going to give it my very best show ever. I felt that I wanted another chance to experience my desire, which deep down must have come from my childhood.

I had always wanted an opportunity like this from my early days. I wanted Auntie Hilda to change, also my father to change, and treat me as a normal child. I wanted my sister Violet to change from being a mentally-handicapped child to a normal child. All the time I was looking for a chance, and now I wanted a chance to join the army. All my ducking and diving, my bravado and my cheekie-chappie personality were hiding my true feelings. I wanted more to make me feel good in myself and to grow into a fine man. Mayford Approved School had taught me a lot. Perhaps now the army could teach me more and I was prepared to try it with an open mind. Bruce was, I could see, quite nervous that something just might go wrong. After all, he had more to lose than me, so I was assuring him there was nothing to lose, but all to gain, thinking of my £250. There were quite a lot of us in the medical centre waiting to have a medical, and most were looking decidedly unhappy, wishing they would fail. I saw one chap with a white stick, obviously pretending to be blind, until one of the medical staff dropped a five-pound note on the floor and he picked it up, so uncovering his scam. He was another Peckham boy. Bruce and I went through the medical tests: chest, heart, eyes, urine test, nothing was missed out. It was the hearing test that was to prove the make or break of our future.

We sat waiting for our names to be called, and this is where Bruce and I had to stick together, remembering I couldn't hear my name or his name being called. And today I am his name, so when Bruce's name is called he would kick my foot indicating that his name had been called.

When my name was called, Bruce got up for his hearing test. After about ten minutes he comes out with a big grin on his face with his thumb up, indicating that I had passed my hearing test. After about six or seven more people had gone in and out for their hearing test, Bruce's name was called. Bruce kicked my foot to let me know that his name had been called to go in, but I did not respond, and the caller shouted his name again. Still I did not respond. I knew his name had been called because he was kicking my foot even harder. The third call was shouted loud enough to bring the building down. I stood up and said to the caller, 'Did you call me?'

'Yes, I bloody did!' the caller said.

Bruce had his head in his hands. I don't know whether he was laughing or crying, but I then entered this room for my hearing test. I was handed some earphones to put over my ears, but of course that could only make it worse for my hearing. The doctor then said something to me that I just did not hear. So I took off the earphones and asked him to repeat what he had said. After repeating himself two or three times, he explained that I was to put the earphones on, and when I heard a sound in them I was to press a button. Of course this was the easy part for me, as I am truly deaf. I am told on high notes with someone with good ears if turned up fully it could blow your brains out, but with me if turned up full I would still be unable to hear, as I don't hear high-pitched notes. At the end of my test the doctor asked why I didn't let them know that I was very deaf, and I said with a surprised voice, 'Am I?' He then looked at me in a sad way and said that I could go. I said, 'Did I pass the hearing test?' and he said, 'I'm sorry, you did not.'

I must have been the only candidate going through that medical building who was as deaf as a doorknob! I returned back to Bruce, who had been waiting for me, and for the next hour in that medical building he was trying to find out how I had got on; but I decided to tease him by saying that I had passed.

'But you are bloody deaf, George! How could you pass?'

'Oh,' I said, 'they washed out my ears.'

'But you still can't hear me now,' he said.

'Can't I?' said I.

'No, you bloody can't! Something is wrong, George. You must go back and tell them that they are making a mistake!'

'Well,' I said, 'it looks like you are going in the Kate Karney [army], don't it!'

Bruce by now was going all colours in his face, and we finally left the medical building. The sweat of fear was running off him. Finally I could not keep calm any longer, or see him suffer in such a way. 'Bruce,' I said, 'I have a confession to make to you.'

'What's that?' he said.

'I bloody failed my hearing test – and you, my boy, are out of the Kate Karney.'

His expression turned from having a nightmare to having won the football pools; it was a sight well worth seeing.

It was now a case of the waiting to see officially if I was to go for my national service, and if Bruce would be excused from his national service. The waiting was worst. It seemed like a lifetime for us both to get the results. Every evening, Bruce came into the Blue Café to see if I'd had any post with my results, and I was just as keen to hear if he'd had his results. The moment came: my call-up papers had finally arrived. I opened up my letter from the army, informing me that I had been accepted into the British army. I put the letter into my pocket and without saying anything to Granddad Fred or Brian, carried on our day's work. At the Blue Café that evening, Leon said as he put our meal on the table, 'Any luck yet, George, on joining the Kate Karney?'

'No,' I said.

'It will be a miracle if you get in, George,' he said.

Then Bruce came in. 'Any luck, George?'

'No, Bruce, no news yet.' I was not going to let on until I knew the results of Bruce's applications.

Two days later Bruce came into the Blue Café as if he had won the pools. 'I have bloody done it – I'm out of the Kate Karney!'

'Now where is my £250?' I said to him.

'Right here, George, as promised. And how did you get on?' he said.

Pulling out my call-up papers from my pocket, I handed the letter to Granddad Fred to read out aloud for all to hear. Then Granddad Fred read it out, saying, 'He's bloody made it, he's joining the Kate Karney!'

'Let me see,' Leon said, taking the papers from Granddad Fred, not believing that I had made it. 'He's bloody right, you know. George has done it!' Then Leon said, 'Listen to this!' and read the attached leaflet, explaining which regiment I was to go into. 'It says here that he is to join the Royal Signals.'

'They have got the "royal" right,' Bruce said. 'After all, he is a pearly king in waiting!'

Leon carried on reading. 'It says here that the Royal Signals is the brains…'

'He ain't got that,' Granddad Fred cut in.

'…and the eyes,' Leon carried on, 'and the *ears* of the British army!'

At that the whole café seemed to burst out laughing. Brian, still holding his stomach with laughter, said, 'The only thing that George has is the eye; the rest is just not there!'

After everyone had fully recovered from the pain in their stomachs from laughing, Leon shouted, 'Drinks on the house, tea for everyone! The British army is about to get its first deaf soldier!'

I knew I had become an accomplished lip-reader, and that I would have to make sure I kept my eyes on everyone's lips in the army in order to stay in. I had about two to three weeks to prepare myself for my national service, and up to the day before joining the army I had worked as usual on the market with Brian and Granddad Fred. I knew that I would miss them and the market life, but at the same time I was looking forward to joining the army. After all, two years in the army is nothing compared with the future in front of me.

Another mate of mine, Leslie, who had been in and out of children's homes for the best part of his life and was blind in his left eye, wanted to do his national service. But in his case he was lucky. His plan was to avoid the eye test to his left eye. When he was asked to cover his left eye to read the wall letters that was OK, but when he was to have his right eye covered, which would prove that he could not be able to read the letters with his left eye, the doctor took a phone call and when he returned to cover Leslie's right eye again to carry out the test, Leslie said, 'You've already done the left eye.' This was just luck on Leslie's side. He was also a Peckham boy, so it was a scam to get in the army.

The night before leaving I said goodbye to all my mates in the snooker hall, the Blue Café, and where people knew that I was off to the army. Everyone said that being deaf I would not last long. The next morning I set out to head for Euston Station, and in tow was Granddad Fred, Brian, Bruce and Leon, who took time off from his café, and three other mates all to see me off and help me find the right train, and make sure that I was still happy at my decision to join the army. But there was no doubt in my mind.

I was wearing my best whistle and flute, with my Peckham Rye (tie) that had a picture of a naked girl on, and a colourful waistcoat around my chest looking like the biggest spiv in Euston Station.

Fred said, 'Come on, George, there's your train!' It was the longest train that I have seen, and there was this big steam engine to pull it at the front. The train seemed to be a special one, as almost everyone about my age was boarding it, and unlike me they all seemed unhappy at boarding it. The time had come to say goodbye to my mates, which for me was sad. I'd had so many good times with them all, and plenty of laughs, so I would be missing them.

Bruce came up to me and putting £10 in my hand said, 'Thanks George I shall always be in your debt, and anytime that you need to buy a car call on me.'

'I want something with an engine in it,' I said to him. Giving his dirty laugh, he assured me that he would have an engine in it.

Then it was Leon's turn. 'Here,' he said, 'I've got some sandwiches here for you, George, to eat on your journey.' Catterick in Yorkshire was where I was to do my six weeks' training.

'Thanks, Leon, and give your good-looking wife a kiss for me!'

'Have you been having an affair with her?' he asked, and then laughed it away.

Next it was Brian's turn. 'What are we going to do without you, George?'

'Don't be such a plonker, Brian! You just look after Granddad Fred for me.'

'I will, George, you can bank on me.'

'That's what worries me!' I said.

Then my three other mates came up to me, embracing me and saying how they all were going to miss me. Then finally Granddad Fred, with a tear in his sparkling eyes, said, 'I hope they send you back, George, because I'm going to miss you. Your life is the markets, not the Kate Karney!'

'Sorry, Granddad, but it's only two years, and I feel I want to do this.'

'You take care, George, I'm going to miss you!'

I then said to them all, 'Remember – we are mates, and mates don't part, and I'll be back!'

'The whistle has gone, George!' Bruce shouted, knowing that I had not heard it. 'I hope they don't have whistles in the Kate Karney,' he said.

I jumped on the train like I used to jump on the buses in my childhood so many times, to begin my journey north to the army camp. As I closed the door and opened the window, I leaned out to wave goodbye to my mates, who were still standing there waving to me as the train pulled out of the station. With my mates disappearing from my view, I got a lump in my throat, as I now realised I was on my own. Along the corridors of the train, I started searching for a seat amongst all the other lads who had joined the train and were also about to start their army careers.

As I sat down in between the lads, the bloke next to me, who introduced himself as David, said, 'You had a good send-off.'

Proudly, I said, 'Yes, they are some of my mates.' Then, pulling out a pack of new cards that I had brought, I said, 'Game of cards, anyone? For bees and honey [money] if you like…'

Within a short time the carriage was full of smoke. We were playing for real bees and honey. I had already taken off my jacket to expose my colourful waistcoat that Granddad Fred gave me the night before, as a going-away present. I had never been north of Watford before, so the journey was interesting to me, taking in the full countryside, seeing so many cows and sheep on the way, and hearing the roar of the train's wheels heading towards my army camp. Here, my first six weeks of training would begin, as would a nightmare for the British army – having their first deaf soldier – which they did not wish to be reminded of!

Chapter Ten

At last we all arrived at Catterick Camp to start our army national service. The train journey seemed to take all day, but it was nice to be able to stretch our legs. We were greeted by the refreshing smell of the countryside lingering in the air around us.

It was so unlike the regular smell of smog and smoke that surrounded London at that time, which left you coughing and choking. We were transported from the station to the camp where we were to carry out our training.

The sergeants lost no time in barking their orders, which started with, 'Come on, you bloody lazy bastards, line up!' It was an open camp with billets scattered everywhere and you could not help but notice all the bullshit; with everything being spic and span, it stood out a mile.

We were all lined up on parade like a lot of lost chickens; our names were being called out to see if there was anyone missing. I had not been wearing my hearing aid for quite a time now; if I did it would give the game away that I was deaf. So I was relying more on lip-reading, but that was no good if the sergeant calling out the orders was also chewing gum at the same time! For me it was impossible to try and lip-read the orders. It was a nightmare, because it was like watching a letter box on a windy day. The names were being called out, but I couldn't hear a thing.

When you heard your name called, you had to respond by saying 'Present, sir!' in order to let the sergeant know that you had arrived safely at the camp. The reason for this was that it was not uncommon on some occasions for boys who just could not face it to bottle out and not bother turning up. When this happened, they were later tracked down, and when caught punished for desertion; but there was no chance of that happening to me, as I was glad to be given the opportunity to train in the British army. All the names had been called and ticked off now, but I noticed that the corporals were looking puzzled as they carried out head counts. This must have happened around five times. Then it dawned on me that I could not hear my name being called, so I couldn't have been accounted for.

My name had not been ticked off, which meant the names ticked off did not match the heads counted. As the corporal passed me for the sixth time, I said, 'Excuse me, sir, did you call my name?'

He replied, 'What's your name?'

I said, 'George Major, sir.'

He raised his voice and repeated my name, saying, 'George Major!' He was now shouting. 'We been calling your name dozens of bloody times! Why didn't you say "Present"?'

I said, 'I never heard you, I've got wax in my ears.'

He yelled, 'Well, get the bloody wax out of your bloody ears!' Then he turned to the sergeant who had been calling the names and said, 'I have found the missing one – it's a George Major… Thanks for wasting valuable army time!' he barked back at me.

I had to say I had wax in my ears to cover up my deafness, but how long could I keep this up? I thought that my army career would be short-lived if they found out that I was deaf. We were then frogmarched to the quarter master's stores to collect our bedding and army clothing. I felt good at getting my army uniform and kit; it gave me a sense of pride, knowing that I was part of the British army. We were then taken to our wooden billets, after being allocated an army number that would remain with us throughout our army life. David, whom I had met on the train, had the bed next to me; you could see that he was very well educated, as he was very well spoken with a posh voice. He was of average size, with puffy cheeks full of teenage spots. He was a nice bloke and easy to get on with. After familiarising ourselves with camp and getting to know where everything was and making ourselves known to others, we turned in and settled down to our first night's sleep.

Bright and early the following morning we were woken up by the sound of, 'Come on, you fucking lazy bastards, get up!' being yelled out by the corporal, while he loudly banged on the bottom of our iron-framed beds, letting us all know that this was no holiday camp and he was the boss who called the shots.

We were to be taught how to swing our arms while marching, how to salute an officer, to present arms, and taught everything about army drill, which is all part and parcel of discipline. This I found very difficult to keep up with, as I was deaf.

As loud as the sergeant and corporals shouted, I had to really concentrate to hear or understand what was being said. The further away they were barking the orders, the more difficult it was for me. I would try to concentrate and focus on following what my fellow soldiers were doing. If they did something out of the blue, it would throw me off track. It was on the training ground that most of my problems from being deaf began to be revealed.

I followed my fellow soldiers as they followed the sergeant's instructions, as he shouted out, 'Left, right, left, right.' That was OK, as I would just follow them as the man in front went left, right, left, right. Great, this was easy, I thought, until without any warning the marching soldiers are told to about-turn. But of course I did not hear the command to about-turn, so I was still happily going forward, and in doing so had brought half the parade down on its knees.

Oh no, I thought, I could hear someone shouting, 'Who's that bloody soldier that's brought my parade to its knees?' The sergeant marched towards me with his stick tucked under his arm. His face was just an inch or so away as he said, 'It's that fucking missing soldier again who's got wax in his ears! Now you have gone and brought my fucking army to its knees! Just how much wax do you have in them ears of yours?'

Then he carried on with his instructions of, 'Left, right, left, right…' I was looking out for the about-turn command again. I did not want to mess up the sergeant's parade again and I could not let on that I was deaf, which was proving harder than I'd first thought. 'Left, right, left, right,' the sergeant was barking, then, 'about-turn!' Again I did not hear the command, and again I brought down half his parade to its knees; but this time not so many, because I think some of the soldiers were now aware of me tripping them up.

'That fucking soldier again!' the sergeant barked, now losing his temper. He approached me again, and shouted directly in my face, 'Are you fucking deaf?' – 'No, sir!' – 'Then you must be daft and stupid!'

I was not happy with that comment, as it made my anger begin to rise inside me. I did not want to give the game away about my deafness, as I desperately wanted a chance to be a soldier and fight for queen and country.

'Right,' he said, 'in order to prevent my soldiers from falling to their knees again, I'm going to put you well clear in front of them.'

So there I was some four yards in front of the parade on my own.

Then I looked over my shoulder behind me, waiting to see when they started marching. I went over it in my mind reminding myself what I had to do to avoid another repeat performance. I began to march, swinging my arms, left, right, left, right. The parade ground was about the length of twenty football pitches, if not more, so here I was, left, right, left, right. But again I did not hear the command to about-turn, and by now I had reached the end of the parade ground, totally unaware that the command to about-turn had been given a few minutes earlier. Once again I was in my own little world, doing what I thought was correct during the parade, only to realise that I had left my parade of soldiers far away on the other side of the parade ground, and I had been marching on my own! By now they were in fits of laughter, and totally amused by what I had done. I then had to run back quickly to join them all again. The sergeant came up to me and ordered me to the sick bay to have the wax taken out of my ears. Had that been the true reason for me not being able to hear his orders, my problems could have been solved by having the wax removed; but that was not the case, and I could not tell anyone.

With that day over, on the following morning we found our way to the mess room, where we had our meals three times a day. Having had my mug of tea, I noticed more full plates than empty ones on my table; obviously the army food was not liked. In my case I was still faced with personal eating problem, which was still affecting me eating just about anywhere. Instead, I would buy my own food from the local shop.

When I got back to my billet, David was there packing up his belongings. I said, 'Had enough of the Kate Karney already?'

'No, George, I'm being transferred,' he replied.

I was to meet him as a lieutenant many months later, which was to my advantage. I was not surprised that David was promoted to lieutenant. He was too smart and intelligent to be a signalman.

It was back on parade for the second day, with the sergeant watching me like a bloody hawk. We were learning how to stand at ease and attention, also to present arms, about-turn and much more. I tried my hardest not to upset the sergeant or mess things up again. The sergeant gave the order for attention and so that I could hear he came right up to me and shouted out loud, 'Attention!' But with my type of hearing, things sometimes sound differently and I thought he said, 'Count to ten.' So I started, 'One, two, three…' and so on to ten. He took one look at me and said, 'Just why have you counted to ten? Are you working in a bingo hall or something?'

I responded, 'Pardon, sir, you said count to ten.'

Then he yelled, 'Who the bloody hell put you in the British army – bloody Hitler?'

By now I was becoming the camp jester, and all the signalmen (as we were called) were trying to get next to me, either to help to cover up their own mistakes, or for the sheer fun of being next to me.

When the sergeant called, 'At ease,' I was still stood at attention. By now the sergeant was taking me in his stride and I think maybe he enjoyed telling his mates about the events of the day with George Major; but I found that a lot of my mistakes were being taken lightheartedly. After all, the sergeant must have seen his group of soldiers were more relaxed and happier under his training. The sergeant was still barking and swearing at me, I suppose to get a bit of fun at calling me this and that, with the soldiers laughing in between. I now found wherever I went in the camp the signalmen had now found a new name for me: 'Norman Wisdom'. I was the talk of the camp, and known as the soldier who brought the British army to its knees. My antics on parade gave them a new sense of morale. This helped me to make a lot of friends, and soon I became very popular in the camp, but I was still trying my best to do all that was expected of me.

With my first week's training over, and five more to go, I was wondering if I would make it. I badly wanted to stay in the army and felt that my hearing was letting me down. I felt that I would have to try harder and not let myself down. I had thought about it, and decided that I would have to watch everyone more closely; this did help, up to a point, as the signalmen were out to help me. I don't think that they wanted me to leave, as they were having fun on the parade with me being there to liven it and reduce the misery of joining the Kate Karney. I made it more relaxed for them, with never a dull moment. When you don't want people to know you are deaf, which I did not, it makes life that bit harder concealing it.

It was on the rifle range that I had my biggest problem. I knew that I could shoot good, as I had won many prizes on the fairgrounds with my shooting, but the army rifle range is not a fairground. I can understand why the Kate Karney cannot afford to have anyone in it who is deaf. We were marched to the rifle range, an open field. In the distance were cut-out figures of soldiers and bullseye boards that we were to practise firing on. I had no trouble hitting my target with confidence, but here the army had safety rules. We were told to lie down on our tummies with our rifle facing our targets. There were ten of us at the time, and we were barked an order as to when and where to fire, and given a number. When the corporal shouted your number, you then fired at your target. My number was nine. When the firing had started, they got to five, at which I thought they had said 'nine'. To my hearing it sounded like nine, as they were shouting the numbers at random. So I fired, nearly hitting a bullseye.

The corporal then came up to me and said, 'Who the bloody hell told you to fire?'

'You did, sir.'

'No, I bloody did not! I said "Five, fire," not "nine, fire." Are you bloody deaf?'

'No, Corporal,' I said.

'Now, keep your bloody earholes open, and fire when I command it.'

So once again he called out his numbers when he wanted us to fire. Again he started at random: 'Three, fire... Six, fire... Two, fire... Five, fire.' I then fired, thinking that he had said, 'Nine, fire.'

'He has done it again!' the corporal shouted. 'He could even get the fucking enemy confused, and get us all bloody killed!'

He came up to me and kicked my foot to get my attention. I turned around with my rifle in hand, something that you are not supposed to do, and without thinking I was facing him with my rifle. He stood there frozen, his face going all colours – thinking, I suppose, that I was about to shoot him. Then he said, 'Now take it easy, son. Think very carefully before you do something silly, and put your rifle carefully on the ground.'

I then left my rifle on the ground and got up to my feet, not realising that I had done anything unusual or wrong. Luckily for me, the corporal was a decent bloke and saw the funny side of it later, and I was still holding my cover with my deafness.

Every day we were back on parade with the same sergeant. He was always chewing his chewing gum, which made it almost impossible to read his lips in order to understand what he was saying, even from a short distance away. He was shouting from his stomach rather from his mouth. On parade, I was marching on the left-hand side of a line of soldiers at six abreast. 'Left, right, left, right!' the sergeant was shouting. On the straight I was OK. 'Left, right, left, right…' Then he shouts, 'Right turn!' This I don't hear, so I am still going left, right, left, right ahead, but now on my own. The other soldiers had done a right, and I had gone on ahead! Had I been on the right of the six abreast, I would most certainly have brought the other soldiers to their knees again. When I had realised my mistake I went running back to catch up with the others, and got another dressing-down from the sergeant, who I couldn't hear or understand. I was forever giving the wrong answers to whatever he said to me.

After training of an evening we would do our bullshit, polishing our boots with spit and polish until you could see your face in it, and iron our army suits. On the trousers, we used to rub soap on the inside of the crease so as to give a firm sharp crease to the trousers. Our army suits were to be our pride and joy. Then we would go round to the NAAFI for a drink and a laugh. I had many mates around me, listening to my tales of market life. As I was the only costermonger in our regiment, to the boys it was unique to listen to my tales. A lot of costermongers had managed to avoid their national service, as many of them never gave a fixed address. They were mostly trying to avoid the taxman and authorities, so many of them became invisible. The boys were amazed how I always got away from having jankers or going up before the CO. They felt it was my cheek and patter that saved my bacon. As for the sergeant, who they thought was a bastard who bullied them and ran them into the ground, it seemed that I could get away with anything with him – something they could not understand.

Three weeks into my training at Catterick Camp, I was still enjoying my army career and not bothered at being called Norman Wisdom. In fact I have never minded at being called any nicknames, as long as it wasn't Melsham – the name given to me by my Auntie Hilda.

At our third weekend I had surprise visitors out of the blue, with no warning from them. It was Bruce, driving with Granddad Fred and Brian. 'What a surprise!' I said. 'Have you missed me already?'

'We have come to see if you are all right and if you need anything, George,' they said. Bruce added, 'Would you like to go out for a meal?'

'That's the best words I have heard in three weeks,' I said. Unknown to them, I had not had a proper square meal in three weeks.

Of course, it was Bruce who settled the bill for the meal. I was telling them of all the mishaps on my training, and the problems with my hearing. 'It won't be long before they find out about your deafness, George,' said Granddad Fred, 'and when they do you will be out.'

'They will have a fight on their hands if they do,' I said.

'Paleface has been asking where you are, George,' said Brian.

'Did you tell him?' I said.

'No,' Brian replied, 'but I told him you was training to become a copper and get a beat on Rye Lane, and let all the street traders carry on trading without any disturbance from the Old Bill.'

'Good on you, Brian!' I said.

It was time for them to make their journey back to London, and before leaving Bruce again said that if there was anything he could do for me, just ask. Brian and Granddad Fred were still choked that I was not with them flogging down Rye Lane, but I told them that when I came out of the Kate Karney I would return and carry on where I had left off.

I was in some ways missing my mates, but on the other hand I wanted to do my national service. It had started in 1947, by law, and lasted until 1963, and on average there was 6,000 teenagers a month being called up for their two years in the armed services. It was expensive for the government to maintain the national service, but it could have proved cheaper had they kept it to this day. We would not have had so much crime and there'd be fewer people in prison. The discipline was rigorous, plus the fitness training, and if as a boy you wanted to be a man then the army was the place for you. You were offered a range of full educational courses if you wanted. Anyway, it would make a turning point in your life, and most of all it taught us teamwork, and I was all for that. I was also exchanging letters with Eileen Chase back home, who had become more than a friend to me. This girl wanted to give all her love to me, but I could only accept part of it. It was a problem that I had, and a problem that I was ashamed of. I was still going on parade and being accounted for like all the others on training, and still I was bringing half the army to its knees and becoming a full-time jester amongst my mates. During our training, many of them tried to get next to me, for the fun of it, but I did not mind, as it was all part of serving together and making life fun. We were all being called a load of lunatics by the sergeant. Those six weeks must have been the worst he had ever had in the army; he was often completely out of his mind, so the others actually looked forward to our daily parades, wondering what could possibly go wrong next… When Bruce, Granddad Fred and Brian had come down, they had told me of a deal they had picked up with some watches, a once-in-a-lifetime deal. All 300 of them had been bought only the day before with bees and honey borrowed from Bruce, and for once it was an honest, straight line, which they had in the boot of Bruce's car in a suitcase. They asked me what I thought of them. After looking at them, I said, 'It's about time that you started flogging something of quality for a change!' I was tempted to try flogging some myself, so I said, 'Can I flog a few of them at my camp?' At this, they gave me one hundred to flog at a pound each.

Armed with my watches, I strapped ten of them on each wrist then in my spare time flogged them to the boys. I did well in flogging them. Some of the boys had challenged me to flog one to our sergeant. This challenge I took up, and at the end of our day's training I called out to the sergeant, 'Sergeant, can I interest you in the finest quality men's watch that money can buy?' Then pulling up both sleeves, I showed him my watches on both wrists. 'All British made,' I said, 'and a must for every British soldier – more so for sergeants, who need to be on time for training their soldiers.'

He looked at me, then at my watches, and at the top of his voice said, 'I've been watching you, Major!'

'That's why I am offering you my watches at one pound and ten shillings to you… but because you are my favourite sergeant I am going to let you have them at a pound each.'

Instead on buying one he bought two, and after buying them he said, 'I don't know how the bloody hell you got into the British army, or how long that you will bloody stay, but if I was you I would take up the business of selling bloody watches rather than being a soldier. It would be safer for the British army!'

I think he knew that I was really deaf but just went along with it; but I did manage to flog all my one hundred watches.

The end of our six weeks was up, and the last day was to be our passing-out parade – the final test in front of our CO. All the boys, like me, wanted to put on our best and give our sergeant a final boost of pride because he had trained us to the best; so the boys today were going to make sure that I would not trip them up and signal to me when it was time to about-turn, when to turn right or left, when it was time to salute, and when to stand at ease or attention, and when to present arms. And believe me, we were the best squad that day. Even the sergeant found a smile at the end of the passing-out parade, and his last words were, 'Well done, boys, you done yourselves proud – including the soldier that brought my army to its knees!'

I had marched with my comrades on the passing-out parade, and a moment of sheer pride entered me. *I have done it*, I thought. I was a soldier representing the queen and country, and I was a fully passed-out signalman soldier, the brains the eyes and ears of the British army… where is the sick bag?

From Catterick we were sent to Aldershot, another army camp, to be posted to a permanent camp. On our first weekend we had our first 36-hour leave, and off I went back to Peckham in my full uniform, feeling quite proud of myself.

My first point of call was Rye Lane to meet Granddad Fred and Brian. 'What a dog's dinner!' they both said, seeing me in my uniform. 'Come on,' I said, 'let's go to the Blue Café and have a meal.'

As we had entered the café, everyone gave out a wolf whistle. Leon came from behind the counter to shake my hand. 'You have got some guts,' he said. 'Your meal is on me.'

'What about us?' Brian said.

'George is here to protect us, but he is bloody deaf and will get us all shot dead,' said Granddad Fred.

I gave them the money for the watches, less my part of the profit, and I asked if I they had any more; but like me they had flogged the lot.

'Your bed is still there for you,' said Granddad Fred.

We then talked all about my army training and the cock-ups that I was doing, and how all the other soldiers had covered for me. Then they asked, 'What happens next?' and I said, 'That is anyone's guess.'

Then I was drafted to Germany, to a place called 'Hertford'. The general talk was that we could be heading for Egypt, with the Suez Canal argument hotting up; we were already on our guard against the IRA, but within three weeks I was shipped back to Aldershot. Perhaps the British army thought they'd had enough trouble on the Suez Canal, without me making it worse. Well, that's what my mates thought, anyway.

From Aldershot, after a week I was on another 36-hour leave, and then, on my return, I was posted to Chester. As I entered my new camp,

I had a sense of pride at being a soldier in uniform who carried the badge of my regiment – The Royal Signals – and my spit and polish boots, which looked like a mirror. I had spent many hours putting the black shoe polish on them and with a piece of rag mix the polish with my spit. I would circle the cloth around and around until the shine came through. I was shown my new quarters, greatly different from my wooden billet at Catterick. Here they had red-brick barrack blocks with a sloping roof and black slates, and everything was brick-built. We also had a very large mess room and a cookhouse with an attached dining hall.

There was a large NAAFI where you could buy your fags, sweets and personal items. In all it was a nice camp, with a friendly atmosphere. I settled into my camp very well and soon made a lot of friends. We still had to drill – that's what army life is all about – so on parade it was back to normal. 'Left, right, left, right!' the sergeant was shouting, but as usual I was unable to hear any commands being called out. I was OK following the left, right bit; I just followed the leader. But when the order was changed to 'about-turn', that's when the boys were all on their knees again. However, this new sergeant was not so easy-going with me as my sergeant at Catterick Camp. He came marching over to me, accusing me of deliberately tripping all the soldiers up. That's when my secret was out. One of the boys said, 'He is deaf, Sergeant.'

'What the fucking hell is he doing in the Royal Signals, then?' he said. 'This is supposed to be the ears of the British army, and here we have a bloody deaf mute!'

I was then sent up to the CO to see what should become of me. As I faced the CO, he said that he had looked at my records and agreed that I was suffering with deafness, and that he was recommending a medical discharge; and furthermore I would not be allowed to use a rifle. I made my protest, saying how I enjoyed my army life, and that I would do all I could to complete my national service, so any chance I got to appeal against my discharge I would take.

There is no doubt about it the army found me a big problem. I was just a waste to them, not able to go into battle or even do my drills as they should be done, without tripping everyone up. I think the boys were disappointed, as they saw it all as a joke, and looked forward to having a laugh.

The camp gave me any job to get me out of the way, really. One of my jobs was in the cookhouse doing general duties. I was still under army discipline and had a weekly kit inspection, with our clothing laid out in a pile on our beds just as we did at Mayford Approved School. On the evening I would go into Chester around the city walls with my mates and chase the birds and do some courting, and believe me some of the birds that we were courting was out of this world!

My sister Joyce had contacted me in August to say that she was getting married at the end of September that year, and invited me to her wedding, so I arranged that I could have a 72-hour leave in order to attend her wedding. It was not until a week before my sister's wedding that my request was granted.

I arrived at Joyce's wedding to Allen, whom I had met through Joyce some eighteen months earlier. Allen was a nice bloke, well suited for Joyce. He was tall, slim and a model type of a chap. On the day, all the family was there for the wedding, including all of Allen's family. The only person who was missing was my father. He had been invited, but decided not to come. If he had come to the wedding, other members of the family would not come. At the beginning, Joyce had wanted her father to give her away. Instead, Uncle Fred from Eastbourne took that role. My relationship with my family was no different than what is was as a child, and Auntie Hilda did not speak two words to me throughout the whole time of the wedding. So I just drank myself silly to forget. Why I should have come to the wedding, apart from wishing my sister well for her future, and then get drunk for the first time in my life? Apart from sharing Allen and Joyce's wedding joy, I did not enjoy the other company, and was glad to return to my barracks in Chester. At least I had friends there and enjoyed myself. I had become a very popular soldier, and we were standing up for each other.

We had plenty of jankers, which meant that you were confined to barracks and forced to carry out jobs like cleaning out toilets, sweeping away leaves, and of course peeling potatoes. We got jankers for breaking even simple rules, and if I could talk my way out of doing certain jobs I would, even in the army, I was always out to make extra bees and honey. I would get sugar, milk, tea or anything else from the cookhouse that I could flog to the boys and made a little business out of it; but I never got caught. I would have got jankers if I did. In the cookhouse we had two local civilians working, neither of them liked the cockneys and there was a lot of cockneys in our camp. It is said that cockneys can mix with anyone wherever they go, whether they be from north, east or west of the country or even abroad: black, yellow, red or pink, the cockney could mix with them. But as far as the two civilians were concerned they could not mix, so they would do anything to annoy the cockneys, like make bad jokes about us, or take the piss at the way we talk. They did this on a daily basis, never missing a day, and very few of us would give them as much as they gave. It could have been because of their size, being well built, so a lot of the boys swallowed their pride and left it at that. Of course, I was carrying on with my jobs in the cookhouse having to work with them, and when they took the piss out of me, I would in turn in my cheeky way give them as much as they gave me – and sometimes more, which used to niggle them even more.

On this particular day, having finished cleaning up in the cookhouse and again being subject to more verbal insults shouted at me because I was a cockney, I was boiling up inside as much as the tank of hot water that was next to the gas ovens that was cooking the day's food. The two civilians had not stopped provoking me. I was just as usual giving them as much stick as they were giving me. They must have thought that they were on a losing wicket with me, so they decided to take the piss out of my hearing. Well, they overstepped the mark when they had called me a fucking useless, no good deaf cockney bastard. That did it. They'd hit a soft spot. I had already had it drummed and beaten into me that I was a useless, no good shit by Auntie Hilda and my father, and I was not taking it from two civilians who meant nothing to me, and who just hated everyone with a cockney tongue. I and the other soldiers had put up with this for weeks, and now it was time to put a stop to it once and for all.

I had put all my childhood behind me, as I wanted to forget all those bad memories, but now it all came rushing back to me. The insults, the beatings, my whole childhood came flooding back, and I could take no more. I'd had enough. I then went into a blind rage, not thinking about what I was doing, and with all the strength in my body, which was ten times more now, I picked them both up with each hand and pushed them into the boiling tank of water that was by the oven. I tipped them into it, with the pots of vegetables cooking in the boiling water, and these saved them from really serious injury. They were screaming out in pain, which attracted many soldiers to come rushing over to rescue them. It took several soldiers to hold me back from the civilians.

There had been many soldiers queuing up for their meals and they had seen how the civilians were provoking me. I am not a violent person, but in a split second I had exploded into this blind rage. Just the memory, just a flash repeat of my childhood, had taken me into this towering rage, and I lost control of myself. Afterwards, it frightened me to think that I had got myself into this state, and since then have never repeated it again. I knew that I had made a terrible mistake and was prepared to admit it. The two civilians were given no sympathy by any of the soldiers. As far as they were concerned they got what they truly deserved. But I had broken army rules and I was then arrested by our own military police and placed before the CO. I was charged with GBH (that's grievous bodily harm) then told that I would be court-martialled for the offence. I had a captain who would be my defending officer, and he agreed with me that I should plead guilty to the offence of grievous bodily harm; but I was told that my defending officer had a petition from most of the soldiers who had suffered themselves with insults from the two civilians, and from those who saw the two of them provoking and tormenting me and taking the mickey out of my hearing.

The trial was a short one. It took place in our camp, and due to the fact that I had been provoked and that I had received a signed petition I received fifty-six days in the glasshouse at Colchester. This was the army prison. I was very lucky, as I could have got at least three years with no remission, as there is no remission in the army law. Whatever you were sentenced to is what you served, and if you did not behave yourself while doing your sentence you risked having more time added.

In the glasshouse, just everything is done on the double, from 6 a.m. in the morning to 6 p.m. at night, and after that it is back to your billet, getting your kit ready for inspection. It is a place where you whitewash coal. I was there for the full fifty-six days – about eight weeks. The day that you leave you are in no doubt the smartest soldier in the British army, and just one little spot of dirt on your uniform means you don't leave, so it was in your interest to be spotless.

I was posted to go to another camp at Crowborough in East Sussex, well away from Chester and the two civilians. I was told later by a soldier who was at Chester that they never took the piss again out of the cockney troops, so they had learned their lesson. Crowborough was to be my last camp. It was much smaller than all the other camps that I had been to. The billets at this camp were well spread out, and this soon became my favourite camp. It had a homely atmosphere about it, and was surrounded by flower beds and gardens. Crowborough village was about two miles further down the road towards Tunbridge Wells, and the A22 to London or Eastbourne was two miles down the road in the other direction. Auntie Vi and Uncle Fred lived in Eastbourne with my two cousins, Ann and Richard, who were a little bit younger than me. It was a good half-hour's drive away. Eastbourne in those days was a very clean and smart seaside resort, with its open red paths. It was a place I considered a second home, full of cheerful people with an added friendliness about it. Crowborough camp was the camp where I would have my medical discharge from the army, something I was not looking forward to or very happy about. It had already been proved with a medical examination that I was deaf, and there was no one to take my hearing test this time, but the army medical team were amazed at how I had managed to pass my hearing test in the first place. They wondered if I had got deaf while in the army, but I could not give the game away by saying that my mate Bruce had taken my test.

At this camp I had plenty of time to myself, only being given jobs for the day that only took an hour to do, so in my plentiful spare time I had time to think. I had already accepted that I would be medically discharged, so my thoughts were for the future. What shall I do once back in civilian life? I knew that I would finish up on the markets again with Granddad Fred and Brian, but my mind was on other things as well – my sister, Violet, for a start. How could I help her? Then, I thought about my mother. I intended to carry on searching for her. She must be somewhere; and then there was my pearly suit that I had started to make. This got me thinking deeper. I knew that as for Violet I could help her more if I wore my pearly suit, just as I did when I was a boy, and by wearing it maybe I would jog the memory of someone who knew my grandfather and hopefully lead to finding my mother. All this was getting stronger in my thoughts about my pearly suit, so I kept telling myself to get involved in my pearly tradition, and take up my pearly entitlement that would form another chapter in my life.

As I was walking to my billet to get ready for a night out with my mates, I passed an officer and gave my usual salute, as you do, when he turned around and said, 'Is that you, George Major?'

'It could be,' I said. 'Do you owe me something?'

'Don't you remember me?' he said.

'Cor blimey, yes, I do remember you! You was the bloke I travelled with to Catterick when we first joined, and you had the bed next to mine, but was posted to be trained as an officer.'

'That's right,' he said, 'and you won a lot of money off me playing cards.'

'Ain't come to ask for your money back, have you, David?' I said.

'No, but I am so surprised to see you here,' he said.

'Well, I do get around,' I said.

'I am not here to give you any favours,' he said.

'I ain't asked you for any yet,' I said, 'but I will let you know when I do!'

That evening me and the boys went down to the pub in the village to find some birds and have some fun. We had our sing-song and drank well. Some of the boys – the usual ones – had one too many, as always, and on the way back to the camp they were still singing and shouting. That did not impress the local residents, who were always complaining about our drunken behaviour. I was on the safe side, as I did not drink much, and when I did it was to be sociable and enjoy the company of my mates; but you would never catch me in a pub drinking by myself under the table. I needed to be in control of myself. Perhaps living and sleeping with my drunken father may have put me off drinking like he did, and throwing it up again. I never wanted to live like that. When some of the villagers complained to us about the noise, my drunken mates would shout back, 'Piss off, you old cow!' – or something else more rude. They were still in their army clobber, which brought shame on most of the camp, but there that's boys enjoying themselves. I was given all sorts of jobs to do in the camp. The army gave me any job in order to forget that I was around.

One particular job that I was given was in the sergeants' mess, which had a games room, and it included a snooker and billiard table. My job was to paint the games room. It also gave me a chance to practise my snooker skills. After my practice I would re-cover the table in order to prevent any splashing of paint on the tables. There was no time limit to finish the painting, so I could really please myself; the army did not want me on drill, for fear of tripping everyone up. I was painting the ceiling with the white distemper when I spilt some of it on the billiard table. I tried everything to clean it up; my snooker practice depended on it! I dried as much as I could with a dry cloth, but it still left a stain.

There was only one thing for it. I already had some green paint that the woodwork had to be painted with, so I tried to match the snooker table colour using a bit of green and a bit of white paint. Very gently, I brushed over the stain on the table, hoping that it would not notice. The following day the sergeant barks out my name and comes within an inch of my face, shouting, 'Not only do you trip up the British army, you now also trip paint onto our best snooker table as well!'

Need I say that I was no longer at my job in the sergeants' games room...

I was then found an outside job – perhaps they thought I would be less trouble outside. The job was cutting the grass all around the camp with a motor lawnmower run by diesel. It was a real big bloody heavy thing, and you had to run the engine to move it. It was so noisy anyone could hear me coming. It was a job, and a job that appealed to me, as I was out in the fresh air and no one seemed to bother me. It was also a job that enabled me to earn myself a few bob. I got this idea in my head and I had to go for it. Right outside the camp were very large houses, some with gardens the size of football pitches and beyond, so I had some cheap leaflets made up to advertise my grass-cutting service, with the phone number of the local phone box just outside the camp for callers to ring. I set times so that my mate could answer it. On the leaflets it said, 'Crowborough Grass Cutting Service: for one month only we will cut your grass at half price.' I then waited for my first phone calls, after handing out my leaflets around the suitable houses. As the phone calls came in, I had my mate, Joe, take them and I was in business. I got my first six customers and was hired to cut their lawns. Armed with my lawnmower, in my denim top and trousers, I set out from the camp to start my little lawn-mowing business as the 'Crowborough Grass Cutting Service', and this was to be my little earner. After all, no one at the camp was missing me. From house to house I went with my lawnmower. I was doing so well at one point I thought of recruiting Granddad Fred and Brian on the little earner, but like all good things it came to a sudden end.

A complaint was made to the camp. It had stood out like a mile: on my lawnmower it said 'Ministry of Defence Property', and the user was in full army denims. How could you miss it? So I was put on CO report for the following morning. I had already learned from my market days that if you are flogging something dodgy, have all your answers ready;

the same could apply to my lawn-mowing service. I had learned the script the night before, when I was told that if I was on CO's orders anything was worth a try; so I already had intended to talk my way out of this one.

Next morning I was ready for the test, standing outside the CO's office. I was instructed to remove my army hat before being marched in front of the CO. 'Left, right, left, right…' Now, normally when you get to the CO's desk you are to keep on marching in a standing position until you are told to halt. In my case I had not heard the magic word 'halt', so I was still marching in a standing position until the sergeant, whose snooker table I had messed up, shouted in front of my face, 'Halt!' The CO was sitting at his desk, and my lieutenant friend, David, was standing next to him.

'Major,' the CO said, 'a complaint was made that you, in army time using army property, embarked out to local houses to cut their lawns. What have got to say about that?'

I then started telling the CO from the memory of my rehearsed script. 'As you are well aware, sir, and indeed everyone is aware, the inmates of our beloved camp have a very bad name in the local area as noisy, rude and a load of bloody hooligans. So, as a soldier who is proud of our camp, queen and country, I decided to try and change that very bad image. So I took it upon myself, wearing my denim uniform and army lawnmower clearly showing where I had come from, to change that image for the sake of the camp, thus showing the local neighbourhood how different we really are, and how we care for our neighbourhood, so helping to get a good reputation for our beloved camp, sir. That is my reason, and I ask you to take it into consideration in your decision.'

The CO had a quiet word with my lieutenant friend, David, who was smiling at my story all the time. 'You are dismissed, Major,' the CO said, 'but try and get an image in a different way than cutting lawns.'

I just could not believe that I had got away with this cock-and-bull story. The only other reason that I could think of was either they liked the way that I had put my story together, or felt sorry for me, knowing that it wouldn't be very long before I was discharged; or perhaps my lieutenant friend had put in a good word for me. But whatever the reason, I had got away with it, plus the money that I had made out of it.

I had got away with it and my outside earnings had now come to a halt. I had bought a motorcycle, which was a bike that had an engine on the back driving the rear wheel. It was at the time a very cheap and popular form of transport, so I used to pop down to Eastbourne quite a lot to see Auntie Vi and Uncle Fred and my two cousins. This I had been doing for the last few months at the camp. It gave me a chance to let them know that I was not the boy that Auntie Hilda had always painted me to be, and I slowly started to build a good relationship with them. I suppose it was my way of fighting back at Auntie Hilda. I hated the fact that I was always thought of as the bad one in the family and had set out to prove them wrong.

My army medical discharge papers came through. I know everything has an ending, but to me this was a sad one. I had been in the army about nineteen months, almost as long as I was at Mayford. I had met so many great lads, learning to live with others and working as a team. I had learned about army discipline, which did me good rather than harm. I had the opportunity to learn how others lived and coped with life, and most of all I'd had a bloody good laugh, which was worth all the £250 that I had got. Indeed, had I not been deaf, I daresay I might have made the army my career. But if that had happened, the Pearly King of Peckham may never have been! Life was set out for me, and all this training with others was part of my understanding about how life ticks.

My last night had arrived with my mates setting up a party affair in our billet. I was not in the mood to celebrate, as I was not looking forward to leaving, but I went along with the idea. We had made our own wine, all pitched together for beers. We put on music and sang out of tune to it. Most of us were getting drunk and pissed to the eyeballs, but to me deep down I was once again alone. The noise of the party was gradually slowing down, and one by one each of us lay on our bunks to sleep the drink off.

The following morning I got up in no hurry, but made the effort to get dressed. Unlike being at Mayford, I was in no hurry to leave. Putting on my civilian clothes, and the colourful waistcoat that I had first worn on leaving to go to Catterick, I took a final look around my billet. I left and went to the guardroom to sign myself out for the last time, with my army suit in my suitcase, to head back to Peckham and start another new life in another new suit; but this suit was to be as the Pearly King of Peckham.

Chapter Eleven

The road signs for Peckham were now in view as I made my journey home from my army experience. I was not happy at leaving the army after my medical discharge. I knew that I would be missing the fun that I had, but was happy to be coming home to Peckham and my market life after a twenty-month break. I was now nineteen years old and not many months away from my twentieth birthday. I was making my way to the Blue Café with my suitcases in hand, as I had no chance of leaving them at Granddad Fred's council flat. He would be out working, and I didn't have a key to his flat. So I had decided to take my cases to the Blue Café for Leon to take care of, until I could make proper arrangements for them. When I had arrived at the café, Leon and his wife gave me a good welcome, as if I was a long lost brother. After asking them if they could care for my suitcases for a while, I left to search for Granddad Fred and Brian, who were still working. Not knowing where they were, I decided to visit all the most obvious places that they would be likely to be working.

As I was walking around the most obvious places, I bumped into Paleface, the Old Bill, and asked him if he had nicked Granddad Fred or Brian today, trying to enquire about their whereabouts. 'No not yet,' Paleface said, 'but I am sure I will have the pleasure of seeing them at some point today.' Then he started to make enquires about myself. 'I've not seen you around in a long time, Major. Where have you been – prison?'

'No, I have been on a long course.'

'Really?' he said. 'What kind of course?'

Jokingly, I replied, 'On a course learning how to avoid the Old Bill.'

He then looked at me and shook his head, and his pale face turned even whiter than it usually was. He can't have been at all surprised by my response, because he knew that I was always trying to be one step ahead of him, and only told him what I thought he needed to know, to my advantage.

Then a few minutes later someone tapped me on the shoulder, and a voice that I recognised as Brian's said, 'George, you are back!'

Before I said anything more I told him, 'Old Bill is doing his rounds.'

Brian said that he knew of his whereabouts as he had been watching and seen me talking to him.

'Where is Granddad?' I asked.

'He is back there, George,' said Brian, pointing to a side road off Rye Lane. He started to lead the way to Granddad Fred, and I followed to where he was waiting with his barrow for the all-clear, from Brian.

'Wotcher, George,' said Granddad Fred. 'Nice to see you back, my old b—! It feels like old times already!' He already knew of my medical army discharge and had been expecting my return soon.

'So how is business then, Granddad?' I asked.

'Very much the same – not at all looking very good; but now that you are back, George, it may change, with your luck.'

'First, Granddad, is there any chance of my old bedroom back at your flat? I have nowhere to stay.'

Without any hesitation he answered, 'Of course you can. You know that you are always welcome at my place… Anyway, George, hang about while I just finish flogging the last of my tomatoes. I have only the last two boxes left, then we can get on our way to the café for a welcome-home drink.'

'How much are you expecting for all the remaining tomatoes?' I asked.

Working out the sums in his head out aloud, he said, 'About a quid's worth, and an hour's work.'

'I tell you what I will do, Granddad. Let's call this your birthday, and I will give you the full twenty shillings for them.'

We then called out to Brian, who had been looking out for Old Bill, and told him he had been made redundant, as I had bought the tomatoes from Granddad.

'What do you want a quid's worth of tomatoes for?' he asked,

'You will find out, Brian.'

I picked up the barrow to wheel it to the Blue Café. When we got there, I asked Brian to bring the boxes of tomatoes into the café. Leon was already behind the counter, working.

I approached him and asked if he would like the bargain of a lifetime. 'What have you got then?' he asked. 'I have the best Jersey home-grown tomatoes, priced at three quid, and as a coming home gift you can have the lot for two quid.'

'Great, I'll take the lot for two quid – I'll take them, so you have got yourself a deal, George.'

'No, Leon, it is you who has a deal. It breaks my heart to flog the tomatoes at such a silly price to you!'

I then asked Brian to take the tomatoes into the kitchen for Leon. I then turned to Leon and said, 'As I have given you such a good deal with the tomatoes, how about you throwing in three rosy leas, as a bonus from you, Leon?'

'Sure George, three rosy leas coming up, and I will throw in a meal for you as well.'

Straight away, Brian asked, 'What about me and Granddad?'

Leon said, 'You're not the one who made me the blinding deal with the tomatoes – it was my mate, George.'

We made our way to our table, where Granddad Fred was seated to drink our rosy leas. As we sat there waiting for our meals, Granddad Fred said, 'Well, George, I see that you haven't lost your touch and the patter while you have been away. The way you flogged them tomatoes to Leon, and managed to get the bonus teas and food on top, was fantastic!'

'Nah,' I must be losing my touch,' I said.

Granddad looked at me with a puzzled expression on his face as he asked, 'What do you mean, George?'

'Well, Granddad, I must have lost my touch for a start, because I was mad enough to give you a quid for them rotten tomatoes!' We all had a good laugh about it as we reminisced about our old market tricks.

We were coming to the end of 1958. The fifties have always been known as the golden years. We had almost full employment in the country, and low crime, with very few divorces. I remember that it was a time when we could name all our neighbours around us, and shared our friendship amongst each other, and with the help of the national service boys were made into men – including me – and they were taught the meaning and importance of self-respect. Class divisions were still with us, between the rich and poor, but economic depression was becoming a thing of the past from the war years. We were doing quite well for ourselves. The National Health Service was in good shape, with everyone being treated fairly, but many children were still suffering ill-treatment at home and in children's homes, with no one showing an interest from the outside. So many children were suffering like I had, and young teenage girls who were born during the war were having illegitimate babies or resorting to back-street abortions, as it was still a disgrace to be a single mother. Yes, the country was doing well in many things, but not doing so well for those children suffering in silence. Many fathers had been either killed or gone missing in the war years, which led to the break-up of many families. I thought that. I had to get on my soap box and put that bit in, to let you know how we saw things in them days, and how lucky we were living in a two-bedroom council flat in Peckham at the time.

So here we were again, living in a two-bedroom council flat owned by Granddad Fred, with Brian and myself sharing it with him. We were back just like the old days, working as street traders and trying to earn an honest day's living. I'd had plenty of time to think of my future while I was away, but still kept my past childhood behind me. I had already given up all hope of ever meeting Rosy Lea again. I was now an independent young teenager, doing my own thing. Although it would be nice to see her again, I no longer had that desire to be mothered and cared for like before. When I was younger I needed her and wanted her to replace my evil Auntie Hilda. I was still determined to find my mother. I knew one possible way of finding her would be to wear my pearly suit and hope that while wearing it, it may jog someone's memories.

Someone might know my grandfather, or of his whereabouts. If I was able to find him, then it could lead me to my mother. After all, Fred Tinsley, the Pearly King of Blackfriars, knew of my grandfather, but had not seen him for some time now. Both Auntie Iris and Fred Tinsley said that I looked like him, so there was a chance that if someone saw me in my pearly suit, it would remind them of my grandfather in his pearly suit. So with this knowledge, and the encouragement from Auntie Iris, Granddad Fred and Brian and also Fred Tinsley, it was time to complete my pearly suit and wear it at last. My decision had been made to take my rightful place among the pearly kings and queens, and in doing this I could help Violet and her hospital, and even pass that help further to other people who needed assistance. But first I had to finish my pearly suit in order to accomplish my aim, with people who wanted me to take my rightful place. So I was fully committed now, and no turning back.

Auntie Iris had already taught me how to sew on the buttons, and Fred Tinsley was supplying me with the strong cotton, given to him by other members of the Pearly Guild, an organisation of pearly kings and queens, to which he was secretary. With my unbreakable cotton, I set out to continue my button sewing. I started by putting the cotton that I had threaded into the needle between my thumb and a lump of beeswax, and pulled the cotton between the two. The wax would make the cotton easier to pull through the thick cloth of my suit. That wax would also give extra strength to the cotton. The pattern of the suit is decided by the king. No pearly king has the same pattern as another king. My design was based on my life. I sewed a straight line of buttons across my suit, about two inches apart, which represented my life. Then in between the line of buttons I sewed a pyramid, one after the other, about one and a half inches apart, which represented life's up and downs, which I'd had more than my fair share of. Then, in between the pyramids, I sewed a circle of buttons that represented a neighbour or friend. The neighbour was Auntie Iris and the friend was Peter, who I met at Mayford. Then you finish up all over the suit with straight lines. The line of life, then the pyramid, for life's ups and downs and then the circles of buttons. When you are low or down, your neighbour or friend will lift your spirits again. That is the pattern and meaning of my personal pearly suit. To me it was a picture of my past life. Every button that I ever sewed onto my suit was sewn with love, and every button that I sewed was threaded through the buttonholes six times each. There are thousands sewn on, all with love. There is almost a mile of cotton stitched on my suit and it weighs almost ½ cwt. In total it would have taken me one year to make my full pearly suit. The number of times that I pricked my fingers with a needle was countless.

A pearly suit is no personal comfort to the wearer. After wearing the hat for a while you have a headache. The jacket gives you backache; the weight of the trousers makes your hips ache. In the hot weather you would sweat like a pig, because the pearl buttons push out more heat. In the winter you really feel the cold because the pearl buttons would get as cold as ice. Even in a large meeting hall, summer or winter the buttons attract the heat, and when you are moving about, the sweat from your body becomes a shower. At the end of your pearly job you can take off your shirt and wring out the sweat into a bucket and collect a quarter of a pint of water. But for all that, if you enjoy it, the aches and pain become the least of your worries. When you are busy sewing, it gives you time to think, and my thoughts had travelled back to Auntie Iris, when I was a boy and she made my first pearly suit. It was so small that when dressed in it I looked like a smart little prince. As I got older and bigger I took the buttons off it and sewed them onto my pearly king waistcoat, which has stayed with me throughout the years, securely sewn onto my new pearly king suit. Auntie Iris always told me that being a pearly was God's will. She always gave me good words of encouragement, which I began to take even more seriously now that I had reached this stage of my life. With all the signs that I was having, and all the encouragement, I knew she was right. Being close to the pearly kings and queens made me feel close to my grandfather and mother. Fred Tinsley had already introduced me to other pearly kings and queens. My grandfather's name was William but he was called 'Willy' for short. He was a well-known and respected gentleman within the community. Concern was growing for him, as no one had seen or heard from him for a while, which was quite unusual. Fred Tinsley and Granddad Fred had arranged for my coronation, which was due to take place in the local pub on the Old Kent Road called The World Turned Upside Down. I felt the name of the pub was so significant to my life as a young boy.

My pearly suit was now complete, and I was ready to begin my reign as the Pearly King of Peckham. The final hour was upon me before I was to leave Granddad Fred's flat for my coronation. Bruce, my mate, had agreed to pay for the food and most of the drinks. They all wanted the night to be a night to remember. I told Granddad Fred and Brian that I was going into the bedroom to get changed. I just wanted a little time on my own to gather my thoughts before getting dressed for the occasion. After all, there was no need to rush, as I had many years ahead of me to serve as a pearly king. Unknown to me at the time, I was to meet with many members of the royal family. I also had the pleasure of dining with the Queen and the Duke of Edinburgh. I have attended meetings with cabinet ministers and their wives, also future prime ministers. I have also met and rubbed shoulders with film stars, actors and actresses, famous singers and top criminals. The most memorable group of people that I met was the poverty stricken and down-and-outs, as I was able to associate them with my own past life as a pearly prince, when I used to help my sister and the hospital. I had memories of having to sneak out of the family home in Boswell Road, with my hidden treasured 'whistle and flute'. On every occasion that I did this, I recall the fear of being caught that filled me from head to toe. I knew the consequences I faced should I get caught, but from that young age I had that burning desire to help others, regardless.

Because my father and Auntie Hilda were so critical of me as a child and the teachers at school left me entirely negative about myself I often felt like I had no worthwhile future and was left feeling utterly empty. However, after a while I developed the urge to teach myself to keep this misery at bay by doing more for others in my pearly whistle and flute. This gave me an outlet for my frustration and led me to my first steps upwards through the black clouds to reach the other side.

I am no longer afraid, because I am a man who can make my own decisions. So no one can stop me now. There is no Auntie Hilda or father to punish or intimidate me. They were the ones who needed help. I would have been happy to try and help them, in spite of the way they treated me. I was so lost in my train of thoughts that I did not hear Granddad Fred and Brian banging on the door. 'Come on, George, it's time to get going, or we will be late!'

I started to get dressed, first putting on my trousers. I had to wear strong braces, and a belt, to cope with the weight of them. If I didn't there was no doubt that they would fall to my ankles. Then came my waistcoat, the symbol of my pearly prince suit all those years ago, which would remind me of the importance of helping others. Then my kinsman scarf, a symbol of the costermonger. Then the jacket, with my full title displayed on the back: 'The Pearly King of Peckham'. And finally my cap. Your pearly outfit is not complete without the cap. As I placed the cap on my head I could feel the power of my cheeky market days spilling out of me. That cheeky chappie was about to start his reign and collect millions of pounds for charity.

Granddad Fred and Brian were still hurrying me along. I slowly opened the bedroom door and stood before them. For the very first time that I could recall they were totally speechless. They looked me up and down then broke their silence with a wolf whistle followed by, 'Cor blimey, George, what a blinder!'

Brian then said, 'You look and sound like a totally different person! You went into the room as George, and came out as the Pearly King of Peckham.'

We left the flat to join Bruce, who had been waiting for us at the main entrance to the flat in his jam jar. At last we were on our way, to my long-awaited coronation celebration, and I was to begin my new life and reign as the Pearly King of Peckham.

Chapter Twelve

Right, my old china plates (mates). With my coronation behind me and the box of toys (noise) still ringing in my ears from The World Turned Upside Down, I've and had a chance to sober up and now is the time to rabbit n pork (talk) about the pearly kings' and queens' history. So I am going to tell you it from the horse's mouth. So let me take you on a journey through them pearly gates into that history. Fasten your seatbelts while the journey takes you to the first stop where that history began, which was the foundation of the pearlies and where we sprang from which was the costermonger, who many of you would know as the barrow boy. The costermongers name came from the fact that they were mongers (traders) who hawked custard apples. It was one of the first varieties of fruit sold by the street traders who later branched out to flogging a wide range of vegetables, china, clothing, jewellery and so on. The name costermonger goes back to the mid-fifteen hundreds – clocking on a bit, aren't I? Almost every main street in London had a market place in them days that was jammed-packed with market barrows and stalls on both sides of the frog and toad [road]. Within these markets you could buy almost anything from fruit and vegetables to livestock in cages. Food was the main selling item: fruit, veg, meat, fish, pies, to name just a few. The costermonger's customers were mainly the working class, the sick and the poor. It was the only place where the poor could buy in small quantities, like half or even a quarter of a cabbage or cucumber according to their budget and requirements. The costermonger was seen as the only ones who cared and catered to their working-class needs. They were also seen to take their time to be helpful and friendly and get to know their customers. Shop owners could not give the poor working class cheap food or the friendliness that the costermonger had. The working class had a lot in common with the coster: they were both poor as the coster came from similar families as themselves and knew the hardships the customers were going through. Coupled with that they spoke with the same cockney tongue. Most of the coster's life was living on the street markets with the huge jostling crowds of people spilling over pavements into the road buying their food as the coster shouted his cries to attract the attention of the poor working class. These people would find that even if they wanted to shop in their local shop they would be made to feel unwelcome. In some cases many shops would refuse to serve them. The shopkeepers were not interested in attracting the lower-class shopper simply because they knew that they would be more concerned about watching the pennies and paying close attention to the prices and that would mean they could not juggle their prices like they could with the better-off customer where bees and honey was the least of their worries so they were happy to spend without questioning the prices. The shopkeepers liked this because they were able to line their pockets by making up the prices as they went along. So the shopkeepers would do their upmost to tailor to the upper-class needs at the expense of the poor and needy. The poorer class was discouraged to shop at the local food shop in order to please the better-off customers.

The working class had to rely on the costermonger in order to survive. It was the poorer districts where the costermonger did his busiest trade. Once the Old Kent Road was lined with stall after stall of costers at work on both sides of the road, serving the poor, including the side roads. This was what it was like in all poor areas of London. Right back from the early 1800s the costermongers were mostly hereditary groups of cockneys. That is why it is essential to study the history of the costermonger from where our pearly history sprang from. The markets attracted all types of people from pick-pockets, beggars and buskers to the homeless and even prostitutes, all in search of food or raising cash to survive. It was a breeding ground of hardship and poverty. The homeless children in torn, old, dirty clothes without shoes on their feet would add to this picture of a market life: everyone trying to survive amidst the poverty surrounding them. Also notable was the child labour being exploited by the chimney sweeps, with some children being sent up the chimney by the sweep to clean them and some not returning, or else returning with torn limbs. Most were homeless so their disappearance or injury would go unnoticed. Some of the homeless children had been left as babies at the doors of hospitals, churches, orphanages or workhouses with a note attached to their clothing, which would state their date of birth, name, religion and if they were baptised. This was common in them days when the mother and father could not afford any more than one child to feed and clothe. There was no birth control then, so from the eyes of the costermonger he saw the poverty more than anyone because it was happening around him in the market street. The poor would confide in him, which made him like a welfare officer amongst the working class as well as their listening friend, and with his own personal experience on the steps of poverty what better listener could you get?

In the 1800s working people dressed according to their jobs and you could tell what line of work a person was in just by their outfit. The costermongers created a dress code of their own which they were proud to wear. Let's start with the coster trousers, which were usually made of dark cable cord that was tightly fitted at the knees and cut wide at the ankles where they almost covered the boots and were cut like sailor's trousers ready for sea. The boots of the coster were vital to his profession and his self-respect: that's how you could identify the real costermonger – by his boots. It did not matter how desperate his means were, his boots were the very last thing to be pawned. His boots would protect him from all weathers that they had to work in, together with their long hours at work.

Moving up from the trousers we have his waistcoat, which was his pride and joy. It was made out of corduroy that was buttoned up close to his throat with festooned sleeves. The waistcoat had four long, flapped pockets, which was a good body warmer especially in the winter. Then comes the jacket which is a full three-quarter-length jacket that would also be buttoned up to the throat like the waistcoat with each side of the jacket having three flapped pockets that were very deep and made out of heavy material.

Now we come to the cap. In them days everyone wore a hat, so the coster was no exception. The cap was of a dark colour normally, which would stand out above the cheerfulness of his boat race (face). Then finally – the costermonger's pride and joy – his brightly coloured kinsman in different patterns and colours that he wore around his neck which he had wrapped loosely with the buds dangling over his coat. In the hot days he often used it to wipe up the sweat from his boat race. If you wanted to further your knowledge of the costermonger, try reading Henry Mayhew's book called *London Labour and the London Poor*. This would give you a better insight into the costermonger than I could.

The costermonger who sold fish would wear a very large apron of blue serge, which would be tucked up around his waist. This was still being used in some fish shops in the forties. So, as an individual the costermonger had to be distinguished from others in his dress and appearance.

Now let's turn to our good-looking coster ladies who wore a heavy cotton dress with a shawl over their shoulders. The dress would hang down to their ankles and like the coster men cover the boots. On their legs they would wear white stockings. They also wore a kinsman loosely around their necks. It was known that a coster would declare his love by giving his woman a kinsman (I used to give a lot away myself). Costers were very fussy about the dress of their woman and always expected their woman to be clean and smartly turned out. In them days it was always a girl's wish to marry a costermonger; maybe it was because of their personality and their cheeky patter, which was an all-important part of their trade and survival. It was also a vital part of the future making of a good pearly, as you will find out.

The costermonger lived by three main principles, which were: honour, respect and loyalty, which are very much missing today. The honour was to themselves and others: you only needed their word, which would be as good as a signed piece of paper. Respect would be to each other and others (apart from the Old Bill). Loyalty was to each other: if you picked on one of them fellow costers, you would pick on them all. They stood like concrete piers; they were united together and stood and fought strong together. They had pride; pride of their trade, pride for their coster tradition and they had pride in themselves. They were the most colourful character who knew how to put on the charm with their patter and gift of the gab that could capture and soften your heart and most of all they, and only they, had the art of flogging: they really could flog freezers to the Eskimos. It leaves no doubt that it was this patter that made them some of the finest charity workers. They could charm for the gold where the layman could only get the silver. We are now looking at a breed of people who were always ready to help the poor, sick and needy. They were kind, friendly and considerate to those in need. Their loyalty expanded throughout the markets. As costermongers they believed that they had the right to offer goods on the streets in order to feed the poor for far less than the shops. The shopkeepers were just robbers to the poor as far as the costermonger was concerned. The costermonger was noisy and assertive as he needed to be in order to make a living in a very competitive environment where you had to be able to make your voice heard. Some even used a drum, beating it to drum up the business and to attract attention to themselves. He had to use his personality as well in attracting the buyers; they were in their own right show people who were also chancers and gamblers which was against the law in them days, but it was a brief emotional outlet for some of them to gamble. No one better than the costermonger knew how to give so that the receiver would not be humiliated; in fact no one understood better in them days than they did in the name of charity and the right way to do it. This was to become the powerhouse for the pearlies. It was known that the costermonger was the salt of the earth and that rubbed off for the pearlies for years to come. That came from the concern for their customers, the poor, with a devoted attitude for them: everyone loved the costers.

The costermonger did have problems, and one of them was to have the right to flog freely on the streets without the Old Bill continually moving them on and the council authority trying to clear the streets, backed by the rule of the law. To add to that they had the bullies who tried to force the weaker coster from their pitches to seize the pitches themselves. This led to fights and more trouble from the authorities. The coster could not make the laws but they needed help to protect themselves somehow and that is when they decided to find a leader for his physical strength and as someone to speak for them. A man was picked amongst dozens of costermongers in the street market to be their leader and guide. It was in about 1852 that the first such leader was picked, thought to be Samuel King, who took it upon himself to let it be seen that he was the leader by lining the seams of his trousers and jacket with smoked pearl buttons to include his waistcoat and hat and called himself the Coster King, using both the name of his trade and his surname. This title took off all around, with a leader being picked in other markets, and them leaders also sewing on the smoked pearl buttons on the seams of their whistle and flute. This was the start of the coster kings all around the London markets, and so was born the cockney dress. Cockneys were fascinated by the glamour of titles and regalia, so why not have their own cockney dress? The costermonger was known to adore royalty – now they had their own breed of royalty and cockney titles. Samuel King had started a royal craze that was spreading to the four corners of London, a further advance to helping the poor and sick. Perhaps Samuel King had in mind what had made King Henry VIII of England popular himself at archery, by rewarding the strongest bowman of his bodyguards with honourable titles like the Earl of Hoxton, the Duke of Whitechapel and the Count of Stepney and so on. But remember, this was only purely honourable of course. The cockney loved it.

Samuel King already knew of the love that the poor and sick had for the costers, so adding a title would be good for morale which met with large approval from up to 30,000 men and women costers, with ninety per cent unable to read or write. In order to defend their rights it was quite obvious that leadership was in need. Now the costermongers had their leaders to fight and talk for their rights and in doing so strengthened the cause for the poor, sick and needy. The coster kings were all surrounded by tearful stories in their hard-working poverty-stricken life and now had started something that was to change the history of the cockneys, with the coster kings' royal standing. His wife as his queen and his children as their prince and princesses made a full cockney royal family, which gave us the working man's monarchy which was to become hereditary. Within a short time the music hall stars had started to copy the coster king's code of dress by doing their whistle and flute with smoked pearl buttons and the seams leading to many famous music halls stars such as Albert Chevalier, a coster singer and actor. Kate Carney, the music hall singer, copied the dress of Mary Robinson who was the most famous coster queen. The list went on, all following the cockney traditional dress.

In 1860 the coster kings formed the first meeting in order to voice their anger and resentment against the authorities and Old Bill who they felt were more than restricting their means of a livelihood and chance of feeding the poor, sick and needy, so they formed the costermongers' union whose object was to protect the interest of the members and defend them from any unjust attacks. The committee of the costermongers' union, having been satisfied that a case was a legitimate one, would do all that was possible to get those acts of parliament amended which were antagonistic and palpably unfair to those who have to earn their livelihood in the market street. These were just two main objections from a list of objections that they had for all their members. They had met together in secret to form the costermongers' union and set out a constitution that covered all market traders and their families and the costers who pushed their barrows for miles to serve the poor. It also covered the costers who had no street licence who also needed a change in law to protect their livelihood.

So with the coster kings as their leaders they now felt more protected and safer with their elected coster kings who continued to cry their wares from the unlicensed pitches while the local authorities and police continued to try to dislodge them. Local authorities were obliged to keep roads open to traffic, which was mostly the horse-drawn carriages. It was also law that crowds were not to gather and obstruct the highway and that there must not be any affray, but it is obvious that the costermonger would have a crowd built up around his barrow. That's the only way he could flog his goods. Local authorities seemed to hate giving a licence to the costers to trade, maybe to protect the shopkeeper who always complained about them, or maybe because it encouraged crowds; but what completed a market was the crowds – the bigger the crowd the better the market, and the more fun to walk through. Everyone has been to a market, rich or poor, and not one of them has felt lonely walking with the crowds. A sense of belonging lies with you, with someone ready to chat with you even if it's to throw religion at you.

So now the coster king had control of his market pitch, deciding who should come or go onto his market street to work, and only the best and the fittest survived. Just a succession of wet days could literally mean ruin to many costers. That's why the coster king looked for only the best of the charmers in order to produce the best market street. The word 'king' was catching on in the London markets. We were now hearing of 'corn king, jellied eels king, china king, shirt king, ice-cream king and so on, and like many costers they would push their barrows, so keeping on the move while they were serving under the eyes of the Old Bill, for if they stood still to serve they would be nicked. Some of the costers would travel for miles with their barrows around the London slums, just to serve the London poor at their door. I often wonder if that's why I have had two hip replacements, by pushing my old barrows, as it would take four people to lift a barrow empty, and that's before you put your goods into it. The coster's working hours were long and tiring, from 4 a.m. in the morning to buy his stock then working until nine or even eleven o'clock at night. It was most certainly a very hard life in all weathers and conditions but his patter and charm were still flowing from him till late at night until he had sold out, without a complaint about his long day. The costermonger never made a fortune as the profits were very small after having to pay for the hire of their barrows, and to hire a barrow was as expensive as having to hire a car in today's value. A good coster would give you free entertainment as he flogged to you with added charm, cheek and patter. He could guarantee to bring a smile to your face even on a wet, miserable day. The coster had a strong desire to excite admiration from the poor people with their flogging style and with their cries the coster would attract that attention in order to prove that only they could flog ice to the Eskimos. The coster without doubt had solidarity with each other and stood shoulder-high. We had the coster king who fought for his fellow coster who worked in his market for the poor and cared for the sick who fed the hungry. Just no one cared for them as much as the coster; who else could have cared for them but the costers? Many who were caught trading without a licence were arrested and brought before the courts and imprisoned for the offence of loitering but it was the only honest way of earning a living for many of them and when they were nicked and imprisoned their families were left without a breadwinner. For many it led to some of their daughters or wives turning to prostitution on the streets in order that their families did not go without. This caused more hatred and street fights between costers and the local authorities and resentment against the Old Bill, whom costers regarded as public enemy number one. I know the feeling from my own market days. They saw the authorities and Old Bill as robbing the poor to feed the rich shopkeeper, but little did the shopkeeper know that it was always the markets that brought the crowds with the shopkeeper receiving the benefits. Let me prove a point.

The local shopkeepers complained about the market in Leather Lane, putting pressure on the local authorities to have the market removed because it was taking their trade and the noise was deafening. The shopkeepers also pointed out that they paid their rates whereas the costers did not, After complaining again about the market, the shopkeeper won and the costers and the market were removed from Leather Lane in Holborn. But it cost the shopkeeper dearly, for when the market was removed, Leather Lane became deserted. No longer the vast crowds spilling into the roads, but a ghost town, as the people took their custom to other surrounding markets. The shopkeeper then had to start a full campaign to get the market reinstated. I say don't bite off the hand that feeds you. What better proof do you need? If I had my way and was a councillor in my local authority I would most certainly encourage a street market in a parade of shops and bring a bit of market life and fun into the shopping parade, knowing full well that it would benefit not only the local authority, but would bring in a spirit of local welfare that brings people together and provides a chance to get to know your neighbour, which can make people more aware of those in need. Even the local churches would come along trying to flog religion to the crowds, and find someone who is prepared to mend their ways. There was no National Health Service or handouts to come to your rescue in them days so this is what gave the coster king the power to help the poor and sick. It would be him that could bridge the gap if you were lucky enough amongst the thousands who needed help. The coster kings were good organisers who would organise ways of raising funds for the poor and sick. It may be a barrow race or pigeon – racing, a known favourite sport of the costers. The costers would get up and do a turn with cockney songs or jokes in the local music-hall shows and collect in their collecting tins with all the bees and honey raised going into a central pot held by the coster kings which would be used to help pay for medical treatment of the sick customers. The coster king would get involved in a big leading part with hospital fundraising events or a carnival or just collecting, rattling their charity tins which was the start of the League of Friends at London hospitals which caught on from the hard work of the costers. It was the costers' art of flogging, coupled with their charm and cheek that was transferred into the flair of raising funds for charity.

More than anyone they most certainly had the gift for it, so the pearly king of today quite rightly must see the advantage and headstart that was open to them. Without the coster king and their members a pearly could not have got off the ground. It is the traditional costers' harvest festival that is the symbol of that thanks, so what little the government did for the poor, sick and needy. The coster kings bridged part of that gap, for the government seemed to think that the poor had only themselves to blame. Perhaps that's why the government and local authorities feared street crowds, in case it would cause an affray or protest against authorities. Month by month the coster king was becoming more respected and looked on as a poor man's real royalty and hero, but as tough as the coster king and costers were, their heart was made of gold. They had the softness under their skin in their fight for the poor, sick and needy, just none of them doing it for the glory or a pat on the back. They did it for all their fellow human beings, those genuine breed of men who gave so much for so little to others, their leadership of each market proving to be a great success story. The authorities now realised that the costers were doing much for the local authorities and feeding the poor and helping the sick. After all, who else could feed the poor? The coster kings knew that they were indispensable. After all, the government did little for the poor, nor did the shopkeeper who kept their profit to line their own pockets and the pockets of local government. From all this struggling at the bottom of the barrel and poverty of the costers, some managed to climb out of the barrel and become very successful, like Lord Cohen, the man who started Tesco's, then Marks & Spencer who started the penny stall in the market place and many more.

The coster king also made many friends of well-known people; one of them was the Earl of Shaftesbury. He certainly loved the costers and their coster kings and they liked and trusted him. This would have been a real honour for the Earl of Shaftesbury as the costers never trusted anyone high up. It is believed that the Earl of Shaftesbury first came across a coster king with his line of smoked pearl buttons on the seams of his whistle while passing in the street. A coster king had dropped a sack that he was carrying over his shoulder by accident. As the sack landed at the feet of the Earl, a dead two-month-old baby was exposed before him; the coster king was taking his dead child to a pauper's burial ground. The Earl asked how the baby had died and why was he not having a proper funeral. The coster king explained that the baby had died of pneumonia and that he could not afford a proper funeral, because the rent he paid for the barrow took most of his profit earned in a week. The Earl, who was known to be a caring man was quite upset by what he had heard, and decided to have a special coster's barrow made with his crest painted on the sides of the barrow which he loaned out free of charge to some of the poorer costers. The Earl, being concerned for the welfare of the costers, wanted to help them. Word got around about his good deeds and what the Earl had done amongst the costers who now sought his help in dealing with their struggle with the authorities and Old Bill. It was in 1874 that the Earl managed to almost stop the fighting between the Old Bill and the costers. He had promised the coster kings and their union that he would campaign for better conditions and street license for them, providing they stopped the fighting with Old Bill. He had proved his words as a friend of the costers and the poor. The Earl of Shaftesbury fought for his bill in the House of Lords and amongst his friends on the costermongers' behalf; he was also responsible for the costermongers' mission on 8 October 1885, the month of the costers' harvest festival.

The funeral of the Earl of Shaftesbury took place at Westminster Abbey. The costermongers had lost a good friend in the Earl of Shaftesbury. Out of respect the coster kings arranged a collection just to purchase a donkey, which is their trademark, and gave it to the Earl's estate as a gift of friendship from the London coster. The donkey lived its life out on the Shaftesbury Estate. Today the Lord Shaftesbury charity is still in existence helping the poor.

The costers were set in their ways and had their own rules and way of life. Most of them had their own donkey, which would be bedded down in their own back courtyard of their two-up-and-two-down terraced houses. They would mostly take their donkey through the house to the back. Their love for their donkeys was part of their everyday life and they cared for them more than themselves. The donkey would be used to pull the decorated barrow that had a floral design and colours on the side panels. The donkey's harness and bridle would be polished to a very high standard. After all, it was their trademark.

The costers not only looked after their donkeys but also each other. Should one of them fall ill others would take it in turns to care for him and would club together to give food to his family. While on hard times it was a life of looking out for each other, which is lacking today. Then, there were many of them who just learned to pick themselves up and start all over again when trade had been bad. Charles Dickens wrote a lot about the costers in 1812 to 1870, which showed how poor the costers were and how they were part of London's everyday scene. When Dickens travelled around the London streets in search of stories he got to know and understand the costers, and from his childhood he understood the feelings of the costers and wrote plays based on their background. He of all people knew they provided an essential service to the London poor – we owe a great deal to our ancestral costermonger for their fight was long and hard.

One of the busiest times of the week was a Saturday night for the costermonger. The reason was that people were paid their wages on the Saturday so it was known as the costers' night of the week, when their lamplights would light up the dull sky till twelve at night. The poor came to buy the weekend shopping; no one ever brought their weekly shopping, as they never had a fridge or freezer to preserve their food.

Another famous writer was Henry Mayhew who wrote extensively about the costers in the 1850s. He above all knew more than any writer about the costers and understood their way of life. He described the costers and how they coped in their poverty. He spent many years learning about this breed and its royalty. The rich and the poor was widening, the poor were growing as London was getting more crowded and the need of the costermonger was becoming greater. In turn their charity was becoming more demanding; the coster kings were using more of their spare time collecting for the growing poor and sick. They were forever looking for new ways to raise funds for the sick with the hospitals seeing the coster kings more and more as the friends of the sick. But for all the bees and honey that was being raised by the costers for those in need, not a penny was banked as the costermonger distrusted the banks and only saw them as the evil of the working class that were only there to misuse your cash. So all the bees and honey raised was either hidden or passed straight to the hospital in cash. Unemployment was now adding to the poverty of the streets of London with the intake of this fast-growing population, with people dying from poverty and disease as there was no sanitation or proper running water. Life was just intolerable and hard for them all, so the fittest would survive and the weakest died. In 1851 Mayhew gave a figure of 30,000 costers, which included women and children who worked on the market streets. However, he said it was most likely double that as costers would avoid the censors for their distrust in authority and most of them were unable to read or write but could add up well.

On a Sunday in a typical overcrowded two-up-and-two-down terrace house living accommodations that the costers lived in, a Sunday dinner would have been the real main hot meal of the week, unless the costermonger were unable to afford this main meal of the week due to poor earnings. He would ask the whole family to clatter their knives and forks on the empty plates so that neighbours would think that they were eating their Sunday dinner, and not starving which proved just how much personal pride the costers had. Yet they still went out to raise bees and honey for the poor and sick. The costers spent very little time at home due to their long working hours so most of their working life was spent on the streets. Even their fights and quarrels were on the streets, so really the streets were their home, and winter was their worst nightmare with the air polluted with smog, caused by the smoke from burning chimneys and oil lamps and industrial smoke being a high risk to their health. Their respect, honour and loyalty still lived on amongst them; there were no stories of 'look after my stall' or jumping into each others' beds or the battles between families that you see in *EastEnders*: that is just fantasy. The cockneys are not like that at all; they are a race unto themselves who are happy-go-lucky and would stand with you, give you their last if you needed it, all with a sense of humour. I see the soap *EastEnders* as the final insult to the real cockney. It provides a very bad public relations for the real East Enders. I know that you have got to have a good story line but it should not be at the expense of the cockneys.

Now I have got that off my chest let's move on. So the costermongers' life was hard with some landing up in prison for trading on the streets without a license. Many could not pay for their fines and at the end of the day all they were doing was earning a living for themselves and helping the poor. Some would pawn whatever they had (which was little) due to failed business. Their final act was to be forced to appeal to the unions for charity. It would have been so easy for him to ask another coster for help as they would have willingly passed round the basin to collect bees and honey for him or even give some of their own stock to help him out or would have organised a concert for him to raise some stock cash so that he could get back on his feet. But again, for many, their pride was stronger than asking for a handout amongst their own ranks. Many of them would rather fight the Old Bill who had put them in this position in the first place so they would consider it more honourable to finish up in prison. At least they would be fed and bedded; but to others it would mean the workhouse, which was humiliating for a coster. But that was when all else failed. The workhouse separated them from their wives and children so it was a lot of pride for the coster to swallow. By applying to the union he would be allowed a limited period to get back on his feet, or another way out for the coster would be to borrow from a money-lender whom he would find in the public house for the next day's stock cash but at a very high interest rate and after his long day's work he had to pay the money-lender back, then borrow again for the following day's work, and so it went on. As leaders of the street markets, coster kings did everything they could to keep a good coster from going down that road to ruin and into possibly the union workhouse. The coster king also made it his duty to give a good coster member a good funeral send-off and avoid a pauper's grave. As poor as the coster may have been when he died he knew that his coster king and other costers would give him a good send-off in style; after all, he was a coster who had done his bit on the markets, who had helped the poor and sick and that did deserve the reward even in death, which was done in full cockney style and honour. There were a large number of writers from America and the Continent coming to seek out the costers and their kings in the late 1800s, trying to find out how they lived and what made them so special to the poor and sick and why they did so much for the community, and most of all trying to find out about the cockney humour mixed with the development of their own secret language (the back slang and the cockney rhyming slang) to good effect that confused the Old Bill. The writers also wanted to know about typical cockney cheek – how did they get away with it? More was to be learned over the years about the coster king who enjoyed dressing in his smoked pearl button whistle and flute, who had done his turn at the carnival, who supported the hospitals, who was raised with the poor and sick and fought for them to understand the hardship of life, and who prided himself on the amount of bees and honey he could raise. So if you was to ask me what I call a good market I would reply in truthfulness: to start at the beginning of a market and on reaching the other end buying back the clothes that you started with and yet feeling contented that you had met the coster king who had the patter and the cheek. For that was his gift, and what better candidate than the coster king could there have been to be transformed into a full blown pearly king. The coster king was a hard act to follow. Would the pearly king of the future be strong enough to compete? We will see.

Chapter Thirteen

It took a humble road-sweeper and rat-catcher to make a further contribution for the coster king to change into a full-blown pearly king. On 24 May 1862 Henry Croft was born. He too developed an affinity with the costers and their charitable outlook on life. He was from a poor family in north London in the days when the poor could barely afford to bring up one child. He, like many, was taken into an orphanage in St Pancras that was better known as a workhouse. He had been left on the doorstep with his name and age and religion, in his rugged clothes. The living conditions are best described as you may have seen in the film *Oliver* – it was a very grey, dull, heavy-handed workhouse. The roof was full of leaks and the windows were broken, allowing the rain and winter to spread more misery. They all had very little food and as a result they were always hungry, conditions that were widespread throughout London workhouses. He slept on sacking laid out on a concrete floor that formed beds in this rat-infested workhouse. There would be forty to sixty children sharing just one room that had no warmth or source of heating. The rats would often bite the children and the kids would grow up with no education or love. He was brought up with the criminal class in which they often ended up. It was a home with four walls rather than none and it was a home and the only one that he knew. It took the suffering of Henry like the costers to fully understand what charity meant and it's that suffering that they experienced that brought something out of it to create the cockneys' greatest history: the pearly kings and queens. So when you see a pearly shaking his charity tin, think what it took to get that tin in his hand.

Each child was given a job in the orphanage workhouse; it was washing the stone floors, washing up, sweeping, or polishing. The list would go on. Henry was given the job of sewing torn garments, sacking that was used as blankets and sewing on missing buttons on the children's clothing.

This was to become useful to him later in his life. Henry the orphan had seen some of his orphanage friends who were not as lucky as him taken from the orphanage by the chimneysweeps who had paid the orphanage a small fee to use them to climb the chimneys with a brush to clean them. Some never returned and others returned with torn limbs, left fully disabled and forced to beg for food for the rest of their lives. Henry was a caring type who thought of others rather than himself, who was learning about the pitiful way of life fast. He had decided in his mind that he would grow up to help ease the suffering that he was experiencing all around him. Henry knew he could not help all the children in this Victorian London, but he could do what he thought was his bit. He wanted to see better sleeping arrangements, fewer rats, and windows that would close, to shut out the rain and cold and the roof repaired and free from leaks. His dream in his young life was to come back when he was a grown man and carry out all the necessary repairs and improve these social ills. This was his ultimate goal in life.

It was in 1875, when he was thirteen years of age, that he was given his first job as a road-sweeper and rat-catcher. He had the experience as far as knowing the habits of the rats was concerned. He had lived with them long enough so that part of the job was easy for him. He had problems with his shovel and broom, however, since they were much bigger than him. He was only a small lad who never grew taller than five foot, so for a small, weak, skinny boy it was not so easy lifting the shovel and using the overgrown broom or pushing the dust cart that weighed in at half a ton around the market streets which were part of his round to sweep. It was while he was sweeping around the market streets that he would watch and listen to the costers in full admiration, but unlike most costers he never drank or smoked. For many years he held down his job as a road-sweeper and rat-catcher and for just as many years he learned the habits of the costermonger. Henry Croft and the costers he so grew to admire were similarly surrounded by this full-scale poverty day to day. Henry had watched the pick-pocketers going about their trade in amongst the market crowds and heard the costers shouting their wares. These remarkable, down-to-earth people also recognised that they had much in common with others in taking care of their own kind and in the pearly tradition of raising bees and honey for the sick and poor. He also saw that they collected and gave help to those in need, without a hint of pity or condescension. Henry also learnt the secret language of the costermonger's cockney rhyming slang that was being used to confuse their public enemy number one, the Old Bill. He was also influenced by the coster kings' dress in his smoked pearl whistle and flute. Henry never gave up telling the costers of the orphanage and the plight of the children, which was still fresh on his mind, hoping that the costers would help him in supporting the orphanage and workhouse that he was raised in; but the coster king had no time for his tales and passed him by. After all, he did have a job, and many people were not as lucky as him. Why should they want to know of his tales of the orphanage that he had so many times explained to them? They already had the poor and sick to help.

By now Henry had other things on his mind as well. He had a family of his own whom he was struggling to feed (eight children and a wife), but Henry's heart was still close to the orphanage and his desire to help them still strong. It would not have been easy for him having two full-time jobs sweeping around the markets and helping to raise a large family but still he would start up a full conversation with the costers about his desire for helping the orphanage and the conditions in which the children lived, but the costers knew only too well about the dreaded workhouse which was considered a last resort among the costers and as far as they were concerned it was the government's responsibility and not theirs.

So for our five-foot Henry it was a lost cause until the day the crew of a large container ship carrying pearl buttons threw part of their cargo overboard, landing on the banks of the River Thames. By 1896 there were up to 200 factories turning out mother-of-pearl buttons in their millions, with some still being imported from Japan where oyster pearl shell can be found from its waters.

It was part of this consignment of oyster shells and buttons that was washed up on the Thames' banks in 1896. Some give other reasons of Henry's discovery of the pearl buttons, but whatever the true details may be, it is certain that when Henry was walking along the bank of the River Thames he noticed what looked like bright glistening rays of light. At first he thought it was diamonds and if they were he could help the orphanage. As he got closer to this sparkling, glistening light he noticed it was something just as rich as diamonds. It was thousands upon thousands of pearl buttons in all different shapes and sizes. This find was to change thousands of people's lives for ever, and still does to this day. Unable to believe his luck he gathered up as many as he could get into sacks and made his way home to empty them. Then he returned again and again. He already had the idea and plan for the buttons in his mind and now he was going to put that plan into action. The idea was that to fully cover a costermonger's whistle and flute with thousands of buttons, so many that you would not see the cloth between the buttons. The idea was from watching and learning from the coster kings and maybe now he could help the orphanage.

So his plan had started and went into action with his skill of sewing from the orphanage days. Night after night and with all the spare time that he had, he sewed and sewed the thousands of buttons onto the three-piece whistle and flute, a task that took over a year to make. When he had completed the whistle and flute in the shining pearly buttons he took himself to the head of the market that he had swept for so many years, and stood in one place for all to see. This took some guts but it attracted the full attention of the large crowd of people and costermongers around him. Then the coster kings came towards him and as they did so Henry took a gentleman's bow in respect of the coster kings that he admired and respected. In doing so he raised his hat to them, holding it upturned in front of him. His intention was to bow before the coster kings that he admired, but as he took that bow people within the crowds started to put farthings and half pennies into his hat. The coster kings witnessed this collection of bees and honey in his hat and were always on the search for new ideas for collecting for the sick and poor. What the coster kings had seen impressed them and they could see that this was what was missing in their own suits. They needed to copy what our Henry had just achieved but what they wanted to know from Henry was how he had obtained all those bloody buttons and how had he sewn them on without losing any of them. Now they wanted to listen to Henry and wanted to know how he had made such a beautiful whistle and flute and where he had got all the shining pearl buttons from.

Henry didn't give much away but told them that if they helped him to fulfil his ultimate dream to help the children in the orphanage he would in return help them to make and design their very own whistle and flutes. Henry suggested they join together and between them they could raise bees and honey just like they had seen him do in his top hat that day. The coster kings were not going to lose this opportunity and agreed to the proposal that they raise funds for the sick, poor and the orphanage.

In 1897 a marriage took place between the coster kings who adopted the new name of 'Pearly King' which Henry had already put on the back of his jacket written in pearl buttons. What he had written originally ('the pearly king of the world') was later changed to 'Pearly King of Somers Town'. Now the coster kings were using mother-of-pearl buttons on their battered bell-bottom trousers, waistcoats and caps. Their queens wore huge ostrich feather hats and the coster kings, referred to as the pearly kings and 'flash Harry', walked the streets of London rattling their collection tins for the poor, sick and orphanages with their queens and children who had inherited their parents' titles in the same way as the real royals. Later the pearls added titles of their market or town to their backs. The pearly kings were now born to raise funds and spread their cheeky charm. All the pearlies were choosing designs and patterns of their own style to their whistle and flutes but there were some coster kings who did not approve of changing their own original styles; after all, the coster kings had been going strong for many years now and were set in their ways. What made things worse was that Henry was getting his friends to wear the cockney dress as well, and the costers resented this. They considered that the original title and history behind it were more appropriate. They also thought that the title was being misused, so jealousy set in with outbreaks of fighting fuelled by disagreement leading to the first spit of the working man's royalty. This resentment stayed with many costers for years to come.

Henry had over the time made himself seven suits just for the love of sewing. His second suit that he made was considered his favourite one. He put on the trouser legs the words, stitched in pearl buttons, 'PITY THE BLIND' and on the other leg, 'HELP THE POOR'. Henry always admired the coster kings and had that respect for them and to show that respect Henry attended the costers' annual donkey carnivals. He did so in his civvies such was his respect for them and their tradition, not wanting to steal the limelight from them. Henry was given his title of Somers Town not of his choosing but chosen by the coster kings whose title was left vacant by the death of Mary Robinson who was the famous queen of the costers who had died at the age of seventy-one. Her coffin was carried into St Pancras and Islington Cemetery by four coster kings in pure white smocks followed by about twenty or so young coster girls each wearing violet dresses and ostrich feather hats. So it was a great honour to Henry being given Somers Town as his title so now he had an army of pearly kings and queens with their princes and princesses all in the name of charity dressed in their magnetic pulling power to raise thousands of pounds amongst them. There was no doubt about it – the pearlies were becoming the full centre of attention.

People were now loading up the collecting tins for the love of the pearlies. Now the poor were helping the poor as never before and keeping the hospitals and workhouse orphanage in funds. The number of pearlies had now reached 400 including the queens, princesses and princes. Big names and titles were springing up: George Dole, Pearly King of St Pancras; Mike Satwick, Pearly King of Holloway; Henry Tongue, Pearly King of Tottenham; Bert Mathews, Pearly King of Camden; Bill Davison, Pearly King of West Ham; Jim Pomroy, Pearly King of Kentish Town; John Marriott, Pearly King of London (a title many disputed); Fred Tinsley, Pearly King of Blackfriars; Jim Duckworth, Pearly King of the Old Kent Road; and finally Fred Hall, Pearly King of Willesden, who was a deaf and almost blind flower-seller, and a good friend of Henry Croft.

Henry Croft died on the 1 January 1930, knocked down by a horse-drawn carriage outside the Whitechapel Hospital. His collection tin was still in his hand. He had died a pauper although he gave so much richness to others. Here was a man who made a large contribution to others and a man who played a large part in the coster kings' history by introducing them to the first full pearly whistle and flute, and he was just a road-sweeper with a big heart that was also taken into trust by the coster kings who became a pearly king himself of Somers Town for thirty-three years, the same length of time Christ lived in this world. At his funeral 400 pearlies made up the cortège, some in their donkey carts, others on foot wearing black arm bands and carrying their pearl-covered caps in their hands. They walked solemnly behind the carriage, a four-horse-drawn hearse. They were also joined by representatives from a number of London hospitals and orphanages carrying the banners that normally adorned their fund-raising carnivals. This time the edges were in black crêpe and on the coffin was his top hat. The streets were lined ten-deep in St Pancras on the route to his burial ground for this pearly king who softened the hearts of the coster kings. He was given the cockney send-off that he so rightly deserved. His family had long disowned him because of the excessive time he dedicated to helping others. But his coster friends never forgot the humble boy from the orphanage who swept the streets around their feet to become their friend. It was George Dole, the Pearly King of St Pancras and Henry Tongue, Pearly King of Tottenham, two of the original coster kings of the market that Henry had swept who were the main bearers for arranging this state funeral. Together, with a band of Irish pipers playing a lament, they led the long procession of mourners to his last resting place. Although in his lifetime he had raised thousands of pounds for charity, he had died a pauper. It was some time later that a member of the house of Lords, Lady Croft, heard of this tragic story and she arranged a proper grave with funds raised by the pearlies and hospitals, and had a marble statue erected above his grave with him dressed in his pearly suit, complete with top hat and walking stick. Years later it was destroyed by modern-day hooligans. The funeral was highlighted on Pathé News. This funeral highlighted the coster's history. The media had started to write about the costers and pearlies with news travelling far and wide around the world about this cockney dress and now the coster kings and pearlies were fighting for control of this pearly club that started to grow out of control. It was some of Henry's friends whom he had made into pearlies who caused the problem as the coster kings disagreed that those people should try and take over this club who had never worked or struggled in a market or knew of its code of conduct or tradition. It is sad to see a brotherhood fall into anarchy. Looking back on the costers' values and self-respect I do see where they are coming from. You can't have a club and have newcomers change the rules of history, and I see no point in washing your dirty linen in public. It only brings your club to self-destruction. The coster kings saw those newcomers as intruders, trying to grab the glory that they and their families before them had fought long and hard for. This caused a split between the different royal families, a split that still exists today.

The coster kings had been having their harvest festival at St Mary Magdalene Church at Congreve Street adjoining the Old Kent Road and it is on this occasion in which they gather as a group for thanksgiving of their harvest at the markets. It started in 1923 and it became a permanent place in their calendar. They brought offerings of fruit and vegetables with a dressed barrow, which was wheeled into church then distributed amongst the poor and sick. This was highlighted not only to express their trade but to let it be known that the pearly history is that of the famous coster kings. The pearly kings and queens' princes and princesses wore their trimmed round hats decorated with ostrich pummels. James Duckworth, who was then a famous coster king of the Old Kent Road, was often known to read the first lesson at the church. The costers' harvest festival came to St Mary Magdalene as a first permanent place, bringing together the coster kings and pearly kings under one roof. James, who never accepted wearing the full mother-of-pearl pearly whistle, only lined his own at the lapels, pockets and waistcoat with the pearl buttons, the hems of the bell-bottom trousers and their side-seams as well as his cap glistening like a crown.

The costers' harvest festival is still carried out to this day but more in the centre of London, on three different dates and three different churches due to rival groups fighting for power for something that is losing its identity, partly due to fighting. The harvest is no longer held at St Mary Magdalene due to being bombed in the war. Some pearlies say that the pearly king was started in 1875 by Henry Croft which is not correct as he was not born until 1876 and he did not appear on the market in his full pearly suit for the first time until about 1897. Others say the pearly kings had been going for 125 years in the year 2000 when in fact the pearlies had been going 103 years in the year 2000. Had you taken away 125 years when they claimed the pearlies had started that would have made Henry thirteen years old and the coster kings would never have listened to a thirteen-year-old or let him be involved in their proud history.

The pearlies would spend most of their spare time out amongst the public collecting in the name of charity. Pearlies were like a magnet attracting all the needles. Carrying their collecting tin is half their job; the other is up to the pearly. The cheekier a pearly is the more bees and honey he is likely to collect. When people meet a pearly they first expect to find that cheeky chappie with a bit of patter to follow and if a good pearly walks into a community he can melt the hearts of those around him with his fun-loving manner. Pearlies are a London scene and can only hold a London title.

The most influential big names were naturally those who took the leading part in processions of hospital carnivals and the charm and cheek to raise bees and honey for the right causes with the big names of the south being James Duckworth, Fred Tinsley, Bill Golden, Bert Lodge. Then, north of the river, Bert Mathews, Jim Pomroy, John Marriott, George Dole and Mike Satwick.

They were some of the generation of pearls who had little education but were by necessity sociable and who were aware of the desperate poverty around them. They were part of it and lived with it themselves. They knew what kind of charity was needed to help most and how it should be offered. They were determined to raise bees and honey and dispense it. No recipient of their charity was ever going to be made to feel humiliated – it was an attitude that they wanted to safeguard. All this fund-raising took place against the background of drab industrial streets amongst the poor from their own local people. It was self-help from their own local home grounds.

The pearlies were known as natural entertainers from the costers and great performers. They were part of that lively cockney cheeky chappie which was part of the cockney clown who could charm you into parting with your cash or even clothes. The pearly king and queens were being asked to appear everywhere. The Epsom derby was a must with pearlies travelling by train coach and on their own pony and cart. It would take up to four hours in their pony and cart to get there. They were invited to fairs, carnivals and the list went on, but these events were never complete without shaking collecting tins. I never felt dressed without it – that was our symbol and our purpose. The pearlies were becoming a feature of London life. Wherever they went they were admired and photographed by home-grown Londoners and visitors alike, not only in England but worldwide. To record the day that they met a cockney king people would stop and stare to appreciate this cockney character wearing his pearly crown jewels found nowhere else in the world. The pearly kings and queens were seen as a great effect for advertising Britain around the world, sponsored by the British Tourist Authority but also individual companies here and abroad who arranged visits to boost their sales of goods. There had been many visits to North America in store promotions that had British goods and personal appearances to publicise films, and interviews on worldwide television and radio, all to explain the British cockney way of life. George and Rose (Mathew) Smith, Pearly King and Queen of Camden, were involved in about twenty radio interviews, made live television appearances and did store visits to promote British goods and were followed everywhere they went by professional and amateur camera operations to obtain any picture for company or family records. George Hitchins, Pearly King of the City of London, had been to Buffalo and Toronto, Holland, France and Germany to promote the British tourist industry. He was also involved with the London Bridge opening in the Arizona Desert in America. Another visit was made to America by John and Rose Marriott and Canada to publicise the commencement of Qantas' daily Cleveland to London transatlantic service. The list goes on and on but at the bottom of all this commercial advertising the sales world could see that it was that cheeky cockney chappie who could flog anything to the world and they were prepared to put their bees and honey on it.

But the main points of our pearly history is the charity work so away from all the glamour and attractive aspect of our life, the collection of bees and honey is top of the list; it is really the purpose of our life. There is not one charity organisation that I or any other active pearly can say we have not helped, including leprosy, which I found to be the hardest charity to support. The pearlies give free time and help to those charities, that's why I believe that pearlies should lead any charity parade; after all, they are the charity kings. A pearly king and his family in his lifetime can collect over a million pounds for various charities. Should a pearly win the lottery or be given something while on his charity duty, he would be inclined to re-donate it for the charity he was supporting. This would be a typical example of the passing on of any gift that they receive without thinking of themselves. George Hitchin, Pearly King of the City of London, could be found every Sunday in all weathers in Petticoat Lane, rattling his collecting tin for some worthy charity, and all who photographed him would put extra cash in his tin – and there were lots of photos taken of him from all corners of the earth.

The pearlies have travelled the length of England opening fêtes and shaking their collecting tins, receiving letters of thanks and appreciation from secretaries of charity organisations. But it is not only the bees and honey that they famously collect; the other story is impossible to measure, and that is the happiness that they bring with their charm and cheeky character that could melt the ice cap on the north pole. It is the happiness that they have brought to thousands of people by their very love and presence and active participation in every conceivable way and hiding any problems they may have themselves. At first hand, due to their professional style, you may think that the pearlies get something out of it and that they must be on a good thing with perks and commission. Well, they don't, as far as I am aware, but they do it because this is part of their history and they enjoy it. It's the way that history has taught them. I and many other old pearlies have been out of pocket in order to give a public appearance to a charity event. L.O.V.E. is another way of spelling charity. A good pearly can get away with anything, like commenting on how nice that bird's bum is where others would get a slap. A good pearly doesn't have people approach him; he approaches them. Their personality is as glittery as the suits they wear which take the place of jewellery for the poor Londoner. Their caps glitter like crowns. The old music halls were fast catching on to the coster king and pearly character. They were part of the lively cockney folk. Marie Lloyd, Charlie Chaplin, (who tried his hand at costermongering), Fred Karno, who scraped for a living in the London slums, even some of the pearlies were doing their turn. In the old days they were skilled performers, which some members of the public expect to see today. Then there was Albert Chevalier, the singer and actor whose stage costume was that of the coster kings' whistle and flute. We had queen of the East End, Kate Carney, who sang coster songs, one of them being 'Three Pots a Shilling' and who was an idol of the pearlies. The three pots of flowers are still seen on some of the pearlies' suits as symbols, so it was the music hall, which was the extension of the pearlies' cockney pub.

A common question always asked of a pearly is how many buttons there are on a whistle. This can be from a few hundred to 40,000.

The next question: how much does it weigh? This can be from 15 lbs to 75 lbs.

Then you are asked what the pattern means. Well, there are many patterns. In 1930 we had 400 pearlies and not one of them had the same pattern. The first pearly whistle was smothered, to cover the entire garment with close-knit buttons, with some overlapping the other button and no sign of the cloth underneath. The suit was completely covered with a declaration of early royal honour. Every pearly had his own choice, choosing the pattern of his whistle and on his back which made claim to his royal rank. It was written in pearl buttons and would declare his pearly territory. Years ago it was customary for the king of another borough to seek permission to step into another pearly king's territory in his pearly suit. This was out of respect to the other pearly kings. It's something that is not done today. The buttons that were sewn onto the garments were stitched on to make patterns and symbols by pearlies for their own regalia. To make a pearly whistle takes good planning and a gift of ability with a good strong needle and very strong cotton together with plenty of patience and a personal attitude and mind about it and a skill that can only come with plenty of practice. Once the whistle is fully completed there needs to be a story that can be understood by the public at large who will be there to admire it. It is the whistle today that will remain with its owner for years to come to be added in their history. Some pearlies choose their designs by something that they have seen in their life that has inspired them. Henry Croft was inspired by a music-hall comedian who wore a whistle covered with shining brass buttons; others are inspired by happiness in their lives, while with others it could be a childhood such as my own.

Some whistles are made from cardboard templates with the filling around it in buttons; or some may draw in white chalk, which would be folded over and rubbed on to the opposite half of the garment. Others would use a few coloured buttons to highlight the design; even shoes and walking sticks were covered in pearl buttons years ago, and then some even covered their Peckham Rye (tie) in pearl buttons. One of my favourite whistle and flutes was owned and made by Bill Davison, Pearly King of West Ham, the tallest pearly king that we ever had, standing at 6' 2" and who always stood head and shoulders over other pearlies. His whistle was the most outstanding regalia decorated in harlequin triangles of tinted small pearl buttons. He also dyed his pearl buttons in Indian ink, red, blue and green and with his white pearl buttons mixed into his design he almost looked like a Union Jack. Some pearlies choose a design for everyday life, a good luck sign, perhaps a horseshoe; others would take care to stitch their buttons around the borders of their whistle, which meant protection from evil. Part of the design represented the wheel pattern of the costers' donkey cart. Then there was faith, hope and charity, which would be a cross anchor and heart, and also the shape of bells, the sign of the cockney. Then there was the drawing of three pots a shilling, which was the idol of the pearlies. These different designs were the most popular designs used by the pearlies in making their whistle. They used cotton that was tripled and waxed for added strength. Some used coloured cotton to stand out, and to add a bit of colour. The completed pearly suit is most certainly worth plenty of bees and honey; with the cost of the pearl buttons today, the buttons alone can set you back a few bob. An American once offered £60,000 at today's rate to a pearly king for his whistle, which was rightly refused. He told the American, 'Mate, you can't buy love,' an expression from a pearly.

When asked, 'How do you stitch them buttons on?' the old pearlies would reply, 'Every button is stitched on with love.' The value reflects the recognition that the whistles are becoming irreplaceable items of our tradition so therefore the whistles and flute are priceless, and increases in value the longer the wearer wears it. The length of time that it takes to make a good heavy whistle would be anything up to a year. Looking around at today's pearly whistles and comparing with the old pearlies, I found that we have produced a lazy pearlies suit outfit. The effort to make a well designed whistle has gone. The old pearly put so much meaning and time to produce a whistle fit for a king. Looking back at my sixty-two years as a pearly I have seen the highs and lows of our greatest history and some of the whistles and flutes produced today would bring shame to the old pearly. Some that I have seen have no meaning or effort put into them. I have seen better in a fancy-dress shop! Call me what you bloody like but at the end of the day the old pearlies who are no longer with us had pride of place in their whistle and flute and if they were active today they too would agree with me that some of the pearlies don't even know the true meaning of our history. One group of pearlies were asked how Henry Croft obtained his first buttons that made his whistle. They replied that while he was sweeping around the markets he collected buttons that fell off people's garments. Apart from the improbability of this scenario there must have been a lot of loose buttons flying around the market. The buttons would have had to rain like cats and dogs.

There was a time when we had the North London pearlies divided with the South London pearlies. The River Thames became the Berlin Wall between them. I saw this as a beginning of the end of one great band of pearlies. The North and South pearlies had their own agenda; all worked hard for charity but it seemed that it was just the very few who made a fuss in the first place. In 1902 Fred Tinsley, Pearly King of Blackfriars, who was an old coster king formed the first pearly club in The World Turned Upside Down in the Old Kent Road with the pearlies from the coster king's background who came from South London and the East End, the Rotherhithe Tunnel being the opening for the East Ender coster to the south. The club was called the Pearly Kings' and Queens' Guild. Some of its members were Pearly King of the Old Kent Road, Pearly King of Blackfriars, Pearly King of Mile End Road, Pearly King of West Ham, Pearly King of Battersea, Pearly King of Woolwich, Pearly King of Whitechapel, and so on. Their motto was 'The Helping Hand'. Then another rival group in North London started in Kings Cross, claiming all the North London pearlies. I remember Granddad Fred telling me at my coronation in The World Turned Upside Down where his old mate Fred Tinsley, Pearly King of Blackfriars, asked me to join his club, Pearly Kings' and Queens' Guild, not to get involved with the other pearlies; he knew the problems. He said to me that I was my own man and should remain that way. I wished I had taken his advice, for future disputes were to come but even with all the quarrels and arguments each side was doing its bit in adding to the history of the pearlies with Beatrice Marriott, Pearly Queen of London, going to Italy to the launching of the ship *Spirit of London* and Ted Marriott appearing in his pearlies in the film *The Prince and the Pauper* with Tommy Steele. Then the Pearly King of Silver Town, Arthur Balfour, emigrated to Australia, taking with him our tradition of the pearls with a mass of publicity in Melbourne which brought visits to Australia of us other pearlies to promote British tourism and even Bert and Beck Mathews went to Amsterdam in order to raise bees and honey for the Queen Wilhelmina's Cancer Fund. But rather than all this bringing us to the front of our history books, for some pearls it brought resentment and jealousy. Why I don't know, as this can only bring good to our history.

If ever I see a pearly on TV or in the news it makes me feel good and proud to know that I am part of that history. Bringing new blood into the pearly cult does not bother me in the least; in fact, I encourage it and welcome it, providing that they do it as a team and not for self-gain or the glory of it all which some do, sadly. It's a shame, really, for we need to replace the best of the ones that are no longer with us. Part of our history is about morality and a genuine desire to help others; that's what made our history great and makes it special. The newcomers must get our history right and abide by the rules of conduct. If not, how can they be trusted, as it would be perfectly obvious to me that if you no longer reflect and love the pearly history then you can no longer lead it.

There have been many disputes among the pearlies that the national press have taken up. There have been disputes over titles, bees and honey and most of all jealousy, with suspicion still stalking the royals, and rivalries still in evidence. Such disputes have certainly done much harm to their image which breaks my heart to see over the years. I have tried to bring old and young pearlies together, with the reforming of three pearly clubs but without success. The trouble is that the culprits wash their dirty linen in public at their open meetings. They have heated discussions over alleged activities and titles, and rivals are out to outdo each other. Status of appearances and amounts collected for charity and cockney humour are well forgotten. So when you see a pearly slagging off another, you know who is doing the dirty washing. I would rather get on with the job of raising bees and honey for charity and leave the disputes to the knacker's yard. I have always seen the old pearlies as the shop window of the British nation, as its magnificent and historic display of tradition.

If I had to give a role of honour for the pearlies who have done so much for our history and who were outstanding kings, this would be my call-:

George Dole, Pearly King of St Pancras; Bert Mathews, Pearly King of Camden; Jim Pomroy, Pearly King of London; Mike Satwick, Pearly King of Holloway; Ted Mathew, Pearly King of Hampstead; Fred Tinsley, Pearly King of Blackfriars; Harry Tongue, Pearly of Tottenham; Bert Singfield, Pearly King of Whitechapel; Ted Arrowsmith, Pearly King of Chingford; Bill Golden, Pearly King of Woolwich; Jim Duckworth, Pearly King of the Old Kent Road; Fred Hall, Pearly King of Willesden who was a deaf and almost blind flower-seller; Ted Marriott (Wiggy), Pearly King of Lambeth; Alf Dole, Pearly King of St Pancras; George Pinnard, Pearly King of Greenwich; Albert Taberam, Pearly King of Hoxton; John Smith, Pearly King of South-West London; Bert Lodge, Pearly King of Borough; George Hitchins, Pearly King of the City of London; Alf Meader, Pearly King of Hackney; Bill Davison, Pearly King of West Ham; Ricky Conway, Pearly King of Deptford and Greenwich; Bill Cole, Pearly King of Islington; William Emmings, Pearly King of Battersea; Ron Kebble, Pearly King of Shepherds Bush; Fred Hitchins, Pearly King of Westminster; and finally, but by no means least, Eddy Chear, Pearly King of Fulham.

Not to forget our beautiful pearly queens in this order-: Sarah Tinsley, Beatrice Marriott, Lilly Satwick, Avis Shepherd, Beck Mathew, Martha Morris, Liz Cole, Rose Mathew, Sheila Arrow Smith, Marie Rackly, Flo Cheer, Kitty Pinnard, Dot Kebble, Grace Smith, Shirley Tongue, Lou Hitchins, Sarah Golden, Emily Emmings, Ann Davidson May Howard, Mary Dole, and finally my favourite princess, Diane Martin, who will finish up as a top queen.

I have enjoyed working with them and my memories of our laughs will live on. I am proud to have known them; they are not made like that today or could even be replaced. Most of the old pearlies whom I knew had come from hard backgrounds that gave them the full strength to fight for what they really believed in and to understand how to help others in need. They all had the patter and the gift of the gab. So it is with the utmost regret that we see our tradition being eroded and destroyed by a few and their bulldozers. Future generations will have to depend on the tales their grandfathers tell, because unfortunately factual and material proof will no longer be available with the lack of knowledge and respect of the few. There is one aspect of our London life that despite pressures and problems is still withstanding the juggernauts. This is the few old pearly kings and queens who still don their buttons and hold court in aid of charity. Foreign visitors can still go home and tell of the day that they met a real royal from London. Their stories will include recollections of that chirpy chappie who just 'made my day' who had the lips of the costermonger in his pearls. The world's greatest scientists have for centuries tried to make gold from stone without success, yet charity organisers throughout the world recall stories of how some old pearly kings charmed gold from hearts of stone. The pearly kings and queens have had their quarrels and problems and their main one is that they continue their disputes, which threaten the ranks of many making their history thinner on the ground.

I would love to see the pearlies throw their caps in the ring and would be happy if they were picked up by the few and become old friends again to rebuild our history for all to sit on that throne with respect, honour and loyalty, just like the old coster kings. But sadly that is only wishful thinking and the quarrels and disputes will continue till the last soldier falls. As we have moved towards the age of modern technology and the changing of attitude and a less caring society so the number of pearlies has changed from its peak in 1930 of four hundred and is down to a few. There are only about eighteen now. Half of them never bothered to carry on their father's title until a carrot was put before them. In the old days it was a done thing for the children from royal stock to carry on the pearly tradition but now the children are not interested in the history of their father's pride or the pearly history, saying, 'I'm too busy with my life.' The same children have seen the pearly disputes and not wanted to get involved. That is another nail in the coffin of this once great pearly history. The word pearly in the *Oxford Dictionary* states 'clothes adorned with pearl buttons such as worn by costermongers' and in 1897 the *Daily News* defined it as sharp looking individual wearing a complete suit of coster pearlies. With the costermonger fading and that sharp individual cheeky chappie no more, how will the *Oxford Dictionary* and the *Daily News* describe a pearly in the not too distant future?

What is also lacking is that young kids are more self-conscious to even consider appearing in a pearly suit as they grow up. At first they went out with mum and dad because they had to, but once that holding hand has gone and they become too preoccupied with modern life with an attitude of not caring about our national heritage and being taught at schools with a plum in their mouth with the liberal society taking control, what chance is there? No longer is that child brought up the cockney way to charm or throw out the cheek where their school friends have never heard of our pearly history while drinking their cans of Coca-Cola. It did not seem too long ago to me when the cockney pearly princes and princesses would gather around me and watch me throw out the cheek and charm and giggle amongst themselves in respect of their history in the making. Is this another colourful face of London culture slipping into the mist of memory? It was a big personal strain to meet the pressures continually with constant appearances with the need to appear smart and cheerful all the time, including the full weight of your whistle and flute both mentally and physically. The hardest bit was kissing the birds also going out to opening fêtes, attending carnivals, gracing garden parties, crowning of beauty queens (that one I loved), attending funerals, weddings, silver and golden anniversaries, one-hundred years old celebrations… Also christenings, fashion events, films, festivals, cockney shows, opening shops, markets (including pie-and-mash shops) – you name it, we've done it, not counting the times you are called to go abroad, make TV appearances, radio shows worldwide, all in the name of our unique and attractive aspect of the London scene. They were part of the memory of yesterday, but like anything in life time changes and so do people's attitudes. For years ago no self-respecting king and queen would dream of appearing in their whistle decorated with plastic buttons – it had to be the genuine article. But that I have seen disappear in some cases. Is it because the respect is losing its high priority? Even the cockneyism of good humour coupled with happiness is gone and people are not finding it. It is the attitude of today compared with the attitude of yesterday that may explain it, when the old pearlies and coster kings were aware of the poverty and hardships that surrounded them; they had worked with it, lived with it and they themselves was part of it just as the costermonger was aware of it. So what better understanding can you have if you yourself have lived with it and the understanding of how to offer and give the help that was so much in demand? It made them more than determined to raise funds and happiness that was needed from the heart and soul of the cockney charm, cheek and spirit that they could freely give. Yes, the old pearlies did their tasks which were by nature in their role, to give that help to the needy, poor and sick, by taking the basin around without any thought to themselves or an attitude of 'look at me'. Coupled with that there was certainly a sense of tradition, through the true old pearly who was brought up to appreciate what little they had and the customs and the attitude to life that the title demanded. He would turn in his grave if he could see the pearly saga today by a few pearlies showing signs of doing something without feelings.

To our history and tradition then that image fails and they would not survive. There have been quite a few people making a pearly garment who have never come from the traditional coster king or pearly tradition which nobody would object to in order to pump more blood into our history, providing that they perform all the acknowledged duties of a true pearly. But once in the club some of them want to go further and take over a tradition that is alien to them. The result means they become Dickensian in spirit, causing so much bickering and each one trying to better the other and losing the plot. Since the late seventies the pearly cult has run out of control with the few newcomers, with even some of the old pearlies in action today not being recognised by them same people. I don't know if it is the lack of our history or the thought of a threat by the old pearlies who can attract the limelight of publicity to their true history who unselfishly give their time to charitable causes in their own quiet way. So what of the future, apart from their own mass suicide over their bickering and jealousy amongst each other? Hopefully that will not happen but there are other things that have and will happen in time to come. The pearlies are sadly declining in numbers today – the reasons are clearly seen. We have a welfare state that we never had in the old poverty days which has taken away the need for charity for the poor the needy and the sick which was the main purpose of the coster and pearly traditions in the first place. Pearlies have moved out of London to far and wide areas. London has become more affluent to its own needs with the urge to tackle unpaid charity because there are too many charities out there now. There has been a cruel loss of neighbourhood, which the pearlies relied on, with no ready descendants making almost no heirs to the thrones and lack of interest in the pearlies' life. Most of all, as I see it and which really spells the end of the pearly, is loss of strong personalities, ready with cheerful exhibitionism, together with physical toughness.

We have seen the high-rise blocks of municipal flats, offices, supermarkets, ring roads, car parks, all changing the face of London as we knew it and all changing and hiding the pearly royalty with all of us too busy recycling five wheelie bins of rubbish. We are no longer living in a neighbourhood street but a lodging house. I miss my old London market street that is also now losing its identity as we knew it, where they were like funfairs and people would stop and chat, exchange jokes with more time on their hands to think of others. Today everyone is in a hurry with the human touch so clearly absent in London. The life that was once so rich and entertaining for us all has now vanished. I can only mourn my old trade and way of life as I remember it as if it was yesterday. Now the few cockney cultures left in London are seeing waves of immigrants and we are now all struggling to keep our identity and slowly it is slipping on a greasy pole.

As a personal favour to an old china plate I was asked to attend a fête in my pearls to boost funds for the charity so near to his heart. After opening the fête I travelled the four corners of the field meeting first the stall holders who after all do the real hard work at any fête then met the young and old who had come to add their support with their bees and honey. As I had walked around with the cockney grin set across my boat race (face) I started my usual chat up lines: 'Nice looking bum you have, ducks,' to my first admirer. Then on to the next bird I met: 'Excuse me, darling, could you get my wallet out of my back pocket?'

'Ask him,' she said, pointing to her husband.

'People will think I am bent,' I replied to her.

'All right,' she said, 'I will do it.'

As she struggled to get my wallet out I was screwing up my face in delight and enjoying every minute of it. By now a crowd was gathering and enjoying the show when finally she got my wallet out of my back pocket. I said 'Thanks, ducks,' and put it back again.

'I thought that you wanted to get your bees and honey out,' she said.

'Oh no, ducks. I just wanted to see if I had bees and honey in it.'

Then everyone clapped. As I walked away this posh woman who had been watching the whole show smiled at me. I could see by her dress and jewellery and her grooming that she had loads of bees and honey apart from smelling of it.

'You rich bitch,' I said to her and kissed her as I walked away. My friend who had stood nearby said to me, 'How you got away with that is beyond me as she is the most stuck-up woman in this village!'

'Piece of cake,' I replied. Then I passed another bird to whom I called out, 'You are the best-looking bird I've seen today!'

'I bet you say that to all the women,' she said. I had already said it to about fifteen women that day.

'No,' I said, 'no one else has your film-star looks.'

By now I had already kissed dozens of birds with lipstick half-covering my boat race (face). I continued meeting the people and being quite a jester and spent a full six hours doing what is expected of me as a pearly king. You learn from experience to pick the right person to throw out that cheeky chappie style in order to get away with it. If you don't pick the right person you would finish up getting a handbag around your head and I haven't had that yet in my sixty-two years as a pearly.

At the end of my day I needed to go. I was bursting when I went up to one of the organisers who had a plum in his north and south (mouth), a right posh geezer, and said to him, 'Watcher china plate, where is the bog house? I am dying to have a piss.'

Well, that is me, George Major, the Pearly King of Peckham, just an ordinary bloke still helping others to survive and leaving my footprints behind me.

★

Epilogue

Well, there you have it, right up to when I was sweet twenty-one years old which I saw as the foundation of my life, a make-or-break. I made it. When I first met my publishers I suggested that my story would need a good ghost writer, as I was far from a scholar and with all my spelling mistakes I had a lot of help from a good friend who typed it all for me. After many weeks she just about managed to read my handwriting. However, what I had written was good, and all they need to do was put in the full stops, commas and capital letters. At that point I felt quite proud at what I had achieved; not bad for a bloke who could not read or write on leaving school, don't you think? But then I do have a lot of rabbit to say to continue my story. That's why I have had to do it in two books.

In the next book, *The Stolen Whistle and Flute: Stitch Two*, the story will take you on some more ducking and diving on the street markets, and the time I insisted on living amongst the down-and-outs for six weeks, day and night, suffering the same hardships and getting to know the tragic stories of how they had come to be living on the streets so that I could give a helping hand. Then there is my continued search for my mother whom I had not yet met. Then the sad story of Brian, who had worked with Granddad Fred and me on the markets and another tragic story of Eileen Chase, my first love. I have many sad and humorous and inspiring stories to tell during my reign as the Pearly King of Peckham. Then I will tell you how I got my very own street and made it into a street market after being refused a street licence. Then, after being told that a barrow boy could not make a travelling salesman, how I proved them wrong, and was given the title of the top salesman of a well-known national company. Then the time I sat in the Queen's golden coach in my pearly whistle and flute and how I had made the Queen Mother laugh, and why the Queen stopped me in the middle of Oxford Street in her jam jar just to have a chat with me, then what I said in reply to Princess Margaret when she asked me how I went for a toilet with all my buttons on my whistle and flute, and how my own childhood stood up to my hectic everyday life. Then I am going to give you a bit of cockney drama – who was the tea leaf (thief) who nicked my pearly whistle and flute? Why was I dragged through the courts fighting for the rights of our cockney history and museum from people who were trying to take it from me?

These are stories that will make you laugh and cry. So, my china plates, if you liked my first book you will love my second, *The Stolen Whistle and Flute: Stitch Two*.